The Fatal Embrace

BENJAMIN GINSBERG

The Fatal Embrace

JEWS AND THE STATE

The University of Chicago Press   Chicago and London

Benjamin Ginsberg is director of the Washington Center for the Study of American Government and the David Bernstein Professor of Political Science at The Johns Hopkins University. He is the author of several books including, most recently, *Politics by Other Means: The Declining Importance of Elections in America, The Consequences of Consent: Elections, Citizen Control, and Popular Acquiescence,* and *Poliscide.*

The University of Chicago Press gratefully acknowledges the assistance of the Exxon Foundation in the publication of this book.

The University of Chicago Press, Chicago 60637
The University of Chicago Press, Ltd., London
© 1993 by The University of Chicago
All rights reserved. Published 1993
Printed in the United States of America

02 01 00 99 98 97 96 95 94 93   1 2 3 4 5

ISBN: 0-226-29665-2   (cloth)

Library of Congress Cataloging-in-Publication Data

Ginsberg, Benjamin.
    The fatal embrace : Jews and the state / Benjamin Ginsberg.
        p.   cm.
    Includes bibliographical references and index.
        1. Jews—United States—Politics and government.   2. Antisemitism—United States.   3. Jews in public life—United States.   4. Afro-Americans—Relations with Jews.   5. United States—Ethnic relations.   I. Title.
    E184.J5G464   1993   92-43399
    323.1'1924'009—dc20   CIP

⊗ The paper used in this publication meets the minimum requirements of the American National Standard for Information Sciences—Permanence of Paper for Printed Library Materials, ANSI Z39.48-1984.

For Sandy

Contents

Preface

I have long been convinced that one of the reasons that so many Jews pursue careers in the social sciences is their conscious or unconscious concern with the great question of Jewish history. That question is, of course, Why is it that during so many different times, and in so many different places, Jews have achieved enormous status, wealth, and power only to be cast down, driven out—or worse? The usually unspoken question is, Can it happen here or, for the pessimists, when will it happen here? As a student at the University of Chicago and during the course of my academic career at Cornell and Johns Hopkins, I often found myself reflecting on these matters even when my manifest scholarly interests were in other areas.

Increasingly, I came to be convinced that Hannah Arendt was correct in her view that the key to understanding the rise and fall of the Jews was to be found in the relationship between Jews and the state. Historically, in response to the hostile attitudes and actions of their neighbors, Jews frequently sought the protection of the state. For their own purposes, rulers often were happy to accommodate the Jews in exchange for the services that the latter could provide. Much followed from the relationship between Jews and states, and, as an outgrowth, some of the most important states in the modern world were built or strengthened. As a result of this relationship, moreover, Jews sometimes achieved great power. Their relationship with the state, however, also exposed Jews to new hatreds and antagonisms. For the Jews, under some circumstances, the embrace of the state proved to be fatal. These considerations are not simply of historical interest. They are also central to understanding the past—and potential future—of Jews in America.

In writing this book, I received help from a number of individuals and institutions. First, by appointing me the Exxon Foundation Lecturer in Social Thought, the University of Chicago's Committee on Social Thought gave me the opportunity to present my ideas in a series of talks in April 1992. I am grateful to Francois Furet and Shmuel Eisenstadt of the committee, and to John Mearsheimer, chair of Chicago's political science department, for introducing the lectures. I am also grateful for the postlecture comments I received from

John Hansen, Stephen Holmes, Norman Nie, and Bernard Silberman. My thanks also to Rabbi Elliot B. Gertel of Chicago's Congregation Rodfei Zedek for sharing with me the detailed critique of my lectures that he presented to his congregation in a sermon entitled, "Preparing for Passover with Professor Ginsberg—a Response to the Fatal Embrace Lectures at Swift Hall."

I also had the opportunity to present some of my ideas to members of the political science department at the University of Houston. Here, too, I received a number of very useful comments. My thanks to Christian Davenport, Robert Erikson, Mark Franklin, Joseph Nogee, Bruce Oppenheimer, Susan Scarrow, Alan Stone, and Kent Tedin.

My colleague Jeremy Rabkin was kind enough to read and comment on sections of the manuscript. Even more important, Rabkin spent a good deal of time discussing and, indeed, arguing vigorously with me about some of my major points as I sought to formulate them.

Arielle Hecht and Jason Lowi were wonderful research assistants.

As always, I learned a great deal while teaching. In this instance, I benefited from my discussions with the students in my 1992 "anti-Semitism" seminar at Cornell as I was completing this manuscript. The students were Mark Bailen, Tahl Ben-Yehuda, Davina Buivan, Giles Cohen, Brett Dorfman, Benjamin Falk, Deborah Feinstein, Andrea Freedman, Arielle Hecht, Neil Kammerman, Sheri Rabiner, Michelle Rhee, Marina Rolbin, Jeffrey Rosier, Riva Syrop, and Seth Weinstein. I hope they profited from the seminar as much as I did.

John Tryneski of the University of Chicago Press functioned more as a valuable colleague than as an editor. I learned that John's suggestions on matters of intellectual substance were as good as his editorial opinions. John also had excellent judgment in his choice of anonymous readers. I am extremely grateful to the two readers appointed by the Press. Their advice was simply superb, and I was almost always happy to take it. Lila Weinberg was a wonderful manuscript editor. Her efforts have made the book much more coherent.

Finally, I want to recognize my intellectual debt to my close friend and colleague, Martin Shefter. Originally, Shefter and I had planned to collaborate on this project as we had on many others in the past. Unfortunately, this was precluded by the serious injuries Shefter suffered in a bicycling accident and the time and energy he needed to complete his recovery. Though we could not write this particular book together, I am proud to acknowledge that most of my views on politics and society have been shaped by my conversations and collaborations with Shefter over the past twenty years.

1   The Jews: Social Marginality and the Fatal Embrace of the State

S ince the 1960s, Jews have come to wield considerable influence in American economic, cultural, intellectual, and political life. Jews played a central role in American finance during the 1980s, and they were among the chief beneficiaries of that decade's corporate mergers and reorganizations. Today, though barely 2% of the nation's population is Jewish, close to half its billionaires are Jews. The chief executive officers of the three major television networks and the four largest film studios are Jews, as are the owners of the nation's largest newspaper chain and most influential single newspaper, the *New York Times*. In the late 1960s, Jews already constituted 20% of the faculty of elite universities and 40% of the professors of elite law schools; today, these percentages doubtless are higher.[1]

The role and influence of Jews in American politics is equally marked. Jews are elected to public office in disproportionate numbers. In 1993, ten members of the United States Senate and thirty-two members of the House of Representatives were Jewish, three to four times their percentage of the general population. Jews are even more prominent in political organizations and in finance. One recent study found that in twenty-seven of thirty-six campaigns for the United States Senate, one or both candidates relied upon a Jewish campaign chairman or finance director.[2] In the realm of lobbying and litigation, Jews organized what was for many years one of Washington's most successful political action committees, the American Israel Public Affairs Committee (AIPAC), and they play leadership roles in such important public interest groups as the American Civil Liberties Union (ACLU) and Common Cause. Several Jews also played very important roles in the 1992 Democratic presidential campaign. After the Democrats' victory, President Clinton appointed a number of Jews to prominent positions in his administration.

Their role in American economic, social, and political institutions has enabled Jews to wield considerable influence in the nation's public life. The most obvious indicator of this influence is the $3 billion in direct military and economic aid provided to Israel by the United States each year and, for that matter, the like amount given to Egypt since it agreed to maintain peaceful relations with Israel.

That fully three-fourths of America's foreign aid budget is devoted to Israel's security interests is a tribute in considerable measure to the lobbying prowess of AIPAC and the importance of the Jewish community in American politics.

At least until recently, another mark of Jewish influence was the virtual disappearance of anti-Semitic rhetoric from mainstream public discourse in the United States. As a general rule, what can and cannot be said in public reflects the distribution of political power in society; as Jews gained political power, politicians who indulged in anti-Semitic tactics were labeled extremists and exiled to the margins of American politics. Similarly, religious symbols and forms of expression that Jews find threatening have been almost completely eliminated from schools and other public institutions. Suits brought by the ACLU, an organization whose leadership and membership are predominantly Jewish, secured federal court decisions banning officially sanctioned prayers in the public schools and crèches and other religious displays in parks and public buildings.[3]

American Jews secured their position of power quite recently. During the Second World War, the Jewish community lacked sufficient influence to induce the U.S. government to take any action that might have impeded the slaughter of European Jews.[4] As recently as the early 1950s, public officials such as Representative John Rankin of Mississippi felt free to make anti-Semitic speeches on the floor of Congress. In 1956, during the Suez crisis, President Dwight D. Eisenhower could refuse even to meet with American Jewish leaders who sought to discuss U.S. policy in the Middle East.[5] Into the early 1960s, elite universities including Harvard, Yale, and Princeton maintained quotas limiting Jewish enrollments.[6]

Not only is the extraordinary prominence of Jews in American politics a relatively recent development but, during the past several years, there have been some indications that Jewish influence might already be waning. In 1992, for example, former President George Bush resisted and ultimately defeated efforts by AIPAC and other Jewish organizations to secure American loan guarantees to assist Israel in the construction of additional Jewish settlements in the territories it occupied after its 1967 war with the Arab states.

In a nationally televised press conference during the loan guarantee struggle, Bush seemed to question the legitimacy of American Jews' efforts on Israel's behalf. The president later denied that this had been his intention. The effect of the Bush press conference and subsequent comments, however, was to intimidate American Jewish organizations and weaken their support for the loan guarantees. The

Bush administration's larger goal was to undermine Israeli Prime Minister Yitzhak Shamir's Likud government, which was viewed as an obstacle to the realization of American policy aims in the Middle East. By cowing Israel's Jewish supporters in America, the White House hoped to weaken Shamir and replace him with a more compliant Israeli government. This American effort was successful. The Likud bloc was defeated in Israel's 1992 elections by a labor coalition led by Yitzhak Rabin. In the fall of 1992, having secured the election of an Israel government more to its liking, the White House gave its support to a new loan guarantee package as an inducement to the Israelis to toe the American line in the Middle East. Then, having nominally improved its relations with Israel, the Bush administration made a token effort to mend its fences with Jewish voters and contributors in America. The administration made it clear, however, that, having humbled the once-powerful Jewish lobby, it would not permit its Middle East policies to be shaped by the wishes of the Jews.[7]

Another indication that the influence of American Jews may be waning is the resurgence of anti-Semitic—sometimes veiled as anti-Zionist—rhetoric in American political discourse. On the liberal left, opposition to Israel is commonplace. During the 1991 Persian Gulf War, for example, some liberal activists charged that the Israeli occupation of Arab lands was a major underlying cause of the conflict. Indeed, the Persian Gulf War opened major cleavages between Jews and other elements within the American liberal community. Liberal groups ranging from the National Council of Churches through the Friends of the Earth argued against the use of force to dislodge Iraq from Kuwait, leaving liberal Jewish advocates of a military solution such as Ann Lewis, former political director of the Democratic National Committee, isolated from their usual allies. In its statement opposing American military action in the Persian Gulf, the National Council of Churches also endorsed the creation of a Palestinian state.[8]

African Americans, for their part, usually do not bother to hide their attacks on Jews behind the smoke screen of opposition to Zionism. In recent years, some black leaders, including Nation of Islam Minister Louis Farrakhan, former U.S. Representative Gus Savage, and Democratic presidential candidate Jesse Jackson have made anti-Semitic comments of the sort that had all but disappeared from American politics. At the same time, anti-Semitic black speakers have become the wandering minstrels of the college lecture circuit. Curiously, some of the very same student and faculty groups that vehemently assert that the first Amendment does not protect speech deemed to be racist, homophobic, or sexist cheerfully dabble in anti-Semitic rhetoric.

To be sure, liberal forces are sufficiently dependent upon Jews for their power in American politics so that anti-Semitic rhetoric on the part of blacks and other liberals is not a *direct* threat to the Jews. The influence of Jews within the liberal camp may be reduced somewhat by an alliance of blacks and other left liberals. Barring some cataclysmic restructuring of political forces in the United States, however, Jews could not be jettisoned from the contemporary liberal coalition in the way that they were, say, from America's nineteenth-century industrialist coalition—a phenomenon we shall examine in Chapter 2.

Nevertheless, the use of anti-Semitic rhetoric on the part of nominal allies of the Jews—and the inability of the Jews to do much about it—*is* a signal to other forces that Jews are now fair game. This signal has not been missed by forces on the political right—forces that are *not* dependent upon Jews for their own political power. Among some groups of conservatives, anti-Semitism has become sufficiently noteworthy that an entire recent issue of the *National Review* was devoted to the topic.[9] The prominent conservative commentator and recent presidential aspirant, Patrick Buchanan, barely bothers to deny his anti-Semitism, while a number of other conservatives are pleased to flaunt theirs.[10]

In 1991, prior to the Persian Gulf War, Buchanan asserted that men named Rosenthal, Kissinger, Perle, and Krauthammer—a group he called Israel's "amen corner" in the United States—were beating the drums for a war in which "kids with names like McAllister, Murphy, Gonzales and LeRoy Brown" would be the ones to die. Later, as a candidate in Georgia's March 1992 Republican presidential primary, Buchanan attacked a group of Jewish hecklers by saying, "This is a rally of Americans, by Americans, and for the good old U.S.A., my friends."[11] During the same rally, Buchanan responded to a question about his anti-Semitism and racism by referring to his First Amendment guarantee of free speech.[12]

In addition, radical populists, who until recently had been viewed as part of the lunatic fringe, have become much more active over the past several years. The most notorious of these, of course, is David Duke, a neo-Nazi who captured 55% of the white vote in the 1991 Louisiana gubernatorial election. For radical populists like Duke, anti-Semitism is an important drawing card, even if they sometimes choose to keep it face down—but still in a prominent spot on the table—when appealing for middle-class votes. Duke failed to win much support in the several 1991 primaries he entered, mainly because he was overshadowed by Buchanan. Nevertheless, the brute fact remains that a Nazi very nearly was elected governor of an American state in 1991.

Many surveys suggest that, except among blacks, popular anti-Semitism in the United States is still at a relatively low level.[13] Contrary to the views of the pollsters, however, surveys are a barometer or reflection of what *has* taken place in political life, not a predictor of what is politically *possible*. If anti-Semitic appeals or rhetoric began to figure more prominently in political discourse among whites, as they already have among blacks, then in due course the polls would undoubtedly reflect this change by recording more popular anti-Semitism. Just as the public cannot be in favor of a political candidate they have not yet heard about, they cannot support a political ideology that has not yet forcefully been presented to them. Ideas, like candidates and products, need to be marketed before they can gain adherents. As Joseph Schumpeter once put it, public opinion is the "product rather than the motive power of the political process."[14]

Could anti-Semitism be promoted successfully in contemporary America? Some social historians have maintained that American "exceptionalism," that is, the unusual strength of liberal values in the United States, precludes the emergence of major anti-Semitic movements in this country.[15] The validity of this optimistic view, though, is open to question. Certainly, liberal democracy has been more firmly rooted in the United States than anywhere else in the world. It is extremely important to understand, however, that the strength of liberalism in America is not a function of some immutable ideological commitment on the part of Americans. Liberalism, rather, has prevailed in the United States as a result of the victories won by liberal forces in political struggles—sometimes pitched battles—against opponents whose values were decidedly illiberal. The triumph of liberal democracy was, by no means, preordained in, say, the 1860s or the 1930s. During both these periods liberal values prevailed because, *and only because*, the political—and military—forces controlled by the proponents of those values won after long and heroic conflicts whose outcomes remained in doubt for many years.

Understanding liberalism as a doctrine that has prevailed, rather than one that has never been challenged in the United States, helps to illuminate the place of Jews and anti-Semitism in American history. First, over the past century, Jews have generally supported liberal values and been linked to liberal political forces in the United States. In turn, the opponents of those forces and values have upon occasion sought to make use of anti-Semitism to discredit them. Far from being excluded by liberalism, during several periods in American history, including the 1880s, 1930s, and 1950s, anti-Semitism played a significant role in attacks launched against liberal regimes in which Jews participated. Anti-Semitism was used, in part, to delegitimate liberal democracy by exposing it as a creature of, or cover for, the Jews. For example, many readers will, no doubt, recall that some right-wing opponents of the New Deal labeled it the "Jew Deal" as a prominent component of their effort to undermine the Roosevelt administration.

Second, during these periods—the 1930s and 1950s in particular —anti-Semitism was defeated by liberal forces rather than precluded by liberalism. Groups espousing anti-Semitic ideologies were vanquished by Jews and their allies in liberal coalitions after long and arduous political struggles whose favorable outcomes were in no sense guaranteed. During these struggles, Jews were important members of the liberal camp. Indeed, as we shall see, Jews helped to defend American liberalism from its foes as much as liberalism protected the Jews from anti-Semitism.

Finally, far from excluding anti-Semitism, American liberalism has, itself, not been entirely free of antagonism to Jews. At the end of the nineteenth-century, as we shall see, the liberal forces of the day, led by Northeastern industrialists, found it politically expedient to respond to their patrician and populist opponents' use of anti-Semitism by distancing themselves from the Jews. As a result, nominally liberal forces participated in a campaign to extrude Jews from American political and social life. Paradoxically, it was precisely the strength of liberal groups that allowed them to jettison their putative Jewish allies. The triumph of liberalism in the aftermath of the Civil War made Jews superfluous to the liberal coalition. A parallel to this experience, as we shall see, is to be found in the relationship between blacks and Jews today.[16]

Thus, anti-Semitism has played a role in American history despite and, in some instances, *because* of the strength of American liberalism. It follows that there would seem to be no a priori reason to believe that American exceptionalism precludes the reemergence of anti-Semitism in the United States. In point of fact, there is certainly ample precedent in American history for an era of Jewish success to be followed by a period of decline—even anti-Semitism. During the Reconstruction era, Jews achieved a considerable measure of influence, but beginning in the 1880s they were systematically extruded from many key institutions in American society. Jews played important roles in Wilsonian Progressivism, but then were assailed through the post–World War I Red Scare and the immigrant restriction movement. The influence of Jews rose during the New Deal era, but institutions in which Jews were prominent, such as government bureaucracies, labor unions, and the entertainment industry, came under attack—at times manifestly anti-Semitic in character—during the McCarthy period.

In this way, the experience of Jews in America echoes the more general pattern of Jewish history. In a number of places and times, for example, fifteenth-century Spain, the Ottoman Empire, Weimar Germany, and postrevolutionary Russia, Jews achieved great power only to lose their influence and find themselves under assault.

Most theories of anti-Semitism seek to identify the roots of ethnic prejudice.[17] Some theorists locate these in economic relations. Others emphasize the role of religious institutions. Still others look to cultural differences and misunderstandings. No doubt, all of these explanations have some validity. It is not clear, however, that there is any mystery here to be explained. Whatever its psychological, social, economic, or even evolutionary basis, suspicion of strangers is the norm in all societies, while it is acceptance of outsiders that is unusual and generally ephemeral. When times are good and foreigners play a recognized and useful role in the community, they may be tolerated. On the other hand, when times are hard and outsiders seem to compete with their hosts, any latent popular xenophobia is more likely to manifest itself, and foreigners may become useful targets for rabble-rousing politicians. Recent events throughout Western Europe are unambiguous examples of this phenomenon.

Certainly, everywhere that Jews have lived, their social or economic marginality—their position, "outside society," as Hannah Arendt put it—sooner or later exposed Jews to suspicion, hostility, and discrimination. Even in multiethnic societies, Jews have usually been the most successful and visible—and, hence, the most exposed—outsiders. In America, Jews currently appear to be accepted by the larger community.[18] Nevertheless, at least in part by their own choosing, American Jews continue to maintain a significant and visible measure of communal identity and distinctiveness in religious, cultural, and political matters. At the same time, most gentiles continue to perceive Jews to be a peculiar and distinctive group.[19] Though Jews have learned to look, talk, and dress like other Americans, they are not fully assimilated either in their own minds or in the eyes of their neighbors. Even in America, the marginality of the Jews makes them at least potentially vulnerable to attack.

In America as elsewhere, moreover, Jews are outsiders who are often more successful than their hosts. Because of their historic and, in part, religiously grounded emphasis on education and literacy, when given an opportunity Jews have tended to prosper. And, to make matters worse, Jews often, secretly or not so secretly, conceive themselves to be morally and intellectually superior to their neighbors. Jews, to be sure, by no means have a monopoly on group or national snobbery. In contemporary America every group is encouraged to take pride in its special heritage and achievements. The problem is that Jews as a group *are* more successful than virtually all the others. Indeed, Jews are extremely successful outsiders who sometimes have the temerity to rub it in. As one outraged right-wing columnist noted recently, a Yiddish synonym for dullard or dope is "goyischer kopf," that is, someone who thinks like a non-Jew.[20]

The question with which this book is concerned, however, is not so much the roots of anti-Jewish sentiment as the conditions under which such sentiment is likely to be politically mobilized. As we shall see, where an anti-Semitic politics becomes important, usually more is involved than simple malice toward the Jews. In politics, principles—even as unprincipled a principle as anti-Semitism—are seldom completely divorced from some set of political interests. In the case of anti-Semitism, major organized campaigns against the Jews usually reflect not only ethnic hatred, they also represent efforts by the political opponents of regimes or movements with which Jews are allied to destroy or supplant them. Anti-Semitism has an instrumental as well as an emotive character. Thus, to understand the cycle of Jewish success and anti-Semitic attack—and to understand why the United States is not exceptional—it is necessary to consider the place of Jews in politics particularly, as Hannah Arendt noted long ago, their peculiar relationship to the state.[21]

Jews and the State

For nearly two thousand years, Jews lived as scattered minorities while preserving a considerable measure of communal identity and cultural distinctiveness from the societies that surrounded them. Their distinctiveness was maintained by Jews' religious and communal institutions and was often reinforced by the hostility of their neighbors and the antipathy of Moslem and Christian religious institutions. Jewish religious practice required male participants to read prayers and other texts, and hence Jewish men received a measure of education that made them considerably more literate and numerate than the people among whom they lived. Their geographic dispersion and literacy combined to help Jews become important traders in the medieval and early modern worlds. Jewish merchants, linked by ties of religion, culture, and often family, played an important role in international commerce.

At the same time, however, their literacy, commercial acumen, and even their social marginality often made Jews useful to kings, princes, and sultans. Into the eighteenth century, rulers regularly relied upon Jews as a source of literate administrators and advisors. European monarchs, moreover, depended upon Jewish financiers to manage their fiscal affairs and relied heavily upon Jewish merchants and bankers for loans. In addition, because Jews remained outsiders to the societies in which they lived, sovereigns found them useful instruments for carrying out unpopular tasks, notably collecting taxes.

For their part, Jews, who like Sikhs and other ethnic minorities offered the state's protection in exchange for services, have usually conceived it to be to their advantage to undertake these tasks. Indeed, Jews often saw this as their only viable alternative. Social marginality made Jews the objects of popular hostility at times shading into violence, and kings could offer a Jewish community protection in exchange for its services. At the same time, the crown could provide Jews with financial opportunities and allow them to enter commercial fields that would otherwise have been closed to them. This exchange of protection and opportunity for service was the foundation for a centuries-long relationship between Jews and the state. Such alliances were responsible for the construction of some of the most powerful states of the Mediterranean and European worlds, including the Hapsburg, Hohenzollern, and Ottoman empires.

These patterns persisted into the nineteenth and twentieth centuries. Jews have maintained a sense of distinctiveness from surrounding societies and have, as a result, continued to experience a measure of suspicion, hostility, and discrimination. Concern about their neighbors' attitudes toward them has continued to lead Jews to seek the protection of the state. At the same time, modern Jewish secular culture, like its religious antecedents, has emphasized education. This has enabled Jews to acquire professional and technical skills that can make them as valuable to presidents, prime ministers, and commissars as they had been to monarchs.

Where Jews have been unable to obtain protection from existing states, they have often played active roles in movements seeking to reform or supplant these regimes with new ones more favorably disposed toward them. Thus, in the nineteenth century, middle-class Jews were active in liberal movements that advocated the removal of religious disabilities. At the same time, working-class Jews were prominent in socialist and communist movements that sought the overthrow of existing regimes in the name of full social equality. In some cases, including Wilhelmian Germany and Hapsburg Austria-Hungary, regimes provided access to a small number of very wealthy Jews while subjecting the remainder to various forms of exclusion. In those cases, Jews could be found both at the pinnacles of power and among the leaders of the opposition.

Over the past several centuries, then, Jews have played a major role both in the strengthening of existing states and in efforts to supplant established regimes with new ones. Their relationship to the state has often made it possible for Jews to attain great wealth and power. At the same time, however, relationships between Jews and states have also been the chief catalysts for organized anti-Semitism.

Even when they are closely linked to the state, Jews usually continue to be a separate and distinctive group in society and, so, to arouse the suspicions of their neighbors. Indeed, in the service of the state, Jews have often become very visible and extremely powerful outsiders and thus awakened more suspicion and jealousy than ever before. As a result, the relationship between Jews and the state is always problematic. An identification with Jews can weaken the state by exposing it to attack as the servant of foreigners. Correlatively, Jews' identification with the state invites political forces that are seeking to take over or destroy the established order to make use of anti-Semitism as a political weapon.

In contemporary America, for example, radical populist fringe groups such as "The Order" and the "White Aryan Resistance" refer to the administration of the United States as the "ZOG," or "Zionist Occupation Government"—a corrupt tool of the Jews who are so prominent in the American political elite. Not so differently, Patrick Buchanan has referred to the United States Congress as "Israeli occupied territory," in this way defining a political institution controlled by his liberal Democratic foes as nothing more than a Jewish front.

It is in these struggles between regimes and their enemies that popular supicion of Jews is often mobilized by contending political forces and transformed into organized anti-Semitism. This is when the embrace of the state, initially filled with so much promise, can prove to be fatal.

In the remainder of this chapter, we shall first examine the centuries-long history of the relationship between Jews and the state in Europe and the Middle East. Second, we will look at the ways in which this association can give rise to organized anti-Semitism. In subsequent chapters, we shall examine the relationship between Jews, the state, and anti-Semitism in American history.

Chapter 2 will treat the period between the Civil War and the great Red Scare that followed World War I. Chapter 3 will focus on the New Deal, the Kennedy and Johnson periods, and the era of the "New Politics" in the 1970s. At the turn of the century, Jews had been extruded from American political and social life. By the 1970s, however, Jews had attained enormous influence in the political process. Chapters 4 and 5 will examine two of the major threats to that influence. Chapter 4 will discuss the contemporary conflict between Jews and blacks, while Chapter 5 will analyze the rise and fall of the Jewish/Republican alliance of the 1980s. Chapter 6 will assess the prospects for a revival of anti-Semitism in contemporary America. As we shall see, the Jewish experience in America has not been exceptional, even though the embrace of the state has not been fatal—at least not yet.

Jews, States, and Anti-Semitism

Jews played key roles in constructing a number of the most important states to emerge in the Mediterranean and Atlantic worlds over the past 700 years. These have included an extraordinary variety of regimes running the gamut from absolutist through liberal to Socialist governments. For many of these states, Jews were crucial in building and staffing institutions of extraction, coercion, administration, and mobilization. As we shall subsequently see, these relationships between Jews and the state have been the chief catalysts for organized anti-Semitism.

As a foreign minority, wherever they lived Jews have faced disabilities and dangers. The protection of the state, therefore, has for centuries seemed to represent opportunity and safety. For example, in both Europe and the Middle East during the medieval era, Jews were eager to induce rulers to grant them privileges and provide them with protection from potentially hostile neighbors. Because Jews tended to stimulate commerce and were a useful source of tax revenues, rulers were often happy to oblige.

The bishopric of Speyer is a typical example. During the eleventh century, the Jews of Speyer asked the ruling prince-bishop to grant them a charter of privileges and to build a defensive wall around their quarter. Because the Jews were economically valuable and he wished to induce more to settle in his city, the bishop agreed. Subsequently, the bishop protected the Jewish community from rioting crusaders, going so far as to hang the ring leaders of the mob that sought to attack the Jewish quarter.[22]

Similarly, in twelfth-century Germany, in the wake of crusader pogroms, Jews sought and were granted royal protection under the "Land Peace" of the German king. Here, too, the activities of Jewish merchants were deemed economically useful.[23] It is an interesting fact that the yellow badge Jews were required to wear in Nazi Germany and German-occupied Europe during the 1930s and 1940s originated as a symbol of the official protection Jews enjoyed in Muslim lands during portions of the Middle Ages. The badge was a visible reminder to Moslems that it was not permissible to attack Jews.[24]

Frequently, Jewish communal leaders sought an alliance with the state for still another reason. Not only did they offer protection and opportunity for the community, but the Gentile authorities could bolster the position of their Jewish colleagues by providing them with what they otherwise lacked: coercive powers through which to enforce their commands. In turn, the Gentile authorities welcomed a cooperative relationship with Jewish communal leaders because this facilitated the collection of taxes from the Jews. Thus, the Gentile government and Jewish communal authorities could serve one another's interests.

For example, in seventeenth- and eighteenth-century Poland, the verdicts of Jewish courts were enforced by the royal authorities, sometimes even in cases involving non-Jews. In exchange, the Jewish authorities ensured the proper collection of taxes from the Jewish community.[25] For a similar reason, in medieval Spain, edicts of the Jewish authorities, even in matters pertaining strictly to religious practice such as the wearing of a hat on the Sabbath, were enforceable by the crown's officials.[26] In the Byzantine empire, the state recognized Jewish courts of law and enforced their decisions.[27] In the Muslim Middle East, the alliance between the Gentile state and the Jewish leadership could sometimes be very strong, indeed, with the leaders of the Jewish community serving, simultaneously, as officials of the host state.[28]

Partly as a consequence of this historic experience, Jews often continued to look to the state for protection even when it was the state itself that was the source of their problems. Thus, in his famous work, *Shevet Yehuda,* written in the wake of the Jewish—and his personal—expulsion from Spain, Solomon ibn Verga sought to portray the rulers of Spain, including Ferdinand and Isabella who ordered the expulsion, as the allies of the Jews.[29]

In a similar vein, as Arendt and others have observed, to the very end many German Jews could not believe that the German state would fail to protect them from the excesses of Nazi fanatics.[30] The historical dependence of Jews upon the state also gave rise to a Jewish philosophical tradition, beginning in the seventeenth century with Spinoza and continuing through the *maskilim* of the eighteenth and nineteenth centuries, in which the state is glorified and venerated and seen, essentially, as a kind parent worthy of total obedience.[31]

As we shall see, Jews have continued to look to the state for protection and opportunity through the modern era. And, for their part, rulers have continued to see advantages in allying themselves with Jews. A confluence of three circumstances is most likely to encourage rulers to cultivate alliances with Jews. These are the desire to strengthen the powers of the state, substantial opposition to this endeavor from established elites, and the absence of alternative sources of financial, intellectual, and administrative talent. The latter consideration has also led many liberal and socialist movements to draw upon the support of Jews.

Jews and the Absolutist State

Despite the severe disabilities to which religious minorities were typically subject, Jews played a remarkable role in the building of a number of absolutist regimes in both Christian Europe and the Muslim Middle East. Rulers were most likely to turn to Jews when they sought to expand their domains at the expense of foreign princes or centralize their power over the opposition of domestic magnates. The Jews who served absolutist regimes secured riches and power for themselves and protection for their communities.

In Europe this pattern was especially notable in Christian Spain from the eleventh through the fifteenth centuries. Medieval Spain consisted of a number of independent kingdoms containing large numbers of Muslims as well as more than 300,000 Jews in a total population of about 5 million. Throughout Spain, Jews were active in the crafts, trade, scholarship, and in the learned professions, especially medicine. Jews were so prominent in the economies of the Spanish kingdoms that their tax payments were major factors in royal treasuries, sometimes accounting for half of all royal revenues.[32]

In sharp contrast to England and France where clerical orders played an important part in the royal administration, the Spanish church and clerical orders had been militarized during the centuries-long war against the Moors, and had come to be more closely linked with the territorial nobility than the crown. As a result, kings had little alternative but to draw heavily upon the talents of Jews as administrators.[33] Spanish kings also depended upon Jews as tax collectors and financiers, particularly in Castile, the most powerful and populous of the Christian realms where, as John Crow has noted, royal power in essence was sustained by Jewish money, industry, and intelligence.[34] Jews played a particularly important role in the efforts of Alfonso X (1252–1284), Pedro the Cruel (1350–1369), Juan II (1406–1454), and Henry IV (1454–1474) to centralize royal authority at the expense of the nobility as well as in the efforts of these monarchs to expand the boundaries of the Castilian state.[35]

To be sure, Jews were ineligible to serve in the very highest offices. The number of literate and educated Christians in medieval Spain, however, was small. Consequently, to secure administrators with the requisite talents, Spanish kings often found it necessary to appoint Jews who had nominally converted to Christianity—so-called conversos or New Christians—to high administrative positions. At the end of the fifteenth century, for instance, the occupants of the five highest administrative offices in Aragon were all conversos.[36] Indeed, even the Spanish church was heavily dependent upon this source of administrative talent. A particularly notable example is the career of Salomon Halevi. Though he served as chief rabbi of Burgos, Halevi was converted to Christianity in 1390, adopting the name Pablo de Santa Maria. Soon thereafter, as Henry Kamen reports, Halevi took holy orders and became in turn bishop of Cartagena, bishop of Burgos, tutor to the son of Henry II, and papal legate. One of his sons, Gonzalo, became bishop successively of Astorga, Plasencia, and Siguenza. Another son, Alonso de Cartagena, succeeded him as bishop of Burgos.[37] As we shall see, the extraordinary position that Jews occupied in the Spanish kingdoms was directly linked to their later expulsion.

Jews also played a major role in state finance and administration in the medieval Muslim world. As the Umayyeds expanded their control of the Iberian peninsula in the tenth and eleventh centuries, they depended heavily upon Jewish administrators and diplomats. Hasday b. Shaprut (905–975), for example, was a major figure in the courts of the caliphs Abd al-Rahman III and al-Hakam II.[38] In the eleventh century, Jews attained the highest levels of political power in Muslim Spain, including the viziership of Grenada, a position held by Samuel b. Naghrela (Samuel ha-Nagid), a Jewish soldier and politician, from 1026–1056. Other powerful Jewish administrators included Yequtiel b. Hasan (d. 1039) in Saragossa and Abraham b. Muhajir (d. ca. 1100) in Seville.[39]

In Fatimid North Africa during the tenth and eleventh centuries, Jews were important bankers, financiers, and advisors to the caliphate. During the reign of al-Mustansir, who succeeded to the caliphate in 1036 while still a small boy, the power behind the Fatimid throne was the Jewish financier and courtier, Abu Saed Ibrahim al-Tustari.[40] Dhimmis, or nonbelievers, were precluded from holding the very highest Fatimid offices, such as the vizierate. Paralleling the case of Christian Spain, however, several nominally converted Jews became viziers.

One such official, Yaqub b. Killis, converted to Islam specifically in order to advance his political career and, as vizier, helped to plan the Fatimid conquest of Egypt in 969. Subsequently, he reorganized the new province, revamping its fiscal system and currency, and prepared Egypt to become the seat of Fatimid government.[41] Other converts who became Fatimid viziers included Hasan b. Ibrahim al-Tustari and Sadaqa b. Yusuf al-Fallahi. The Ayyubids (1171–1250), who succeeded the Fatimids. also employed large numbers of Jews and Jewish converts as administrators.

During the fifteenth and sixteenth centuries, Jews came to play a major role in the fiscal affairs and administration of the Ottoman empire. After the expulsion of the Jews from Spain in 1492, the Ottomans accepted thousands of refugees because they valued the financial, administrative, and manufacturing skills that the Jews brought with them. Sultan Bayazid II is reported to have remarked that King Ferdinand was foolish to have expelled such talented subjects. Jews were particularly useful to the Ottomans because they lacked ties to any of the subject populations of the multiethnic empire and, thus, could be entrusted with unpopular tasks such as tax collection.

Jews dominated the imperial revenue system, serving as tax collectors, tax farmers, tax intendants, and tax inspectors. Jews also created and operated the imperial customs service. Indeed, so complete was Jewish control over this segment of the Ottoman state that Ottoman customs receipts were typically written in Hebrew. Jews also accompanied provincial governors or "pashas," as financial advisors and fiscal administrators. In the latter days of the empire, when provincial governorships became hereditary or quasi-independent, local Jewish financiers continued in this capacity. For example, the Farhi family of Damascus directed the financial affairs of Syria from the eighteenth century through the termination of Ottoman rule after World War I.[42]

A number of Jews also became important advisors to the Ottoman court. The most famous was Joseph Nasi, who was the principle counselor to two sultans and was ennobled as the duke of Naxos. Nasi used his influence to secure the sultan's support for the reestablishment of a Jewish homeland in Palestine, then under Ottoman rule. With the sultan's help, a Jewish settlement was created in Safed, in the upper Galilee, that became a center for rabbinic study. Unfortunately, not all of Nasi's advice was sound. It was his plan that helped to bring about the Turkish naval defeat in the battle of Lepanto in 1571, and, as a result, his influence at court declined.[43]

Another major Ottoman state institution that relied upon Jewish administrators was the imperial army—the janissary corps. Jews dominated the position of ocak bazirgani, or chief quartermaster for the corps. This became the hereditary possession of a small group of Jewish families in Istanbul and Salonika. In addition, each provincial janissary garrison had its own quartermaster, virtually always a Jewish merchant.[44]

Absolutist regimes were constructed throughout Europe from the sixteenth century. Some state-building monarchs, most notably those of France, England, and Tsarist Russia were able to make use of the church or to co-opt segments of the aristocracy for this endeavor. The church was a particularly important source of literate and experienced administrators. Cardinals Richelieu in France and Wolsey in England are notable examples.

Where, for one or another reason, monarchs were unable to make use of established institutions and elites in this way, they often found it useful to turn to Jews. For example, to finance his conquest of England, William of Orange turned to the Dutch Jewish financiers who, descended from Spanish exiles, had helped to make Holland a major commercial center and played an important role in the finances of the Dutch state. In 1688, William obtained a loan of two million gulden from the Lopez Suasso family. After he secured control of the English throne, William encouraged a number of Jewish financiers, most notably the Machado and Pereire families, to move to London where they financed William's effort to form a military coalition against Louis XIV.[45]

In the less heavily urbanized and commercialized European periphery, the savings of Jewish merchants and traders represented one of the few sources of liquid capital. Jewish financiers could mobilize this capital and provide monarchs with loans to underwrite war making and state building. Thus, in Central Europe, so-called Court Jews served as administrators, financiers, and military provisioners.[46] The Hapsburg emperors of Austria relied upon Jews for these purposes from the late sixteenth century and, in return, provided Jews with protection from riots and pogroms. For example, when a mob attacked Frankfurt's Jewish quarter in 1614, Emperor Matthias moved forcefully against the rioters and hanged their leaders.[47]

After the Thirty Years War broke out in 1618, the Hapsburg emperor, Ferdinand II, turned to financier Joseph Bassevi of Prague to finance the war effort. Bassevi was allied with the most powerful figure at the imperial court, Prince Liechtenstein, and with General Wallenstein, commander of the imperial armies. In exchange for loans to finance the war, Emperor Ferdinand leased the imperial mint to Bassevi, Liechtenstein, and Wallenstein. The three men recouped their investment by debasing the coinage.[48] Bassevi also established a network through which to supply the imperial armies with food, fodder, arms, and ammunition. During and after the Thirty Years War, virtually all the major states in Central Europe and Scandinavia found it necessary to make use of the resources and talents of Jews to compete with their rivals. The Hohenzollern rulers of Prussia relied initially upon Israel Aaron and then upon the Gomperz family. The Behrends served the court of Hanover and the Lehmans Saxony, while the Fuersts served Schleswig-Holstein, Mecklenberg, and Holstein-Gottorp. The Danish royal family employed the Goldschmidts, while Gustavus Adolphus of Sweden relied upon Jewish contractors to provision his army.[49]

Jews continued to serve absolutist states in these ways through the nineteenth century. The most prominent of these Jews, of course, was the Rothschild family whose name came to be synonymous with international finance. The founder of the dynasty, Mayer Amschel Rothschild of Frankfurt, was the chief financial agent for William IX, elector of Hesse-Cassel. During and after the Napoleonic wars, Mayer dispatched his sons to the major financial capitols of Europe—London, Paris, Vienna, and Naples. Nathan Rothschild, who headed the London branch of the family, saved William IX's fortune by investing it in England and served the British government by transferring millions of pounds in gold to the British army in Spain.

In the decades after the war, governments became increasingly dependent upon foreign borrowing—an activity that the Rothschilds came to dominate. Between 1818 and 1832, Nathan Rothschild handled 39% of the loans floated in London by such governments as Austria, Russia and France. Similarly, the Vienna and Paris branches of the family raised money and sold bonds for the Hapsburgs, Bourbons, Orleanists, and Bonaparts. By mid-century, the entire European state system was dependent upon the international financial network dominated by the Rothschilds.[50]

In the 1860s and 1870s, another Jewish financier, Baron Gerson von Bleichroeder, was a principal figure in the creation of a united German state. Bleichroeder helped Bismarck obtain loans for the war against Austria after the chancellor failed to secure financing from the Prussian parliament. Subsequently, Bismarck entrusted Bleichroeder with negotiating the indemnity to be paid by France after its defeat in the Franco-Prussian War in 1871 (on the French side, negotiations were conducted by the Rothschilds). During Bismarck's tenure as chancellor of a united Germany, Bleichroeder continued to serve as his chief confidente and fiscal advisor.[51]

Jews and the Liberal State

Absolutist regimes provided a small number of Jews with the opportunity to exercise considerable power and acquire great wealth. Liberals in the nineteenth century, by contrast, advocated legal equality and national citizenship for all Jews, holding out the promise of economic opportunity for broad segments of the Jewish community. As a result, Jews supported liberal movements everywhere and benefited from their success. Where liberal forces were strongest—in France, Britain, and, of course, the United States—this Jewish support was not critical to liberalism's success. Jewish participation, however, was important in Southern and Central Europe where liberal movements faced their greatest obstacles.[52]

Jews in substantial numbers supported Mazzini's "Young Italy" movement and took part in the uprisings of the 1830s. In addition, Mazzini received considerable financial aid from the Jewish banking firm of Todros in Turin. Subsequently, the Jewish banking houses of Rothschild, Bendi, and Tedesco financed Cavour's efforts to unify Italy. Jews were also important in Cavour's inner circle, serving as publicists for his cause and members of his cabinets. From early in his career, Cavour was a staunch advocate of Jewish emancipation.[53]

Significant numbers of Jews participated in the liberal revolutions of 1848 in central Europe. In Germany, Jews fought at the barricades in Berlin and helped to lead the Prussian national assembly and

Frankfurt parliament. Such intellectuals as Heinrich Heine and Ludwig Borne were major publicists and propagandists for the liberal cause. In Austria, Jews participated in the Vienna uprising and helped to formulate a new liberal constitution. In Hungary, 20,000 Jews enlisted in the national army formed by Louis Kossuth. The constitutions of most of the liberal regimes established in 1848 provided for emancipation of the Jews. After these regimes were overthrown by conservative forces, however, many of the Jews' new privileges were rescinded. Central European Jews continued to support liberal movements even after the revolutions of 1848 were defeated.[54] In the 1860s and 1870s Austrian and German rulers were compelled to make concessions to liberal forces, and Jewish disabilities were removed as they had been earlier in France and Britain when liberal regimes were consolidated in those countries.

If the distinctive contribution of Jews to the construction of absolutist states lay in the realm of finance and military provisioning, their characteristic role in the development of liberal regimes was in the domain of political mobilization and opinion formation. Liberal regimes removed religious disabilities and opened up opportunities for Jews in business and the professions. This cleared the way for a great expansion of the Jewish business class and fostered the emergence of an important urban Jewish stratum consisting of lawyers, journalists, writers, physicians, and other professionals. These businessmen and professionals became important figures in the popular politics of the liberal era as publishers, editors, writers, politicians, political organizers, and party financiers. In these capacities, Jews were staunch supporters of the liberal state and important allies for those leaders who sought to strengthen it.

In France, Jews supported the liberal revolution of 1848. Two prominent Jews, Adolphe Cremieux and Michel Goudchaux, served the Second Republic as ministers of justice and finance, respectively. The accession of Napoleon III brought an end to this short-lived regime, and Jews played little role in the Second Empire that followed. After the rout of French forces in the Franco-Prussian War and the collapse of the Second Empire in 1870, Jews were active in the founding of the Third Republic. The Rothschilds organized the payment of the German war indemnity, and a number of Jews participated in the early republican governments. Cremieux once again served as minister of justice; Eugene Manuel, Narcisse Leven, and Leonce Lehmann occupied important government posts; and several Jews served in the Chamber of Deputies. Throughout the history of the Third Republic, until its destruction at the hands of the Germans in 1940, Jewish politicians, financiers, and publicists were active participants in the defense of the Republic against those institutions and forces in French society—the army, aristocracy, and clergy in particular—that sought its downfall.[55]

A small number of Jewish financiers had become wealthy during the period of the Second Empire. On the whole, however, most French Jews lived in relative poverty in Alsace prior to the 1870s. With Germany's annexation of Alsace in 1870, thousands of Jews moved to Paris. Under the auspices of the Third Republic economic opportunities opened to Jews, and they used these to make significant places for themselves in banking, commerce, and the professions.

Between the Franco-Prussian War and the First World War, Paris was a major international banking and financial center, and Jews were among the dominant figures in French finance. In the late nineteenth century, roughly one-third of all Paris bankers were Jews. Among the most prominent were the Rothschilds, the Camondos, the Leoninos, and such financiers as Bamberger, Reinach, Stern, Deutsch, Heine, Ephrussi, Goudchaux, Lippmann, Pereire, and Bischoffsheim.

These bankers were heavily involved with the development of railroads and industry within France and also loaned large amounts of money abroad, especially in the Middle East and North Africa. Their clients included the rulers of Egypt, Tunis, Turkey, and Morocco, Louis-Raphael Bischoffsheim, a prominent Jewish banker, was typical of this group. He financed a number of railways in the south of France as well as provided funding for both governments and private ventures in North Africa. He served as a director of the Banque des Pay-Bas, the Credit Foncier Colonial, the Franco-Egyptian Bank, and the Société du Prince Imperial.

Similarly, the financiers Emile and Isaac Pereire founded the Credit Mobilier, one of the first investment banks in France. Isaac's son Eugene, also a banker, developed railroads in the Midi and in Spain. Isaac Pereire had interests in the Middle East as well, and at one point he served as France's honorary consul in Persia. Isaac Camondo, whose father immigrated from Turkey, was a major figure in French industrial development, serving as head of the Banque de Paris et des Pays-Bas as well as president of a number of railroad, natural gas, and cement companies.

Jews were very active in the political life of the Third Republic. Before the First World War, they were most closely identified with

Leon Gambetta's liberal "Opportunist" faction of the Radical Republican party. Prominent Jewish Gambettists included Cremieux, Leven, and Lehmann as well as Isaie Levaillant, Edouard Millaud, Joseph Reinach, and David Raynal. Cremieux was Gambetta's first political mentor; Reinach was the owner and editor of the Gambettist newspaper. Jews figured so prominently in the Gambettist faction that its opponents often charged that Gambetta himself must be a Jew. After Gambetta's death, Jews continued to be closely aligned with his most prominent political heir, Jules Ferry.[56]

Early in his career, Gambetta had been something of an economic radical. By the late 1870s and 1880s, however, the Gambettists had come to be identified with a probusiness position similar to that of American Republicans during the same period. In addition, the Gambettists were the chief proponents of anticlerical legislation and, especially under Ferry's leadership, pursued a policy of French imperial expansion in Africa, the Near East, and Asia.

These positions were congenial to the interests of French Jews. The Gambettists' anticlerical legislation reduced the political power of the Catholic church, an institution that by definition excluded Jews. Jewish businessmen welcomed the Gambettists' program for promoting domestic economic development, which included a protective tariff, tax incentives, and support for railroad construction. Gambettist colonial policy served the interests of those who sought protection for the investments in North Africa and the Near East.

Through their political activities, Jews helped to strengthen the liberal state vis-à-vis its opponents. In particular, Jews threw their weight behind the anticlerical campaign, thus helping to undermine the power of a leading bastion of opposition to the Republic. In alliance with the army, the aristocracy, and the administrative corps, the Catholic church opposed the Republic and sought the restoration of a monarchy.

The church's control of the nation's educational system made it an especially important member of this alliance. Thus, from the perspective of republican forces, it was critically important to strip the church of its educational functions. Joseph Reinach, Alfred Naquet, and Georges Mandel, along with other Jewish politicians and journalists, played a leading role in the republican anticlerical campaign. Jews helped to formulate the educational program of the Ferry government which, in 1882, broke the church's educational monopoly by establishing a system of free primary schools where religious instruction was forbidden. This reform of the educational system, followed in 1884 by the Ferry government's enactment of a law permitting divorce, was seen as a major blow against the political power of the Catholic church and, hence, the entire antirepublican coalition.

In Britain, Jews did not figure in the creation of the liberal state. However, Jewish politicians, publishers, and financiers helped to strengthen the liberal regime and expand its popular base between the Crimean War and the First World War. During the mid- and late nineteenth centuries, British Jews achieved considerable wealth, status, and political influence. The Rothschilds were one of the two most important banking families in Britain. Other important Jewish financiers included the Sassoons, the Cassels, the de Hirsch family, and the Semons. By the First World War, though Jews constituted only 1% of the total population of Britain, 23% of Britain's non-landed millionaires were of Jewish origin.[57]

In the middle decades of the nineteenth century, Jews also came to be a major factor in British journalism. The Reuters News Agency, founded by Paul Julius Reuter (whose name was originally Israel Beer Josaphat) in 1848, was the chief purveyor of information on world events to the entire British press and, at times, the government as well. The Sassoons owned and edited the *Sunday Times*, Harry Marks founded the *Financial Times*, and Sir Alfred Mond controlled the *English Review*. Jews were especially important in the popular press. The *Daily Telegraph*, controlled by the Levy Lawson family, was London's first penny newspaper and, in the 1870s, had a circulation of just under 200,000. The *Telegraph* appealed mainly to a lower-middle- and working-class audience and specialized in sensational coverage of both domestic and foreign events. Harry Oppenheim had a major interest in another mass circulation daily, the *London Daily News*. Sir Alfred Mond published the *Westminster Gazette*, a paper that provided its popular audience with dramatic coverage of the exploits of British military forces in the far-flung reaches of the empire.[58]

During the same period of time, a number of Jews served as members of Parliament and rose to positions of considerable influence in the British government. Obviously, the most notable example is Benjamin Disraeli, a converted Jew who served twice as prime minister between 1868 and 1880, and along with William Gladstone was the dominant figure in British politics in the late nineteenth century. Other prominent Jewish politicians in the pre–World War I era include G. J. Goschen, who served as chancellor of the exchecquer from 1887 to 1892; Farrer Herschell, who was lord chancellor in 1886 and again in 1892–1895; Sir George Jessel, solicitor general from 1871 to 1873; Rufus Isaccs, who served as solicitor general in

1910, attorney general from 1910 to 1913, and lord chief justice in 1913; and Edwin Samuel Montagu, who served as under-secretary of state for India.

These Jewish political and business elites helped to consolidate the liberal regime in Britain by reconciling conservative forces to democratic politics and by expanding the resources and popular base of the British state. The key figure in this process was Benjamin Disraeli. Disraeli helped develop the techniques of party management and electioneering that ultimately restored the competitiveness of the Conservative party in the aftermath of the expansion of the suffrage in 1832. Moreover, Disraeli himself engineered a further expansion of the suffrage in 1867 that brought portions of the lower-middle and upper working classes into the national electorate. By showing Conservatives how to win in this new political universe, he cemented their attachment to the liberal state.[59]

In addition, Disraeli helped to fashion an imperialist program that, in the latter decades of the nineteenth century, bound together the aristocracy and the military and administrative establishments with segments of the financial community, the press, and the middle class in a coalition that would support his efforts to strengthen the British state. The Disraeli government's policy of imperial expansion in India, the Middle East, and Africa yielded important political and economic benefits for the participants in this coalition. The aristocracy, the military, and the administrative elite secured positions of influence and control over a larger share of the nation's resources. At the same time, for members of the middle class lacking family and social connections, the work of building and administering the empire offered career opportunities often superior to those available at home. These benefits provided the members of the imperialist coalition with strong reasons to favor expansion of the British state's scope, sweep, and power.

Jewish financiers and newspaper publishers were important participants in this coalition. In the late nineteenth century, more than one-fourth of all British capital was invested overseas. Long-established financial interests invested primarily in North America and Australia where property owners could rely upon the protection of local laws and authorities. Newer banking houses, a number of them Jewish, were more heavily invested in the Middle East, India, Asia, and Africa where local laws and authorities offered little security for foreign property. Here, British investors had to depend upon the protection of their own government and its military forces. This dependence gave Jewish financiers a stake in the creation of a strong national government able and willing to project its power throughout the world.

Jewish financial and business interests were important participants in the imperialist enterprise. For example, the Indian railroad network that the Sassoons helped to finance was closely integrated into the imperial administration, and Julius Reuter's wire service functioned as the command and control mechanism of the colonial government. Upon occasion, the British government also turned to Jewish banking houses to finance imperial expansion. Disraeli's purchase of the Suez Canal in 1878, for example, was made possible by Henry Oppenheim's extensive contacts in Egypt and a four million pound loan from Lionel Rothschild. The role played by Jewish capital in the creation of Britain's nineteenth-century empire was not lost on its critics. In his classic work, which became the basis of Lenin's theory of imperialism, J. A. Hobson argued that "men of a single and peculiar race, who have behind them centuries of financial experience," formed "the central ganglion of international capitalism."[60]

This theme also was prominent in the work of Goldwyn Smith, a noted scholar and opponent of Disraeli's imperialist policies. Smith frequently charged that the Disraeli government's foreign policies were motivated more by Jewish than British interests. He often extended his attacks to Jews in general, claiming that no Jew could be a true Englishman or patriot. Indeed, Smith asserted that Jewish emancipation had itself been a tragic error.[61] Eventually, Smith left England—refusing to be governed by a Jew—and joined the faculty of the newly established Cornell University in rural New York. Today, one of Cornell's major buildings honors Smith's memory, and excerpts from his writings and speeches are reprinted often in official university publications.

For its part, the Jewish-owned popular press worked to rally public support for the government's imperialist endeavors. The press depicted the conquest and subjugation of foreign territories as a great adventure. Generals like Kitchener and Gordon were portrayed as heroic figures. Journalists captured the popular imagination with accounts of the exploits of British forces in faraway lands. The *Westminster Gazette*'s vivid depiction of a minor British military expedition in the Sudan is typical:

A large number of the Tommies had never been under fire before . . . and there was a curious look of suppressed excitement in some of the faces . . . Now and then I caught in a man's eye the curious gleam which comes from shedding blood—that mysterious impulse which, despite all the veneer of civilization, still holds its own in man's nature, whether he is killing rats with a terrier, rejoicing in a prize fight, playing a salmon or potting dervishes. It was a fine day and we were out to kill something. Call it what you like, the experience is a big factor in the joy of living.[62]

The Reuters news service was particularly important in popularizing imperialism. Reuter's specialized in the collection and dissemination of news from the furthest outposts of the empire. Its dispatches, upon which all British newspapers came to rely, emphasized the positive, "civilizing" aspects of British colonial administration and military campaigns. The steady diet of campaigns, battles, and raids in Reuter's dispatches, along with news of the more mundane details of colonial rule, maintained popular interest in the empire and made it an accepted part of British life.[63] The press benefited in a direct way from its coverage of these matters. The British popular press, like its American counterpart during the Spanish-American War, discovered that exciting tales of empire building gave an enormous boost to circulation and revenues.

Jews also played a major role in German liberalism. Before the First World War, though Jews comprised barely 1% of the German population, they constituted a major segment of the bourgeoisie and an important base of support for liberals. Jews had been particularly important in the liberal press. Two of the most important liberal newspapers, the *National-Zeitung* of Berlin and the *Frankfurter Zeitung*, were owned and edited by Jews. Of the twenty-one daily newspapers published in Berlin during the 1870s, thirteen were owned by Jews and four had important Jewish contributors. All three newspapers specializing in political satire were controlled by Jews.[64]

In the aftermath of World War I, Jews strongly supported the creation of the liberal Weimar Republic. Indeed, a Jewish socialist, Hugo Preuss who served as minister of the interior in the provisional government established after the collapse of the monarchy, was primarily responsible for drafting the Weimar constitution. Throughout the life of the Weimar regime, Jewish businessmen, journalists, and politicians were among its most active and ardent supporters.

Through their commercial and banking activities, Jews contributed to the substantial economic development and reconstruction that took place during the Weimar era. Jewish firms accounted for nearly 80% of the business done by department and chain stores, 40% of Germany's wholesale textile firms, and 60% of all wholesale and retail clothing businesses. Almost half of all private banks were owned by Jews, as were the largest and most successful of the credit banks. The most important was the DD bank, formed from the merger between Arthur Salomonsohn's DiscontoGesellschaft and the Deutsche Bank. The DD bank helped to revive and rebuild Germany's heavy industry and merchant navy after World War I. The equally important Dresdner Bank was directed by Eugen Gutmann until his death in 1925 and then by Henry Nathan. The Darmstadter and Nationalbank, directed by Jakob Goldschmidt, was largely responsible for obtaining major loans of working capital for German industry from Holland, Sweden, and the United States.[65]

In a continuation of the pre–World War I pattern, Jews were influential in the liberal press of the Weimar Republic. Three of the nation's most important liberal newspapers, the *Berliner Tageblatt*, the *Vossiche Zeitung*, and the *Frankfurter Zeitung* were owned by Jews. Jews also owned the two largest publishing houses in Germany, the Ullstein and Mosse concerns, as well as many smaller publishing firms.

In addition, Jews were extremely important in the professional, intellectual, and cultural life of Weimar Germany. Approximately 11% of Germany's physicians and 16% of its lawyers were Jews. Jewish academics, intellectuals, and artists were the leading figures in German theater, literature, music, art, architecture, science, and philosophy during the Weimar era. Jews were also the most influential critics of drama, art, music, and books as well as the owners of the most important art galleries and theaters.[66]

Their central place in the economy and cultural life of Weimar Germany gave Jews a major stake in the liberal regime. The commitment of the Jews to this regime was, of course, greatly increased by the rise of the Nazis and other anti-Semitic movements seeking to overthrow the Weimar Republic. The virulent anti-Semitism of these groups provided Jews with a very strong incentive to fight for the survival of the Republic.

Although Jews had participated in the creation of the German Communist party (KPD), the overwhelming majority of German Jews backed parties and politicians who supported the Republic against its enemies on both the left and right. Most Jewish voters identified with the moderate Democratic party. A smaller number belonged to the Social Democratic party (SPD) which had largely abandoned its more radical prewar stance and given its support to the liberal regime. Many important Jewish politicians were liberals independent of party ties. These included Walter Rathenau, minister of the interior who was assassinated by right-wing extremists in

1922, and Curt Joel, the leading figure in the Reich ministry of justice from 1920 to 1931.

Because Jews constituted only 1% of Germany's population, their electoral weight was slight. Jews, however, were important financial contributors to liberal parties, and the political influence of the Jewish legal establishment, press, publishing industry, and other media was substantial. Jews were a major source of financial support for liberal parties including the Center, Democratic, and Social Democratic parties as well as the Bavarian People's party. As the militancy of the Nazis and other anti-Semitic parties on the political right grew after 1930, Jews also helped to fund the paramilitary "Reichsbanner" units formed by the Social Democrats to defend against violent attacks from right-wing thugs and paramilitary groups.

The Jewish legal establishment, too, played a role in opposing right-wing opponents of the Weimar Republic. Politicians of the right specialized in arousing their followers with inflammatory speeches that often provoked violent action. Lawyers funded by the Jewish Centralverein adopted the tactic of pressing charges of disorderly conduct or slander against such speakers and their followers. As a result of this technique, a number of prominent right-wing politicians, including Julius Streicher, Gregor Strasser, and Pastor Munchmeyer, were compelled to pay fines or serve short jail terms.[67]

Jewish journalists, writers, dramatists, and intellectuals were among the most determined opponents of the institutions and forces associated with the antirepublican political right. Writers like Kurt Tucholsky and Ernst Toller enraged conservative opinion by mounting fierce attacks on the Junkers and the army—the twin pillars of the old regime. Similarly, Jewish journalists were relentless in their criticism of the right-wing political parties and politicians that emerged after the war. In the end, of course, the exertions of the Jews on its behalf were not sufficient to save the Weimar regime. As we shall see, moreover, their strong identification with and defense of Weimar helped to make the Jews a more inviting target for the Republic's foes.

Jews and the Communist State

In Western Europe, middle- and upper-class Jews gave their support to liberal states that provided them with equality before the law, the right to participate in politics, professional opportunities, and protection for their investments. In nineteenth-century Eastern Europe, however, most Jews lived in poverty and faced a constant threat of violence from their neighbors and, often, from the authorities as well. Socialist movements spoke most directly to their concerns. They held out the hope of a state that would improve the economic conditions of the Jews and protect them from violence. Jewish subjects of the Russian and Austro-Hungarian empires were a major base of support for socialism. When millions emigrated to Central and Western Europe and the United States at the turn of the century, they often carried their socialist commitments with them.

In addition to the Jewish proletariat, middle-class Jewish intellectuals were often drawn to socialism. Particularly in Central Europe, many Jewish university graduates found that their career opportunities were not commensurate with their educational qualifications. In Germany, Jewish students were able to gain access to higher education; indeed, the proportion of the population attending universities was far greater among Jews than any other group. In Prussia, the largest German state, the proportion of Jews receiving university educations was ten times greater than the percentage of Protestants and Catholics. At the same time, however, Jewish university graduates were effectively barred from the civil service careers that attracted many of their fellow students.

Those Jews who sought to pursue academic careers found that their opportunities to attain secure professorial appointments were limited by the anti-Semitism that pervaded German universities. Before the First World War, nearly 20% of the part-time and temporary teaching staff at German universities were of Jewish origin. However, less than 7% of the full professors were Jews. At the most prestigious university, Berlin, there was not a single Jewish full professor. Examples of the difficulties faced by Jewish scholars are numerous. Georg Simmel, one of Germany's most brilliant sociologists and philosophers, was not awarded a full professorship at the University of Strassburg until four years before his death at the age of sixty. Similarly, Ernst Cassirer, Germany's leading neo-Kantian philosopher, could only secure a professorship at the new and struggling University of Hamburg.[68]

This lack of appropriate career opportunities often bred alienation among Jewish intellectuals and encouraged them to imagine a social and political order that allowed fuller play for their talents. As a result, members of the Jewish intelligentsia figured prominently, both as theoreticians and activists, in socialist and communist movements. For their part, such movements found that Jews' intellectual skills made them useful propagandists and organizers. Thus, in the late nineteenth century, Jewish intellectuals came to be a major element within the leadership of left-wing parties and movements.

In pre–World War I Germany, for example, Jews were extremely important in the Socialist party. The SPD was founded by a Jew, Ferdinand Lasalle, and Jews, including such individuals as Eduard Bernstein and Otto Landsberg, were among the party's most prominent parliamentary leaders. In addition, the party's leading journalists were Jews as were its most notable theorists—Bernstein, Adolf Braun, and Simon Katzenstein; its leading expert on municipal administration was a Jew, as was its expert on electoral law and its chief youth organizer, Ludwig Frank.[69]

Socialists dominated the provisional government established in Germany in the immediate aftermath of World War I. Two of this government's six cabinet members, Otto Landsberg and Hugo Haase, were Jews. Other Jewish Socialists also played important roles during this period. Kurt Eisner was prime minister of Bavaria in 1918–1919. Georg Gradnauer was prime minister of Saxony from 1919 to 1921. In Prussia, Paul Hirsch served as prime minister from 1918 to 1920 and Kurt Rosenfeld as minister of justice in 1918. As noted earlier, Hugo Preuss formulated the Weimar constitution and served as minister of the interior. After the creation of the Weimar Republic, Jews continued to play important roles in the leadership of the SPD. About 10% of the party's Reichstag deputies were Jews, including Rudolph Hilferding, who was minister of finance in 1923 and from 1928 to 1930.

Among the most vehement opponents of the Socialist provisional government was the German Communist party, whose leadership also included a number of Jews. In 1919, under the direction of party chief Paul Levi, the KPD staged a revolt against the Socialist provisional government. One of the most prominent leaders of this revolt was Rosa Luxemburg, who was later captured and murdered by rightist paramilitary forces. Jews were also among the leaders of the Communist government that the KPD briefly established in Bavaria after the murder of Kurt Eisner. Eugen Levine was head of the short-lived Bavarian Soviet Republic, Gustav Landauer was its commissar for propaganda and cultural affairs, and Ernst Toller commanded its "red army." This regime was crushed in May 1919 by free corps forces.[70]

Jews were also important in Socialist and Communist movements in a number of other nations including Britain, France, the United States, and most of the nations of East Central Europe. In Hungary, for example, Jews were prominent in the prewar Socialist movement and in the "Galileo Circle," the center of Budapest student radicalism. The Hungarian Communist government established by Bela Kun in 1919 was dominated by Jews. Twenty of the regime's twenty-six ministers and vice-ministers were of Jewish origin. This government was overthrown after one hundred days by French-backed Rumanian forces.[71]

In Russia a number of Jews, most notably Paul Axelrod and Lev Deutsch, were among the founders of the Social Democratic party in the 1890s. In addition, the Jewish Socialist Bund organized tens of thousands of workers in the Pale and played a major role in the unsuccessful 1905 revolution. During the period leading up to the 1917 Revolution, Jews were active in both the Menshevik and Bolshevik leaderships.[72]

After the Revolution, among the first official acts of the victorious Bolsheviks was outlawing the pogroms and anti-Semitic movements that Russian Jews had feared for centuries. In a radical break with the Russian past, moreover, the new regime provided Jews with the opportunity to participate fully in government and society. They quickly came to play a major role in the ruling Communist party and Soviet state. Jews were among the few supporters of the Revolution with even a modicum of education and literacy. Thus, they soon assumed positions of leadership in areas requiring such skills—foreign affairs, propaganda, finance, and administration.

Three of the six members of Lenin's first Politburo—Trotsky, Kamenev, and Zinoviev—were of Jewish origin. Trotsky, in addition, was commissar of defense and organized and commanded the Red Army during the civil war that followed the October Revolution. Kamenev and Zinoviev became members of the triumvirate (along with Stalin) that ruled the Soviet Union immediately after Lenin's death in 1924. Other prominent Jews in the early Soviet government included Yakov Sverdlov, president of the Communist party central committee, Maxim Litvinov, commissar for foreign affairs, and Karl Radek, who served as press commissar. In subsequent years, Jews continued to play major roles throughout the Soviet state. Lazar Kaganovich, for example, was one of Stalin's chief aides, commissar of heavy industry during the Second World War, and a member of the Politburo.

If the distinctive contribution of Jews to the absolutist state was in the realm of finance, and their singular role in liberal regimes was the mobilization of opinion, the special contribution of the Jews to the Bolshevik state involved the organization of coercion. From the beginning, the Soviet state relied heavily upon military, police, and security services to sustain itself, and Jews were active in these agencies. Like Sikhs and Gurkhas in British India, Jews had traditionally been at the margins of Russian society and, hence, prepared to staff and direct the coercive instruments upon which the state relied to control its citizens.

During the 1920s and 1930s, Jews were a major element in the secret police and other Soviet security forces. Genrikh Yagoda, for instance, served as chief of the secret police during the 1930s. Yagoda had been a pharmacist before the Revolution and specialized in preparing poisons for his agents to use in liquidating Stalin's opponents. Other high-ranking Jewish secret policemen included Matvei Berman and Naftali Frenkel who helped to expand and institutionalize the slave labor system. Slave laborers working under Frenkel's supervision built the White-Sea Baltic Canal in 1932. As many as 200,000 workers perished while completing this project. Another Jewish security officer, K. V. Pauker, served as chief of operations of the secret police in the 1930s. Lev Inzhir was chief accountant for the Gulag. M. T. Gay headed the special secret police department that conducted the purges of the 1930s. In what came to be called the "Great Terror," he supervised the mass arrests, trials, and executions of Stalin's opponents. Two other Jewish secret policemen, A. A. Slutsky and Boris Berman, were in charge of Soviet terror and espionage abroad during the 1930s. Jews were also important in the Red Army. In addition to Trotsky, prominent Jewish generals included Yona Yakir, who was a member of the Communist party central committee; Dmitri Schmidt, a civil war hero and commander of the Kiev area; and Yakob Kreiser, a hero of the defense of Moscow during the Second World War.[73]

Another domain in which Jews were particularly visible was the Soviet cultural and propaganda apparatus. Semyon Lozovsky was deputy chief of the Soviet government's information bureau and chief Soviet press spokesman during World War II. Jews dominated the Soviet film industry, which Stalin viewed as an especially important propaganda instrument. Prominent Jews in the film industry included directors Sergei Eisenstein, Mikhail Romm, Mark Donsky, Leonid Lukov, and Yuli Reisman.[74]

One important Soviet propaganda agency operated entirely by Jews, albeit under Stalin's overall direction, was the Jewish AntiFascist Committee (JAC), established during the Second World War to propagandize on behalf of Soviet causes. Leading members of the JAC included the famous actor-director Solomon Mikhoels, writer

Ilya Ehrenberg, violinist David Oistrakh, and film director Eisenstein. The JAC helped to mold a positive image of the Soviet Union among American and Western European intellectuals.

A third area in which Jews played a particularly noteworthy role was the governance of the Soviet Union's Eastern European satellites after World War II. Indigenous Jewish Communists provided the Soviets with a useful leadership cadre in Czechoslovakia, Poland, East Germany, and Hungary. Many of these individuals had received training in Russia, survived the war years in the Soviet Union or with Soviet-sponsored partisan forces and, as a result, had strong ties to the USSR. A typical case was Hirsch Smolar, an important postwar Communist party leader. Smolar had been born in Poland, was trained in Moscow as a Communist party agitator, and sent to Poland in 1936 to organize underground party cells. During the war, Smolar fought against the Germans as a member of a Soviet-sponsored partisan unit. With the defeat of the Germans, he returned to Moscow but was soon dispatched to Warsaw to assist in consolidating Soviet rule. Smolar was active in organizing the Polish Worker's party and directed the Central Jewish Committee, through which the Communist party sought to dominate the Jewish community.[75]

As in Russia, the social marginality of Eastern European Jews made them useful instruments for the imposition of Soviet rule over reluctant populations during the postwar period. Jews were, on the one hand, willing to organize and administer unpopular programs. At the same time, because Jews were often shunned by the local populace and dependent upon Soviet power for their positions and even personal safety, they could be trusted to remain loyal to the Soviet Union.

Czechoslovakia provides a notable example of the prominence of Jews in Eastern European regimes after World War II. Fewer than twenty thousand Czech Jews, out of a prewar community of several hundred thousand, had survived Nazi extermination camps. Despite these small numbers, however, Jews were a major force in the Czech Communist regime. Rudolph Slansky was secretary general of the Czech Communist party. Within the government, Jews effectively ran the ministries in charge of foreign affairs, foreign trade, planning, and propaganda.

Similarly, in Hungary, Mathias Rakosi served as head of the Communist party while General Peter Gabor commanded the secret police. In addition, Joseph Revai served as minister of culture and chief Communist party propagandist while other Jews headed the state planning office, the ministry controlling industry and commerce, and

Radio Hungary. Similar situations prevailed in Romania, where from 1947 until 1952 Ana Pauker served as Communist party secretary and minister of foreign affairs, and in Poland and East Germany as well.[76]

The role played by Jews in the governments of the Soviet satellites after World War II is one reason that during the 1980s and 1990s, in the wake of the collapse of the Soviet Union, anti-Semitic sentiments were often voiced by nationalist forces in these countries. By the 1980s, hardly any Jews remained in Eastern Europe, so this outburst of hatred was often labeled "anti-Semitism without Jews." Nationalists, however, were appealing the continuing memory of Jewish association with the Soviets. Of course, in large measure, Jews had been associated with the Soviets because of the brutal treatment they had previously received from their own countrymen.[77]

Anti-Semitism

Historically, alliances between Jews and states or state-building movements have been the chief catalyts for organized anti-Semitism. Typically, of course, anti-Semitic campaigns proceed from a mixture of motives. Pure hatred of Jews obviously is one important animus for the participants in anti-Semitic groups and movements. However, as was noted earlier, in societies where an anti-Semitic politics becomes important, usually more is involved than simple dislike of Jews. Anti-Semitism, as we shall see, has an important instrumental aspect.

There are three circumstances under which anti-Semitism is likely to become an important political factor. First, political forces that oppose a state in which Jews are prominent may seek to undermine the regime and its supporters by attacking its Jewish backers and depicting the government as the puppet of an alien group. Typically, in this circumstance, anti-Semitic appeals are used to create what might be termed coalitions of the top and bottom. In the modern world, these are associated with Nazism, but in early modern Europe they were sometimes associated with efforts by the church or aristocracy to rally popular support against the crown. They are used by forces that attempt to mobilize the masses while avoiding threats to the interests and property of elite strata. Thus, anti-Semitic ideologies are typically espoused either by radical populists who court elite support or by a segment of the upper class seeking to arouse and mobilize a mass base for an assault on the established order.

Elites are normally fearful of popular mobilization, especially to the level of excitement and, perhaps, violence associated with the overthrow of a regime. They are, moreover, fearful of the rabble rousers with whom they may have to ally themselves in such coalitions of the top and bottom. As a result, such coalitions are only likely to emerge when elites face the most severe economic crises or political threats. The French Third Republic and Weimar Germany are major cases in point.

The destruction of a regime associated with Jews by a coalition of the top and bottom is sometimes followed by the continued use of anti-Semitic appeals to attack and discredit institutions and social classes affiliated with the old political regime. Attacks on the Jews can help the new regime clear away the vestiges of the old order and prepare the way for the construction of a new one. Early modern Spain and Nazi Germany are the most important cases. In both these cases, regimes were able to institutionalize the anti-Semitic fervor they had mobilized. In Spain this was accomplished through the mechanism of the inquisition, and in Nazi Germany through the SS and the incorporation of anti-Semitic principles throughout the civil administration. In this way, both these regimes were able to simultaneously discourage sporadic anti-Semitic agitation—a source of turmoil and instability—while using anti-Semitism as a source of state power.

Second, anti-Semitic campaigns often emerge from the internal politics of a regime linked to Jews. Campaigns against the Jews may develop when Jews' erstwhile allies feel that they can consolidate and enhance their own power by casting off their former Jewish associates. Stalinist Russia, as we shall see, is a case in point. Often, rival factions within a governing coalition endeavor to displace their nominal Jewish colleagues and, so, to aggrandize their own power. This was typical of court politics in the medieval Middle East.

In a similar vein, when a regime linked to Jews comes under external attack, Jews' allies may feel compelled (or see an opportunity) to throw the Jews to the wolves to save themselves. Thus, for example, in twelfth-century England. Jewish financiers provided the funds that supported the crown's efforts to expand its authority vis-à-vis the aristocracy. As a result, when the barons moved to restrict the powers of the crown during the thirteenth century, the Jews were among their chief targets.

In the *Magna Carta* of 1215, for example, the barons compelled King John to accept limits upon the capacity of the Jews to recover debts from the landed gentry. The king was also forced to agree to accept limits upon his own ability to acquire and recover debts that members of the gentry originally owed to the Jews. The acquisition of such debts had been a significant—and hated—mechanism through which the crown extracted resources and enhanced its power over the nobility. Subsequently, the crown distanced itself from the Jews, first imposing severe disabilities on them and later expelling the Jews from England—though not before expropriating as much of their capital as could be found.[78]

The case of Hungary is a more recent example. In pre–World War I Hungary, the Magyar governing class was closely allied with the Jews who dominated business and the professions and extended Magyar influence in the provinces. As a result of this alliance, Hungarian Jews enjoyed complete political freedom and social acceptance. Indeed, Jews were sometimes given access to noble status. Between the wars, however, the Magyar elite's relationship with the Jews came under attack from radical populists within Hungary as well as from Hungary's German allies. To save itself, the Magyar aristocracy agreed to restrict the political, economic, and civil rights of its former partners. Ultimately, large numbers of Hungarian Jews perished at the hands of the Germans.[79]

Similarly, in the seventeenth-century Ukraine, Jews were aligned with the Polish nobility, whom they served as estate managers, tax collectors, administrators, and the operators of such enterprises as mills and breweries. When in 1648, however, the Ukrainian peasantry led by Bogdan Chmielnicki revolted against the Poles and their Jewish subordinates, the Poles sought to save themselves by handing the Jews over to the Ukrainians in exchange for their own lives. Thousands of Jews were killed when denied access to or evicted from the fortified Polish towns where they had sought refuge.[80]

Finally, where Jews play a major role in efforts to supplant an existing regime, the state or social forces under attack may respond with an anti-Semitic campaign designed to protect the established order and discredit its antagonists. Generally, such a campaign involves inciting popular forces by claiming that the government's opponents are unpatriotic and linked to Jews and other foreign elements. Because most governments view rabble-rousing of this sort as destabilizing and potentially dangerous, they generally endeavor to keep the popular forces they mobilize on a short leash and to reign them in as soon as possible. Tsarist Russia is an important example. As we shall see in Chapter 2, moreover, this was an important phenomenon in the United States during the years after the First World War. Let us consider some of the major examples of each of the three conditions under which organized anti-Semitism is likely to emerge and flourish.

Anti-Semitism and the Disruption of Political Regimes

Anti-Semitism was an extremely useful instrument in late nineteenth-century France and early twentieth-century Germany for uniting seemingly incompatible groups from the uppermost and lower ends of the social spectrum around their shared antipathy for the bourgeois order and the liberal state. The fact that Jews play a visible role in a regime, of course, does not mean that the government's opponents will necessarily seek or be able to successfully use anti-Semitism to attack it. The regime and the coalition of forces supporting it may be too strong to be attacked successfully.

Thus, as we have seen, Jews played a visible role in the British state in the nineteenth and early twentieth centuries. In the nineteenth century, the enemies of the imperialist coalition made use of anti-Semitic appeals to attack it, and in the early twentieth century the regime's Jewish connection was attacked by Fascists led by Oswald Moseley. However, the forces supporting the British liberal regime were too powerful to be seriously threatened. The upper classes were generally too secure to consider allying themselves with radical populists and had, moreover, become fully reconciled to the liberal order during the nineteenth century. Moreover, as we have seen, important segments of the upper class and the state bureaucracy were aligned with Jews in the imperialist coalition. As a result, anti-Semitic political movements were unable to make much headway in England.

In a similar vein, forces attacking a regime my find it advantageous to ally themselves with Jews rather than to attack them. For example, in early twentieth-century Italy, Benito Mussolini was able to forge and seize power at the head of a strongly nationalist, antiliberal coalition. Though Jews constituted only a tiny segment of the Italian populace, they had figured prominently among the political and intellectual leaders of the liberal state before the First World War. Leaders of Jewish extraction included two prime ministers, Luzzatti and Sonnino, as well as a number of other cabinet officials and even several important military officers. During the First World War two Jews—Claudi Treves and Giuseppe Modigliani—were not only among the most important leaders of the Italian Socialist party but were also among the leading opponents of the war effort.

Despite the identification of Jews with liberalism and socialism, however, and despite the existence of a measure of anti-Semitic sentiment in the populace, the Fascists made little or no use of anti-Semitic appeals against the liberal order. Indeed, from the earliest days of the Fascist movement, Mussolini welcomed and received Jewish support.[81]

Though Jews played a prominent role in the liberal regime, their principle alliance was with the Piedmontese monarchy, the Italian army (a number of Jews served as important officers), and the coalition of northern industrialists and southern *latifundisti* that served as the backbone of support for Italian national unity and a strong Italian state.[82] In a situation similar to the Hungarian case, this nationalistic elite found the Jews to be useful allies. Jews were enthusiastic proponents of Italian nationalism and the Italian state as antidotes to clericalism. Moreover, Jews strongly supported Italian economic development and served as important importers of capital for Italian industrialization. For example, the Banca Ovazza in Turin was a major factor in financing the growth of Piedmontese industry at the end of the nineteenth century.[83]

As distinguished from the case of the German Nazis, to which it is often compared, this "top" part of the Italian Fascist coalition—a segment allied with Jews—was a far more important force in the Fascist coalition than the radical populist and strongly anti-Semitic "bottom" which dominated the superficially similar Nazi coalition in Germany.[84]

As a result, in Italy, Jews were members rather than targets of the nationalist coalition that supported and bankrolled Mussolini as a politician who could promote national unity, preserve the power of the state, and serve as a bulwark against Socialism. As members of this coalition, Jews participated in the Fascist movement and subsequently served in prominent positions in the Fascist regime. For example, Guido Jung served as minister of finance, Alberto Liuzzi was a commander of the Fascist militia, Giorgio Del Vecchio was the first Fascist rector of the University of Rome, and a number of Jews were important Fascist newspaper editors, journalists, and publicists.

Anti-Semitic sentiment sometimes surfaced among Mussolini's radical populist followers. However, this was a minor theme in the Fascist movement. Anti-Semitism was not a significant part of Italian Fascism until the years immediately preceding World War II and the war years, themselves, when Italy came under enormous pressure from its German ally to cooperate in the Final Solution. At this point, some segments of the Fascist party collaborated with the Germans. Even so, the majority of Italian Jews survived the war.[85]

THIRD REPUBLIC FRANCE

Though it played little part in the assault on Italian liberalism, anti-Semitism played a key role in the politics of Third Republic France. By attacking the Jews, politicians who opposed the Republic sought to unite conservative and radical populist forces that were hostile to the liberal regime but had little else in common. The conservative camp included army officers, elements of the Catholic clergy, and members of the aristocracy. The radical populist group included small tradesmen and shopkeepers, disgruntled and unemployed professionals, and some industrial workers.[86]

The army and aristocracy had strong ties to the old regime and found their status and power undermined by the republican government. Many local tradesmen, merchants, and small shopkeepers fared badly during the 1880s and 1890s because of their inability to compete with the larger national and regional firms and department stores that emerged during this period. The Catholic church, of course, was bitterly opposed to the republican regime's secularism and, especially, to the anticlerical program promoted by the opportunists.

For their part, many young professionals were dissatisfied with the republican government because of the limited career opportunities available to recent university and professional school graduates at the end of the nineteenth century. Under republican auspices, French professional schools had greatly expanded their enrollments leading to the production of large numbers of doctors, lawyers, and engineers for whom there was little or no suitable work. Ironically, these individuals now blamed the republic for their problems. As to industrial workers, the late nineteenth century was a period of intense labor strife in France and, in the eyes of workers and their Socialist spokesmen, the republican regime was an agent of business.

While each of these forces was antagonistic to the Republic, they had little else in common and were certainly not united around any one alternative to the liberal regime. The Catholic church, army, and aristocracy favored restoration of the monarchy, while the forces of the organized working class sought the creation of a Socialist regime. From the perspective of the Republic's opponents, anti-Semitism seemed to be one cause that might bring these forces together behind a common plan of action. After a bitter struggle, anti-Semitism was defeated in nineteenth-century France, but the reasons for its defeat form an interesting contrast to the failure of anti-Semitism to obtain a foothold in Italy and its great triumph in Germany.

In Italy, as we saw, twentieth-century Fascism did not employ anti-Semitic appeals because the conservative portion of the Fascist coalition was allied with Jews. In nineteenth-century France, conservative opponents of the liberal regime were tied to the army and church—institutions that excluded Jews—and were quite happy to make political use of anti-Semitism. As we shall see below, however, anti-Semitism was defeated in nineteenth-century France because radical populists were unable to sufficiently expand the "bottom" portion of the anti-Semitic coalition of top and bottom. It was not until the advent of German Nazism, as we shall see subsequently, that the opponents of a liberal regime were able to perfect the use of the anti-Semitic weapon.

Jews were very visible in the economic and political life of the Third Republic France and had become closely identified with its most controversial policies. Jews were particularly linked to the regime's efforts to reduce the secular power of the Catholic church. Jews also were tied to the rapid commercial and industrial development that took place under republican auspices, generating considerable distress among working- and lower-middle class strata. In addition, prominent Jews were implicated in several of the Republic's most notorious financial imbroglios, including the 1882 Union Generale exposé, the 1889 Comptoire d'Escompte affair, and the 1892 Panama scandal which involved Baron Jacque de Reinach. The prominence of Jews in republican politics and, especially, their association with the more unsavory aspects of the republican regime made it a simple matter for opponents of the Republic to attack it by assailing its Jewish ties.

The emergence of anti-Semitism as a political force in France was initially associated with the nationalistic and antirepublican Boulangist movement of the late 1880s and early 1890s. General Boulanger, himself, disavowed anti-Semitism. Maurice Barres and other Boulangist politicians, however, saw anti-Semitism as a potentially unifying force in French politics. "Boulangism," wrote Barres, "must be anti-Semitic precisely by virtue of its being a party of national reconciliation."[87]

Barres viewed anti-Semitism as an especially useful instrument for bringing the lower classes, or as he put it the "ardent and suffering masses," into the Boulangist camp. Barres continually charged that the Republic was controlled by Jewish financiers and stock market speculators who were ruining honest French workers, tradesmen, and merchants. Through such charges, Boulangists hoped to capitalize on the hardships faced by both urban workers and members of the petit bourgeoisie during a period of rapid industrialization and economic change and to unite these groups against the liberal state. The prominence of Jews in the leadership of the liberal Opportunist faction was a particular target of the Boulangists. Barres charged that a "Jewish party," Opportunism, was "enslaving" France to "the Semites."[88]

In a similar vein, Edouard Drumont, author of the 1886 anti-Semitic best-seller *La France juive*, argued that the Republicans, especially those led by Gambetta, whom he described as an Italian Jew, were corrupting French society and impoverishing French workers through their financial manipulations. Drumont sought particularly to appeal to Catholics by denouncing the anticlericalism of the Third Republic as one more chapter in the Jews' never ending war against the Church.[89]

Drumont's anti-Semitic party, the Ligue Antisemitique, became a major force in French politics during the 1890s. The Ligue played a role in the organization of anti-Semitic riots throughout France in 1898, as well as in the election of a number of parliamentary deputies. After 1898, the Ligue received much of its financial support from the duc d'Orleans, pretender to the French throne. The duke's advisors hoped that an association with the Ligue would help to expand his popular base and provide the House of France with an organization capable of fomenting violence in the streets of Paris on behalf of the monarchist cause. The duke issued a violent anti-Semitic proclamation, known as the San Remo Manifesto; he subsidized the publication of two new anti-Semitic newspapers, and provided the Ligue with funding for the construction of a grand and heavily fortified new headquarters building in Paris.[90]

Efforts by the Third Republic's opponents to use anti-Semitism to undermine the regime culminated in the Dreyfus case of the late 1890s.[91] A Jewish army officer, Captain Alfred Dreyfus, was found guilty in 1894 of selling French military secrets to the Germans and sentenced to life imprisonment in the French penal colony on Devil's Island. The evidence against Dreyfus had almost certainly been fabricated, and the army's handling of the entire case reflected the bitter and pervasive anti-Semitism of the French officer corps. Efforts by Dreyfus's supporters to have his conviction overturned and a new trial conducted, however, quickly sparked a bitter struggle between the defenders and foes of the Third Republic.

The Republic's enemies sought to use the example of a Jewish traitor to symbolize the regime's corruption and to stigmatize its defenders as betrayers of the French nation. Republican forces rallied

behind Dreyfus seeking, for their part, to establish Dreyfus's innocence in order to demonstrate the cruelty and duplicity of the regime's opponents. In 1898, Emile Zola published his famous open
letter, "J'accuse," charging that the army had framed Dreyfus and
destroyed the evidence that could have established his innocence.
Zola's letter sparked a battle that raged in the courts, in the press, in
parliament, and in the streets of Paris for more than two years before
the pro-Dreyfus forces were able to secure a new trial and begin the
steps leading to Dreyfus's eventual exoneration.

Critical to the ultimate victory of the Republican defenders of
Dreyfus—the Dreyfusards, as they were called—was the decision
of French Socialist leader Jean Jaures to throw his support behind
Dreyfus's cause.[92] During the initial stages of the conflict, the Socialists remained neutral, viewing the Dreyfus affair as nothing more
than a struggle between Jewish and non-Jewish fragments of the
bourgeoisie. Eventually, however, Jaures came to understand that a
victory for the anti-Dreyfusards would enormously enhance the
power and prestige of the forces of the political right, possibly leading
to the construction of a political regime far less palatable to the working classes than the liberal Republic.

Jaures also became concerned with the inroads that anti-Semitic
forces were making in his own working-class base of support. The
Socialist press, organizational structure, and militant street-fighting
forces were thrown into the fray on the side of the Dreyfusards.
Jaures explained to his followers that the Republic was engaged in
a struggle against a military conspiracy seeking to encircle it. Under
the circumstances, he asserted, the working classes must come to the
Republic's assistance. The result of Jaures's decision was to deprive
the anti-Semitic and anti-Republican coalition of much of its potential popular base. The coalition of top and bottom was left to rest on
too narrow a bottom and toppled.

Jaures's support for the Dreyfusard cause not only played an important role in its eventual victory but also laid the groundwork for
the emergence of a pro-Republican alliance between Socialist and
liberal forces in France. This alliance helped to immunize the working classes against anti-Semitism and, hence, to diminish the political
utility of anti-Semitic appeals. For decades, French workers were
taught by union leaders and Socialist politicians to understand anti-
Semitism as a ploy by reactionary forces to blind workers to their
true interests. Moreover, the alliance of liberals and Socialists that
emerged from the Dreyfus affair put the Republic on a firmer political
foundation, successfully defending the regime against its domestic

adversaries until its military defeat and destruction by the Germans in 1940.[93]

The political function of anti-Semitism in Weimar Germany was similar to its role in Third Republic France. Anti-Semitism was a theme that could unite the conservative and populist opponents of the liberal regime. Jews were quite visible in the political, cultural, and intellectual life of the Weimar era and, as a result, many Germans identified the Weimar government with the Jews. Indeed, its foes often derisively called the Weimar regime a "Judenrepublik." Some forces in Germany had never been able to reconcile themselves to the defeat and dismemberment of the Empire while others joined the ranks of Weimar's opponents in the wake of Germany's economic collapse in the 1920s. The Republic's various enemies found that they could effectively attack it by attacking the Jews.

Opponents of the regime included traditional conservatives such as Prussian Junkers, army officers, and Ruhr industrialists who feared the influence of Socialists in the government and feared that the regime was too weak to control the forces of the radical left. These groups generally supported such conservative parties as the DNVP (the Nationalist party).

A second set of the regime's foes consisted of middle- and lower-middle-class Germans whose positions had been undermined by the defeat and disintegration of the Empire and the collapse of the German economy in the 1920s. These included former officials of the imperial regime as well as demobilized army officers, ruined smallholder, small businessmen, and students. These groups formed the base of support for parties of the radical right such as the Freiheitspartei, the Deutsche Erneuerungsgmeinde, and the Deutsche Arbeiterspartei as well as the Freikorps and other paramilitary groups. Several hundred radical right-wing parties of this sort, many of them emphasizing anti-Semitic appeals, emerged in Germany in the chaos following World War I. The Nazi party, like the others, appealed primarily to members of the dispossessed lower-middle class.

The Nazis were unique, however, in one respect. Unlike the others, the Nazis were able to mobilize significant support among working- and upper-class forces as well. As to the working class, during the late 1920s, the Nazis developed a network of factory cells and also attracted the votes of large numbers of unemployed workers.[94] Their ability to secure working-class support was a function of the Nazis' organizational skill and the appeal of their methods to some workers. In contrast to workers' established Social Democratic leaders, the Nazis did not speak of complex, long-term solutions to the problems faced by the working class. Instead, the Nazis engaged in direct and violent action against immediate and visible targets—the Jews. Indeed, to a far greater extent than even other parties of the radical right, the Nazis exulted in acts of violence—in beatings, riots, desecrations, pogroms, and murders. As Pulzer has observed, the simplicity of Nazi ideology and the ferocity of their tactics had an enormous allure for desperate and angry workers.[95]

The capacity of the Nazis to appeal to the working classes, in turn, led traditional conservative and upper-class forces to view Hitler as a useful instrument through which they might link themselves to a broader popular base. Moreover, the Nazis appeared to pose less of a threat to traditional elites than other radical populist forces. Most radical-right parties appealing to the dispossessed presented platforms calling for a variety of social and economic reforms in addition to whatever anti-Semitic appeals they might make. The Nazis, however, focused almost exclusively on the issue of the Jews. In Nazi ideology, other social and economic reforms were virtually irrelevant. As Hitler put it, "There are no revolutions except racial revolutions: there cannot be a political, economic or social revolution."[96]

While traditional conservatives were uneasy about all the rabble-rousers, the political and economic condition of Weimar Germany made them desperate. From the perspective of the upper classes, the Nazis' exclusive focus on issues of race meant that Hitler and his followers might be potential links to the masses who had little interest in and posed little threat to their own economic concerns. The resulting support the Nazis received from conservative forces led by the DNVP's Alfred Hugenberg, as well as the financial backing they received from industrialists like Thyssen and Stinnes, were critical to the Nazis' ultimate success. Significantly, though Hitler welcomed this support, conservatives remained the junior partners in the Nazi coalition. Indeed, few individuals drawn from traditional elites were ever admitted to the upper ranks of the Nazi party or, with the partial exception of the military, to positions of power in the Nazi state.[97]

Thus, the Nazis were able to use anti-Semitism and, especially, systematic violence against the Jews to build a coalition of upper-, lower-middle, and working-class forces against the Weimar regime. This coalition rested on a much broader bottom than its nineteenth-century French counterpart. As distinguished from Italian Fascism, moreover, this coalition was dominated by its radical populist rather than its conservative wing. With the continuing collapse of the German economy, this coalition succeeded where its counterpart in Third Republic France had failed.

ANTI-SEMITISM AND STATE BUILDING

The Nazis' use of anti-Semitism, of course, did not end with the destruction of the Weimar Republic. The "war against the Jews," culminating in the systematic murder of the bulk of the European Jewish community, continued to be a central focus of the Nazi party's ideology and program even after it seized power in Germany. This continuing exploitation of anti-Semitism by the Nazis in power was a logical and by no means unique extension of their use of anti-Semitism to seize power. Just as anti-Semitism could help them to demolish the Weimar state, so, too, could it help them to build its successor.

Anti-Semitic campaigns have, over the past several centuries, periodically played a role in state building. Typically, this occurs when forces that initially made use of anti-Semitism to undermine an established regime succeed in creating powerful political coalitions and institutions whose unity and purpose are defined in terms of opposition to Jews. Through a continuing campaign of anti-Semitism, these can be reenergized and used to strengthen the new regime.

Moreover, just as anti-Semitism can function to unite the otherwise disparate opponents of a regime, so, too, can it be used to bolster the cohesion and identity of a regime's diverse supporters. A campaign of anti-Semitism also can help to intimidate a government's opponents including not only Jews but other groups that can be linked to Jews. In addition, under the rubric of the need to deal with the excessive power of pernicious influence of Jews—the "Jewish problem"—a regime may be able to justify the construction of coercive, extractive, and administrative agencies that can expand its reach and power.

Centuries before the advent of Nazism, this is precisely how anti-Semitism came to be an important state-building instrument during the unification and consolidation of the Spanish kingdom under Ferdinand and Isabella. There had been little anti-Semitism in Spain until the fourteenth century, and, as we saw earlier, Jews had achieved considerable influence in Castile and the other Spanish kingdoms. In fourteenth-century Castile, however, efforts by the crown to expand its own power and revenue base sparked bitter struggles with the nobility.[98]

Jews were closely linked to the crown and served, in particular, as its revenue agents. This tie between Jews and royal authority led the Castilian nobility to frame its opposition to the crown and its fiscal demands in anti-Semitic terms. Where the nobility was able to escape increased taxation, the result was to shift the burden of new taxes to the lower ranks of Castilian society who joined the attack on the Jews as a way of assailing the crown and its demands for taxes. The growth of anti-Jewish sentiment was also encouraged by the Catholic church which hoped to increase its influence within the Castilian state by supplanting the crown's Jewish advisors and administrators.

In 1369, dissident members of the nobility helped Henry II of Trastamara to overthrow his half-brother Pedro I and ascend to the Castilian throne. Pedro had been closely identified with the Jews and was supported by them during the struggle with Henry. In the years following Pedro's defeat, Jews became the targets of demonstrations and pogroms. Indeed, anti-Jewish violence throughout Spain in the late fourteenth century led to tens of thousands of conversions, many forced.

These conversions had an unanticipated consequence. Even if they had been converted at the point of a sword,. in their capacity as nominal Christians, converted Jews were entitled to hold royal offices from which, as Jews, they had previously been barred. During the reign of Juan II of Castile (1406–1454) and his successor Henry IV (1454–1474), converted Jews—the so-called conversos—came to occupy key roles in the Castilian government and even began to intermarry with segments of the Castilian nobility. Thus, the ironic effect of fourteenth-century anti-Semitism was to enhance the role of Jews in the government of Castile during the fifteenth century. Jewish converts could become royal officials and members of the nobility as well as advisors, tax collectors, and financiers.

As a consequence, however, of the enlarged role of Jews in the Castilian state, it became easier for the regime's opponents to identify it with Jews and to make use of anti-Semitic appeals to foment resistance to taxation and the expansion of royal authority. This resulted in an upsurge of anti-Semitic activity during the reign of Henry IV and demands by his opponents that the king agree to the establishment of an inquisition, a special ecclesiastical process designed to root out heresy.[99]

Because conversos were nominally Christian, they were subject to the authority of the church and liable to severe punishment if found guilty of a violation of ecclesiastical law. In this way, an inquisition could be used to attack the conversos and the state with which they were linked. Henry was forced to permit the creation of an inquisition but was able to keep it under tight rein. After Henry's death, however, his half-sister Isabella assumed the throne of Castile. Isabella's husband Ferdinand succeeded to the throne of Aragon in 1479, uniting the two most important Christian kingdoms. Ferdinand and Isabella moved to make use of Henry's widespread unpopularity and, especially, the identification of his regime with the Jews to consolidate and expand the power of the newly unified Spanish state.[100] In 1480, Ferdinand and Isabella brought about the establishment of an inquisition to examine charges that many conversos secretly continued to practice Judaism, thereby violating the laws of the Catholic church. By 1481, hundreds of conversos had been found guilty of this charge and burned at the stake as heretics.

Although the inquisition was ostensibly an ecclesiastical institution, the crown maintained virtually complete control over its activities and made use of the inquisition to enhance royal power and national unity. Indeed, the inquisition played a central role in the construction of the Spanish state during the late fifteenth and sixteenth centuries. First, because the lands and property of suspected heretics were forfeit to the crown the inquisition provided the royal treasury with a substantial portion of the revenues needed to prosecute the war against the Moslems and complete the territorial unification of the Spanish kingdom.

Second, the inquisition played an important role in Spanish national unification. The public trials and the terrible spectacle of the auto-de-fé, in which convicted heretics were publicly burned at the stake, were designed to unite Spaniards against the enemies of god and the state while building public support for the regime by demonstrating its power and majesty.

Finally, as it uncovered plots and heresies among the conversos, the inquisition functioned to intimidate the regime's opponents and to subordinate local and regional authorities to the authority of the crown. An enormous number of Spaniards, especially among the nobility and upper classes, were vulnerable to the inquisition. Over the previous centuries and especially during the past fifty years, members of the upper classes had intermarried with Jews and conversos and, as a result, many had or could at least be accused of having some Jewish ancestry. These could easily be denounced by their enemies as secret "Judaisers"—clandestine practitioners of the Jewish religion—and given over to the inquisitors.

Since the inquisition's standards of proof were somewhat arbitrary, there was no guarantee that such a charge could be disproved. The result was to place the upper classes and nobility at the mercy of the crown. In many areas, most notably Aragon, Catalonia, Cordoba, Saragossa, and Valencia, the nobility resisted the inquisition. For example, virtually every noble family in Saragossa was involved in the plot that led to the murder of the chief inquisitor. Such resistance, however, generally proved futile.

At the same time that the inquisition worked to intimidate the nobility, it was also used by the crown to subordinate local councils and representative bodies.[101] Inquisitors claimed that their authority superseded that of local governmental bodies and gradually expanded the scope of their jurisdiction from heresy to more mundane matters such as bigamy, usury, blasphemy, witchcraft, sodomy, and the expression of erroneous religious views by members of the populace at large. Local governments, particularly in Aragon, Catalonia, and Valencia sought to resist this encroachment upon their traditional prerogatives by an agency of the crown. With the help of the inquisition, however, the crown gradually expanded and centralized its power.

Not surprisingly, through the mid-seventeenth century Spanish monarchs continued to view the inquisition as an enormously important instrument for maintaining the unity of the state and the power of the crown.[102] Indeed, so important an instrument of royal power was the inquisition that the one group that was legally not subject to its control—Jews who had refused to convert to Christianity—were expelled from Spain in 1492. The continued prsence of unconverted Jews in Spain was viewed by the crown as a threat to national unity and to the state's authority.

NAZI GERMANY

The Spanish case is a useful backdrop for understanding the role of anti-Semitism as a state-building instrument in Nazi Germany. The Nazis' successful attack upon the liberal Weimar Republic had been organized around and fueled by hatred of Jews. For many of the party's leaders and activists, including Hitler himself, eradicating Jewish influence in Germany was a central and transcendent goal as well as a means to other ends. Some historians have argued that the Nazis planned the "final solution" from the very beginning. When they came to power, however, the Nazis had no clear-cut or coherent Jewish policy. Instead, different forces within the party advocated and, in some instances, implemented diverse and contradictory anti-Semitic programs.[103]

Thus, Ernst Rohm, head of the SA, and Joseph Goebbels, minister of propaganda, were associated with a policy of direct and violent action against the Jews. On the other hand, Hermann Goring, who eventually became Reich counselor for defense, and Heinrich Himmler, head of the SS, were advocates of a more systematic or bureaucratic approach to the destruction of the Jews. This intraparty battle for influence over Jewish policy was an important one. Given the central place of Jews in Nazi ideology, the individuals and agencies able to control the solution to the "Jewish problem" would add immeasurably to their own power and prestige.

Direct action against the Jews began immediately after the Nazis took control of the government in 1933. SA units, acting with little central coordination, staged numerous riots and attacks on Jewish businesses as well as beatings and murders of Jews. These activities were extremely popular among the party faithful. Violence in the streets, however, generally provoked an unfavorable reaction in the German populace, undermined Hitler's claim to be the only man in Germany capable of maintaining law and order, and tarnished Germany's image abroad. Therefore, Hitler moved to limit SA activities to organizing boycotts of Jewish businesses. These, however, were difficult to enforce and were damaging to the German economy.

Violent and direct action against Jews continued through 1938 when it reached its climax in the nationwide pogrom that came to be called Reichskristallnacht. In response to the assassination of a German diplomat in Paris by a Jewish student, Goebbels organized anti-Jewish riots throughout Germany. Synagogues were burned, Jewish stores looted, and Jews beaten in the streets of Berlin and other German cities. In the aftermath of Kristallnacht, however, Goring and Himmler were able to convince Hitler that this sort of action was disruptive to the German government and economy, and conveyed the utterly unfair impression both at home and abroad that Germany was ruled by thugs. As a result, after Kristallnacht, loosely coordinated violence against the Jews abated and a much more systematic form of terror, carried out by bureaucratic agencies rather than hoodlums, became predominant.[104]

All the while that the SA was carrying out its spasmodic campaign of violence, another form of action against the Jews also was taking shape. This was the bureaucratic solution to the Jewish problem. Beginning in 1933, a series of discriminatory laws was enacted limiting the number of Jews in the civil service, in the professions, and in the universities. At the same time, the "Aryanization" and legal expropriation of Jewish businesses was begun. By 1938, virtually all Jewish firms in Germany had been either put out of business or turned over to non-Jews, and Jews were virtually driven out of the professions and the German economy.

In September 1935, the Nuremberg laws were enacted, excluding Jews from German citizenship and prohibiting marriages or extra-marital relationships between Jews and Germans. Under the Nuremberg laws, very strict racial categories were devised. A Jew was defined as someone who was descended from at least three Jewish grandparents or was descended from two Jewish grandparents but belonged to the Jewish religious community or was married to a Jew. An individual who was descended from two Jewish grandparents but did not practice the Jewish religion and was not married to a Jew was defined as a person of "mixed Jewish blood" (a Mischling) of the first degree. An individual with one Jewish grandparent was defined as a Mischling of the second degree. The Mischlinge were not subject to most of the measures taken against Jews, but they did suffer some disabilities.[105]

After 1938, under a series of administrative regulations, Jews were deprived of their driver's licenses, stripped of most of their property, expelled from schools, forbidden to use telephones, banned from many forms of public transportation, allowed only limited rations, exempted from protection by labor and work safety legislation, and subjected to special forced labor and tax laws. Jews were also concentrated in specific residential areas. Beginning in 1941, Jews were required to wear a Star of David on their clothing to make them readily identifiable.[106]

The bureaucratization of the attack on the Jews is also associated with Heinrich Himmler and the SS. During the late 1930s Himmler, a staunch proponent of bureaucratic methods for dealing with Jews, had increased his influence over Jewish policy and by 1939 had won overall control over matters dealing with Jews. By defeating other forces within the party for control over Jewish policy, Himmler greatly expanded his own power and that of the agencies under his command, namely, the SS, the Gestapo, and the Race and Settlement Office which sought to reorganize German society along racist lines.

Since 1934, the SS had organized the emigration and expulsion of thousands of Jews from Germany and, under the leadership of Adolph Eichmann, saw to the emigration of nearly one-fourth of Austria's Jews in 1934–1935. The expansion of the Reich after 1939, however, brought the Jews into the German realm more rapidly than they could be expelled. Himmler's efforts to develop programs that would win Hitler's favor, ensure his own continuing control over Jewish policy and, thereby, expand his own power led to the formulation of ever more grandiose emigration schemes, unsuccessful plans for Jewish resettlement in Madagascar and Ecuador and, ultimately, to systematic murder on an enormous scale.[107]

Arendt was not far off the mark when she described Eichmann and the other Nazi bureaucrats as personifying the banality of evil.[108] In Nazi Germany, the struggle for bureaucratic power and position led to the formulation of bold initiatives by the Nazi equivalents of today's "policy wonks." Just as status and power in Washington often flow to those bureaucrats who are able to generate interesting and innovative programs that please their political bosses, so, too, were there enormous rewards in the Nazi state for the development of programs that excited the imagination of the political leadership in Berlin. Bureaucratic struggle, the most banal of all human activities, bears as much responsibility as anything else for the European Holocaust.

As in the case of the Spanish inquisition more than four centuries earlier, the Nazi campaign against the Jews played a vitally important role in the construction of the Nazi state and the expansion of its power. In particular, the bureaucratic solution to the Jewish problem drew most agencies of the German state and major institutions of German society into the Nazis' anti-Semitic crusade. In this way, the anti-Semitic impulse was transformed into an instrument of state building that helped to strengthen and expand the Nazi regime's control over the German state and penetration into German society. Left unchecked, the anti-Semitic sentiment that the Nazis had so successfully mobilized now threatened to be a source of turmoil and instability for the regime they were seeking to create. Properly institutionalized and channeled, however, anti-Semitism could become an important instrument of state power.

Government agencies of all sorts played important roles in the campaign against the Jews. Violence in the streets could be managed quite nicely by thugs and hoodlums. As Raul Hilberg has observed, however, the implementation of racial laws, the "Aryanization" of Jewish property, the drawing of ghetto borders, the disposition of pension claims by deported Jews, and ultimately the transportation and systematic murder of millions of Jews were matters requiring the involvement of a host of government agencies and the accountants, lawyers, judges, engineers, and other technical specialists in their employ.[109]

Implementation of the Nuremberg decrees, alone, involved the courts and administrative agencies in numerous disputes over whether particular individuals were Jews, Aryans, Mischlinge of the first degree, or Mischlinge of the second degree. What, for example, was to be done in cases where a Jew had acknowledged paternity of an illegitimate child whose paternity could not be established conclusively? What about a half-Jew who had practiced the Jewish religion (and, thus presumptively defined as a Jew rather than a first-degree Mischling), but now claimed to have done so under parental compulsion rather than as a matter of personal preference.[110]

Similarly, the disposition of confiscated Jewish assets required a myriad of decisions by the Finance Ministry. The creation and maintenance of ghettos involved a great deal of work by municipal authorities. Subsequently, the transport of enormous numbers of Jews to concentration and death camps required painstaking planning by the Transport Ministry. As they participated in the Nazis' anti-Semitic campaign, these agencies were gradually drawn into the orbit of and subordinated to the Nazi regime—the SS and other security services in particular—that defined their new missions and priorities and could reward bureaucrats for their cooperation.[111]

In due course, agencies were moved to compete to develop ideas and initiatives in their areas of expertise that would help the Nazis more effectively accomplish such tasks as identifying Jewish property of transporting Jews to death camps. A number of government agencies, including the finance ministry, the transport ministry, and the Foreign Office, created departments and trained specialists in Jewish matters to help them work more effectively with the security services. In this way, the Nazis strangthened their control over the German state.

At the same time, the systematic and bureaucratic solution to the Jewish problem helped to link virtually every major institution of German society to the Nazi regime. The churches were a chief source of birth records and, thus, became enmeshed in the process of racial classification. German banks and businesses assisted with and profited from the Aryanization of Jewish properties. Major German manufacturing firms employed Jewish forced laborers. Thousand of middle-class Germans were happy to accept the positions from which Jews were expelled in the professions, the civil service, and the universities.

In addition, the Nazi system of racial laws and classifications made hundreds of thousands of Germans directly vulnerable to the regime's rewards and punishments. As in medieval Spain, Germans and Jews had intermarried for generations. An enormous number of Germans, especially among the middle- and upper-middle classes, had sufficient Jewish ancestry to be disqualified from desirable positions in the civil service or to be considered Mischlinge and subject to a number of disabilities.[112]

The eagerness of such Germans to upgrade their status led to the creation of a new occupation, that of Sippenforscher, or genealogical researcher specializing in helping individuals prove their Aryan descent.[113] Fortunate Mischlinge might be able to secure reclassifications, or "liberations," thus enhancing their career opportunities while diminishing their fear that the regime might one day decide to consider them Jews.

Moreover, millions of other Germans with no discernible Jewish ancestry had past or present social, business, professional, and romantic relationships with Jews that could bring them to the attention of the authorities. Often, Germans could be denounced to the Gestapo by their enemies, hostile neighbors, or business rivals for such associations, especially if they involved violations of the laws against sexual relationships with Jews. Thus, through its racial policies, the Nazi regime politicized sexual and personal relationships. In this way, as in fifteenth- and sixteenth-century Spain, the campaign against the Jews not only reinforced the Nazis' hold on the German state but also strengthened the Nazi state's grip upon German society.

Ultimately, the use of anti-Semitism as a state-building tool, and its incorporation into the fabric of the Nazi state, made the European Holocaust possible. In the context of a European welfare state, agencies and officials are rewarded for developing more effective ways of providing services to their clients. Similarly, in the context of a state whose construction was so dependent upon and legitimated by the need to solve the "Jewish problem," state agencies and bureaucratic officials could make their marks and enhance their power, status, and claims upon state resources by developing and perfecting means of ridding first Germany, and then the territories conquered by Germany, of the source of this problem.[114] It is an indication of the efficiency of the German state that it very nearly succeeded in this endeavor.

ANTI-SEMITISM AND THE CONSOLIDATION OF POLITICAL POWER

On a number of occasions in Europe and the Middle East, anti-Semitic campaigns have been used by political forces that had been allied with Jews to drive them from the leadership of states and regimes they had helped to build. This may come about when the programs and policies of a regime linked to Jews spark political opposition—especially opposition tinged with anti-Semitism. In response, a government may seek to deflect the assault by distancing itself from the Jews or even joining in the attack upon their erstwhile Jewish confederates.

As we have seen, this occurred in Hungary between the First and Second World Wars. Before 1917, Jews had been closely allied with the Magyar gentry. However, during the interwar years, the Magyar elite's stake in this alliance diminished and the former allies of the Jews acquiesced in the anti-Semitic campaign launched by the forces of the radical right when this began to pose a threat to the regime. In a similar vein, the non-Jewish members of a governing coalition may endeavor to jettison or subordinate their Jewish colleagues in order to enhance their own power and to make room for cadres with stronger roots in civil society who can help the regime consolidate and stabilize its authority.

Stalinist Russia is a notable example of a regime that had been closely identified with Jews, whose non-Jewish leadership turned to anti-Semitism to deflect opposition, subordinate its Jewish allies, and forge new alliances that would help it to consolidate its power. As we saw earlier, in the aftermath of the Bolshevik revolution, Jews played an extremely prominent role in the Soviet regime. During the struggles that followed Lenin's death in 1924, however, anti-Semitic appeals to the Communist party's rank and file were among the weapons used by Stalin to defeat Trotsky, Zinoviev, and Kamenev and seize the party's leadership. Indeed, much of the invective used by Stalin in the intraparty battles of this period was designed to appeal to anti-Semitic sentiment inside and outside the party. For example, the label, "left oppositionist," used by Stalin to castigate his enemies, was a euphemism for Jew. In a similar vein, Stalin's advocacy of the doctrine of "socialism in one country" was partly designed to limit the influence of foreign Jewish Communists who often had ties to Jewish Communists in the Soviet Union itself.

During the 1930s, Stalin moved to consolidate his power by intimidating or eliminating all potential sources of opposition within the Communist party, the army, the secret police, and the administrative apparatus. Jews exercised a great deal of influence within all these institutions and, as a result, formed the largest and most important group of victims of the Stalinist purges. Jews consituted about 500,000 of the ten million purge victims of the 1930s and comprised a majority of the politically most prominent victims.[115]

In a series of show trials, during this period, the key Jewish officials of the Communist party and Soviet state were accused of plotting against the revolution and were systematically killed. These included Kamenev, Zinoviev, Radek, and Rykov. Important Jewish

military commanders such as Yakir and Schmidt were also liqui-
dated. The secret police forces used to implement these purges often
were led by Jews who were killed in their turn, until the influence of
Jews within the secret police was substantially diminished. Those liqui-
dated included Yagoda, Pauker, Slutsky, and the Berman brothers.

Given the paucity of other educated individuals, the Soviet regime
was compelled to continue to rely upon the talents of Jews in the
party and the state bureaucracy. Their influence in the Soviet hierar-
chy, however, had been greatly reduced. Stalin's purges continued
during the 1940s. At the 1941 party conference, for example, Litvinov and Antselovich were demoted from full to candidate membership on the Communist party Central Committee, while G. D. Vain-
berg and Molotov's wife, Zhemchuzhina, were expelled altogether.
In 1939, Jews had comprised 10% of the membership on the Central
Committee. A decade later, they constituted barely 2% of the committee's members. This not only gave Stalin total control of the Communist party apparatus but also allowed the regime to broaden its
political base by increasing the representation of other nationality
groups in the party leadership.[116]

During the Second World War, Jews played prominent roles in
the Soviet government, particularly in the realms of propaganda and
foreign relations. After the war, however, the regime was confronted
with an upsurge of popular anti-Semitism, most notably in areas that
had been occupied by the Germans. The populations of these areas,
who had often cooperated with the Nazis, feared that returning Jews
would seek restoration of their homes, property, and positions. Nationalist movements, particularly in the Ukraine and Lithuania
sought to exploit this popular anti-Semitism to attack the Soviet
regime.[117]

Stalin, who disliked and distrusted the Jews, reponded to the nationalist threat by embarking on a new anti-Semitic campaign of his
own. The Soviet press began to impugn the loyalty of Jews and to
suggest that they might betray the socialist motherland. A number
of the leading figures of the wartime Jewish Anti-Fascist Committee
(JAC) were accused of plotting to transform the Crimea into a Zionist
republic to serve as a base for American imperialism. Shlomo Mikhoels, head of the JAC and director of the Moscow State Yiddish
Theater was murdered by the KGB in January 1948. By the early
1950s, Jews had been effectively barred from the Soviet foreign service, from foreign trade institutes, from positions of military command, and from senior positions in the bureaucracy as well as from
positions of leadership within the party itself. The positions formerly

held by Jews were given not only to Russians but also to members of minority nationality groups as part of the regime's effort to curb nationalist opposition and expand its political base.

Because Jews constituted the best educated and most talented group in the Soviet populace, the regime could not completely dispense with their services in the professions, in scientific research, or in the civil service. The government, however, relied upon a policy of intimidation to check Jewish influence. This was one factor behind the arrest of some of the Soviet Union's leading Jewish physicians in 1953. In the case of the so-called doctors' plot, a number of Moscow physicians were charged with conspiring with American intelligence services to destroy the Soviet leadership. Hundreds of other Jewish doctors throughout the USSR were dismissed from their posts. The accused physicians were saved from execution only by Stalin's sudden death.

After Stalin's demise, the Soviet regime continued its efforts to placate the nation's various nationality groups by increasing their representation in the civil service, the professions, and in institutions of higher education. This was often accomplished at the expense of Jews who were progressively relegated to marginal positions in the bureaucracy, the educational system, and the economy. By the 1960s, Jews exercised little power in the Soviet regime.

A similar sequence of events occurred in the Soviet Union's Eastern European satellites. As indicated above, in the aftermath of World Wat II, Jews played major roles in the puppet governments established by the Soviets in Czechoslovakia, Poland, East Germany, Hungary, and Romania. This prominent Jewish presence allowed nationalist and religious forces to use anti-Semitic appeals to mobilize popular opposition to Communist rule in these nations. For example, in Czechoslovakia, underground anti-Communist groups pointed to the "tremendous influence" of Jews in the Communist party and government. In Poland, the Catholic church fostered anti-Semitism as part of its struggle against the Communist regime. In 1946, for instance, Cardinal Hlond, the Catholic primate of Poland, averred that "animosities" caused by "Jews in the government" were the cause of a pogrom in the city of Kielce.[118]

During the early 1950s, to combat its nationalist opponents and solidify its hold on Eastern Europe, the Soviet Union systematically purged Jewish Communists from their positions of power in the satellites. In Czechoslovakia, Hungary, Poland, and Romania, Jews were replaced by local cadres who had better ties to the dominant nationality groups within each country. Thus, in 1950 and 1951, virtually all Jewish Communists in Czechoslovakia were purged. These included Communist party Secretary General Rudolph Slansky, Deputy Secretary General Otto Sling, and top officials in the Ministries of Foreign Affairs, Foreign Trade, and Information.[119] Several were accused of the crime of "counterrevolutionary Zionism." Similarly, in 1953, many prominent Jews in the Hungarian government were purged and killed. These included General Peter Gabor, head of the secret police, as well as a number of other top military, police, and Communist party officials.[120]

Despite these purges, however, the nationalist and religious opponents of Communist regimes in Eastern Europe continued to attack them as tools of the Jews. This is why, as I noted earlier, a good deal of anti-Semitic sentiment and rhetoric surfaced in Eastern Europe after the collapse of the Soviet empire and the subsequent breakup of the Soviet Union, in the late 1980s and early 1990s.

Conservative Anti-Semitism

A final political use of anti-Semitism is the defense of established regimes. Jews have often played active roles in movements seeking to reform or supplant states to which they were unable to acquire access. Regimes seeking to shield themselves against such movements frequently make use of their Jewish ties to discredit them.

For example, during the late nineteenth century Jews were strongly associated with liberal movements in Germany and Austria. Forces such as the church and aristocracy that defended the status quo as well as anticapitalist parties representing the peasantry and lower-middle classes often found anti-Semitism a useful weapon against liberalism. Thus, in imperial Germany, the court chaplain Adolf Stoecker founded the anti-Semitic Christian Social Workers party in 1878, seeking to appeal to tradesmen, artisans, and other members of the lower-middle class threatened by capitalist development. In the 1880s, Bismarck gave Stoecker a measure of support, hoping to use his party as a weapon against liberal forces. In the Hapsburg empire, the anti-Semitic Christian Socialist party, led by Karl Lueger, mayor of Vienna, united the same lower-middle-class strata with elements of the Catholic clergy.[121]

In Eastern Europe, Jews were more likely to be associated with Socialist or Communist than with liberal groups, and governments sought to use anti-Semitism as a weapon against these movements. In Tsarist Russia, for example, from the mid-nineteenth century, the government sought to attack and discredit revolutionary forces by linking them to Jews.[122] After Alexander II's assassination in 1881 by revolutionaries who included a Jew, Hessia Helfman, the government charged that revolutionaries were part of a Jewish conspiracy and fomented pogroms throughout Southern Russia and the Ukraine. The Ignatiev Report of 1882 recommended that harsh measures be taken against Jews to quell popular protest. The resulting May Laws of 1882 severely limited areas of Jewish settlement, slashed Jewish quotas in schools and universities, and attempted to dislodge Jews from trade and the professions. In 1891, the Moscow, St. Petersburg, and Kharkov Jewish communities were expelled to the countryside.

Tsarist attacks on the Jews continued in the twentieth century. In 1902 and 1903, under the command of the interior minister Wenzel von Plahve, major pogroms were launched in Bessarabia and White Russia. Peter Stolypin, appointed minister of the interior in 1906, vowed to "drown the revolution in Jewish blood." Under Stolypin's direction, the paramilitary forces of the Union of the Russian people, called the "black hundreds," carried out a series of assassinations of liberal and radical opponents of the regime as well as a campaign of terror against the Jews. Stolypin sought to depict opposition to the monarchy as a Jewish conspiracy in an effort to maintain the loyalty of peasants, workers, and lower-middle-class strata.[123]

Anti-Semitism, Jews, and the State

Thus, over the past several centuries, Jews have played important roles in the construction of absolutist, liberal, and socialist states as well as major parts in movements seeking to reform or supplant regimes to which they were unable to obtain access. Jews have traditionally offered their services to the state in exchange for the regime's guarantee of security and opportunity. Ironically, however, precisely this relationship between Jews and the state has often sparked organized anti-Semitic attacks.

To be sure, where Jews forge a close relationship with the state, they may well obtain protection and a considerable measure of power. In ancient Babylonia, all citizens were required to bow before the exilarch, or leader of the Jewish community. During the eighteenth-century heyday of the European court Jew, Shakespeare's *Merchant of Venice* could be performed in Berlin only if preceded by an apology to Jewish members of the audience. In twentieth-century Russia, Jews commanded powerful instruments of terror and repression.

The power and protection offered Jews by the state, however, has

tended to be evanescent. It lasts only so long as Jews' allies in governing coalitions continue to find them useful and "their" state continues to have the capacity to defend them from attack. In the meantime, by employing the state to hold off their enemies, the Jews add
its foes to their own.

This is the great dilemma of Jewish history, and it is a dilemma
that has no solution. Should Jews eschew the protection and opportunity afforded them by a connection with the state in order to avoid
the dangers inherent in the relationship? This is not truly possible.
Jews are trapped by the logic and structure of their situation. They
want to maintain their identity while securing protection and opportunity. Thus, they can hardly be expected to resist the embrace of
the state. As we shall now see, this dilemma is a useful backdrop for
understanding the history of Jews and anti-Semitism in the United
States.

2 Jews, State Building, and Anti-Semitism in Nineteenth-Century America

Prior to the Civil War, the Jewish population of the United States was small and its role and visibility in American life minimal. Although anti-Semitism occasionally manifested itself in such incidents as General Ulysses S. Grant's famous order barring Jewish peddlers from his military district, hatred of Jews was not a significant phenomenon. Indeed, in the years before the Civil War, American racist and nativist concerns were focused primarily on the much larger and more visible Catholic minority as well as, of course, upon blacks.

In the decades following the Civil War, however, Jews came to be important factors in American banking and finance and became politically influential. In this period, German-Jewish merchant bankers, usually recent immigrants to the United States, marketed American government, municipal, and corporate securities in Europe and served as major conduits for European—especially German and French—capital into the United States.

As important dealers in securities and major investors in their own right, Jewish financiers became involved with all aspects of American fiscal and monetary policy as well as with corporate organization and reorganization and even with American foreign policy in the late nineteenth century. In short, Jews became factors in planning and implementing American economic development, political reconstruction, imperialism, and state building during the latter half of the nineteenth century.

In these endeavors Jews developed close ties to the new, fabulously rich stratum of Northeastern financiers and industrialists who effectively governed the United States during the Gilded Age. Jewish bankers helped to finance the corporate expansions, mergers, and acquisitions that made this stratum so wealthy and participated, as well, in their efforts to dominate the political processes of the era. As a result of their alliance with Northeastern industrialists, the prominence and influence of Jews in the United States increased substantially. For example, at the start of his first administration, President Grant invited Joseph Seligman, a German-Jewish financier, to serve as secretary of the treasury- -an offer Seligman declined.

The close and visible relationship between Jews and the ruling industrialist elite, however, led at least some of the forces that opposed the new industrialist order to turn to anti-Semitic appeals in an effort to undermine and delegitimate the regime by identifying it with the Jews. Two groups, in particular, made use of such themes: old-stock New England patricians from America's founding families, and agrarian radicals in the South and West organized in the Populist movement. These two groups, dissimilar in so many other respects, were united in an intense opposition to the industrialist order that was simultaneously subverting the status and political influence of the patricians and the economic position of the agrarians.

They united in attacking the parvenu Jewish banker as the symbol par excellence of the greed and excess of the Gilded Age. Patricians and Populists united also in the immigration restriction movement which made use of vitriolic anti-Semitic appeals. The proponents of a restrictive immigration policy attacked Jews as well as other immigrants from Southern and Eastern Europe as undesirables who were destroying America's culture and society and threatening to overwhelm the morally superior Anglo-Saxon race. This nascent union of Populists and patricians might have become the American counterpart of the coalition of top and bottom that began to make very effective use of anti-Semitism to mount major attacks upon European liberal regimes during roughly the same period of time.

In America, however, anti-Semitism failed to become a significant political threat to the industrialist order. It would be tempting to ascribe this failure to the capacity of the American liberal ethos to prevent European anti-Semitic doctrines from taking root in the tolerant soil of the New World. America's "liberal tradition," of course, at one time or another has been used to explain the relative weakness of socialism, fascism, anti-Semitism, and almost every problem in this country.

The failure of anti-Semitism to become an important political force in nineteenth-century American politics, however, is less a tribute to the strength of America's liberal capitalist creed than it is a curious result of the strength of capitalist political forces in America— a strength that, paradoxically, allowed them to deflect anti-Semitism by ridding themselves of the Jews.

In nineteenth-century Europe, Jews were too important an element in liberal coalitions and regimes to be dropped by their allies. The supporters of liberal regimes, whatever their personal views of Jews, were compelled to oppose anti-Semitism to preserve liberalism. Thus, for example, in France, Socialist leader Jean Jaures eventually felt compelled to give his all-out support to the pro-Dreyfus forces, despite a considerable history of anti-Jewish sentiment within the French Socialist party, because he understood that the victory of the anti-Semites might fatally weaken the liberal regime.

The indispensability of the Jews meant, however, that anti-Semitism could continue to serve as a weapon against liberalism. In a sense, the Jews were an albatross needed to keep the ship afloat. Their support was important to the liberal state, but their presence, as evidenced by the French and German cases, allowed the regime's political opponents to use the issue of anti-Semitism to unite the upper- and lower-class foes of liberalism and capitalism against the bourgeois political order.

In the United States, by contrast, the industrialist regime had defeated and subjugated its most dangerous foes during a long and bloody civil war. It was well able to survive and prosper without the support of Jews, and if an association with them was troublesome they could be jettisoned. Here, the services of the albatross were *not* required to keep the ship afloat. As we shall see, beginning in the 1880s, the industrialist stratum with which Jews had been allied responded to its attackers by disassociating itself from the Jews and linking itself, instead, to one of its former foes—the patricians. At the end of the nineteenth century, a new American elite was formed which united elements of the old New England aristocracy with the new captains of industry and finance. Jews were categorically denied membership in this new ruling class and suddenly found themselves excluded from the nation's key political and social institutions.

Paradoxically, however, the result of this process of elite formation and Jewish exclusion was to greatly reduce the effectiveness of anti-Semitism as a political weapon. By the turn of the century, the industrialist stratum had vigorously and visibly disentangled itself from its Jewish connection and had linked itself to the patricians. Thus, the upper-class component of a potential American coalition of the top and bottom now was tied to the industrialist order which, in any case, could no longer be plausibly identified with Jews. Anti-Semitic appeals continued to be used by the Populist "bottom" of the nascent coalition, but after the movement's defeat at the national level in 1896, agrarian anti-Semitism became primarily a weapon of regional defense against industrialist encroachment into the South.

After their exclusion from the established industrialist order, Jews aligned themselves with a major coalition of forces seeking to reform that order, namely, the Progressives. Jews gave their enthusiastic support to Theodore Roosevelt and Woodrow Wilson and played important roles in the Wilson administration. This alliance between Jews and native-stock Progressives, as we shall see below, however, was disrupted during the great Red Scare of 1919–1920.

Jews in the Gilded Age

The period following the Civil War was one of great industrial and commercial growth in the United States. Huge fortunes were made in banking, railroad construction, and manufacturing. The government, under the influence of the business wing of the Republican party, strongly supported economic and industrial expansion through such programs as land grants, amounting to some 100 million acres, to subsidize railroad construction, and the development of monetary policies aimed at ensuring the availabity of an adequate supply of money and credit for commercial purposes.

German-Jewish bankers, financiers, industrialists, and merchants achieved remarkable economic success and a considerable measure of political influence during this period. German-Jewish millionaires included the manufacturer Philip Heidelbach; bankers Joseph Seligman, Lewis Seasongood, and Solomon Loeb; railroad magnates Emanuel and Mayer Lehman, and Jacob Schiff as well as the Warburgs, the Lewisohns, and the Guggenheims. During the Gilded Age, these Jewish entrepreneurs made millions of dollars in real estate, finance, and commodities investments.[1]

Joseph Seligman was the most important member of the group. During the Civil War, like a number of other American bankers, Seligman had made a great deal of money helping to create a secondary market for U.S. government bonds. After the secession of the South, the Rothschilds and other major European financiers had little confidence in the ability of the American national government to win the war and were reluctant to participate in loans to the federal treasury. Indeed, European investors moved to redeem their American securities as quickly as possible fearing that they would soon be worthless.[2]

In response, the national government turned to domestic bankers who were able to sell more than $2 billion in federal securities mainly in small blocks within the United States iself. Their participation in the primary and secondary markets for the Civil War era debt provided financiers based in America with a great deal of marketing experience and a much stronger financial base than they had previously possessed.[3] The Civil War, in effect, created a new class of powerful American financiers, among them a group of New York German-Jewish bankers.[4]

After the Civil War, these German-Jewish bankers played major roles in four great national projects: refunding the national debt; establishing the fiscal foundations for the creation of Republican governments in the former confederate states; economic development and expansion; and, finally, American imperial expansion.

The Federal Debt

Like their counterparts in Europe, Jewish financiers in the United States became important collaborators of the government as it became dependent upon the maintenance of a stable and reliable international market for its securities. European regimes during the late nineteenth century depended heavily upon financiers such as the Rothschilds to sustain their revenue needs mainly because their enormous military expenses outstripped the incomes they could generate through the rudimentary systems of extraction available to them. In the United States during the period after the Civil War, by contrast, governmental expenditures were low and public revenues, generated mainly by customs duties, theoretically were more than adequate to meet them. Nevertheless, state finance and debt also became important problems in the United States in this era.

First, at the conclusion of the Civil War, the government was compelled to deal with the matter of the enormous debt that it had built up to prosecute the war. Between 1860 and 1866, the national debt had increased from a mere $65 million to nearly $3 billion, a sum amounting to roughly 30% of the gross national product of the Northern states. This mountain of debt curtailed private investment by absorbing capital that might otherwise have been used to finance private endeavors, such as railroads. At the same time, much of this debt had been acquired when the fate of the Union was still in doubt and, hence, were obtained at rates of interest well above current market levels.[5]

As a result, the national government needed to move expeditiously to develop some mechanism for repaying or refunding its outstanding obligations. This was accomplished through the issuance of new U.S. government securities bearing considerably lower rates of interest than the securities marketed during the war. Some of the proceeds from the sale of the new bonds were used to retire the old debt. At the same time, to increase the availabiliy of funds for investment in industrial and commercial development, a strong effort was made to sell these new securities in Europe and, so, to bring new capital into the country.

Sales of government securities also became important because the U.S. government's revenues in the post–Civil War era were derived largely from customs duties. These duties, which provided roughly two-thirds of the government's annual receipts, unfortunately did not provide a smooth and uniform flow of income. They were mainly collected in the spring and summer when most imports entered the country, but then fell off sharply. Federal government expenditures, unfortunately, did not have the same pattern as revenues. For example, interest payments on the public debt came due in January and July. Many other government expenses were quarterly. Thus, for several months at a time, the federal government might be forced to save money for future disbursement. During such periods, however, the nation's money supply would be contracted, with adverse consequences for business and trade. As a result, the government moved to sell short-term notes to meet its expenses during periods when its income from customs receipts dropped.[6]

As was also the case in Europe, the exigencies of state finance during the postwar period impelled the national government to rely heavily upon bankers able to create a market for its securities. Especially useful were those bankers whose international connections allowed them to sell U.S. bonds abroad and, thereby, bring European capital into the United States. With their connections to Jewish banking houses in Europe, the Seligmans and other German-Jewish financiers became valuable agents in government securities transactions.[7]

Thus, for example, when $15 million in new U.S. bonds were marketed in Europe in August 1871, the European bankers who took the notes were overwhelmingly Jews. Major participants included the houses of Cohen, Seligman, Bischoffsheim and Goldschmidt, Bleichroeder, Wertheim, Erlanger, and Oppenheim. Similarly, in 1874, the Seligmans worked with the Rothschilds to market some $25 million in U.S. bonds in Europe, and in 1875 the Seligmans, again working with the Rothschilds, marketed $55 million in U.S. bonds in England and on the European continent.[8]

With participation in state finance, in America as in Europe, came political influence. As noted above, when President Ulysses Grant took office in 1869 he offered Joseph Seligman the position of secretary of the treasury. Though Seligman refused the offer, he continued to be consulted closely by the administration on the refunding of the public debt, currency stabilization, and methods for strengthening American credit abroad.[9]

Seligman's influence continued during the presidency of Rutherford Hayes. In 1877 the Hayes administration adopted many of Seligman's suggestions for refinancing the government's debts. Seligman and other German-Jewish bankers played a major role in marketing U.S. bonds in Europe during the 1870s.[10] Indeed, by the late 1870s Seligman, working together with August Belmont (one of the few German-Jewish bankers to convert to Christianity), the Rothschilds, and J. P. Morgan, dominated the sale of U.S. government securities in Europe.

The Southern State Debt

German-Jewish bankers were also heavily involved in marketing the securities of Reconstruction-era Southern state governments. After the Civil War, radical Republicans sought to drastically alter the social and political structures of the states of the former Confederacy. They sought to establish a regime that would break the political power of the planter class that had ruled the region prior to the war. Republican radicals attempted, moreover, to create a new governing coalition of newly freed and enfranchised blacks, such loyal whites as could be identified, and Northern immigrants—the famous carpetbaggers—who came to the South hoping to find political and economic opportunity. Southern Republican state governments were, of course, closely linked to the national Republican party and were designed to serve as Republican bulwarks in national politics.[11]

The radical Republican regime in the South was, of course, supported by a military and administrative apparatus that included the federal army, the federal court system, U.S. commissioners, internal revenue collectors, postmasters, and customs officials.[12] This federal apparatus by itself, however, was never sufficient to guarantee the stability of the Republican state governments. Especially as the U.S. army began to withdraw its troops from the South in the 1870s, Republican state administrations were compelled to turn to their own resources to maintain their power. Many of the state governments developed spending programs designed to bolster their political support by giving a variety of groups a stake in their preservation. These programs included a substantial expansion of state patronage positions, economic development, particularly railroad construction, and elaborate public works projects.[13]

Because the economy of the South had been devastated by the

Civil War, the Republican state governments were never able to create tax bases that could adequately support these programs, though several introduced onerous new taxes. High tax rates, however, tended to undermine the political support that the states needed. Moreover, high tax rates were fiscally not very useful in a region whose market economy had been shattered and where money was scarce. This meant that many of the radical governments had to turn to deficit spending and borrowing to finance their ambitious development and public works programs.[14]

The South, itself, was capital-poor. Thus any effort by state governments to borrow money meant the importation of capital from either the North or abroad. Northern capital in huge quantities, during this period, was being absorbed by railroad construction and industrial development. As a result, Reconstruction-era Southern governments often found themselves turning to sources that had access to European capital. This, of course, included the German Jews.

Joseph Seligman was thus heavily involved with Alabama state debt. Similarly, Jacob Schiff, the head of Kuhn, Loeb and Company, was involved with Georgia securities. In general, these bonds were poor credit risks because of the corruption and inexperience of Southern state officials during this period and could eventually not be sold anywhere in America or in England where investors were likely to be familiar with American conditions. However, through their connections to Jewish firms in Paris, Frankfurt, and Amsterdam, German-Jewish bankers in the United States were often able to market even the most questionable securities. Thus, the Jewish firms of Erlanger and Company and J. H. Schroeder and Company in Paris came to be among the most active European participants in the marketing of Southern state debt.[15]

For example, in 1870, two Boston financiers formed the Alabama and Chattanooga Railroad Company and persuaded the Alabama state legislature to endorse nearly $5 million in bonds issued by the company for the construction of about 300 miles of track. The state's endorsement entitled it to a first lien on the property of the road in the event of a default on the notes. The legislature also authorized a $2 million state bond issue to fund a state loan to the railway company. None of these bonds could be sold in the United States. Within thirty days of their issue, however, all the bonds had been marketed in Britain, France, Germany, and The Netherlands by the Schroeder and Erlanger companies, though usually at a steep discount. The railroad company defaulted on its debt payments within the year amidst charges of fraud.[16]

In this instance, the foreign bond holders were able to recover some of their losses after 1876, when a state debt commission established in the wake of the Democratic return to power decided to maintain the state's credit worthiness by refunding rather than defaulting on the state debt. In most instances, foreign bondholders were not so fortunate. After the end of radical Reconstruction and the restoration of Democratic rule in the South, many state governments refused to honor their predecessors' debt issues, claiming that the bonds were tainted by fraud and illegal procedures. The repudiation of the Reconstruction-era debt, of course, led to decades of litigation.[17]

It is interesting that the importance of Jews in state finance during the Reconstruction period helped one Jewish politician play a more direct role in a Southern Republican state administration. One of South Carolina's most prominent Republican politicians during the 1870s was Franklin Moses who served, successively, as a delegate to the South Carolina constitutional convention, speaker of the South Carolina House of Representatives, adjutant and inspector general of the militia, a trustee of the state university, and, in 1872, governor of the state.[18] Moses was a scalawag, that is, a Southerner who supported the Republicans. South Carolina's Republican government, like some regimes in premodern Europe and the Middle East, had a very narrow pool of talent from which to draw. Its political base consisted of uneducated, newly freed slaves and a very small number of whites. Hence, the Republicans were eager to have Moses's services even though he was a Jew and former Confederate.[19]

Like the other Reconstruction-era Southern state governments, South Carolina was forced to borrow heavily to finance its administration and internal improvements. Moses proved to be especially adept at raising money through the sale of state securities and was able to make use of this talent to further his political career.[20] Between 1868 and 1871, the state legislature, led by Speaker Moses, issued or guaranteed some $23 million in bonds. As in the case of other Southern state bonds, many of these securities were marketed on the European continent by Jewish banking firms. Most, unfortunately, quickly declined in value to less than fifty cents on the dollar and were ultimately repudiated after the Democrats returned to power.

Franklin Moses's administrative talents extended beyond the

realm of finance. While speaker, Moses organized a 14,000-man state militia composed mainly of black troops and led by white officers. Subsequently, Moses personally traveled to New York to purchase arms and supplies for this force.[21] In the American South during Reconstruction, as in the Third World today, election outcomes depended as much upon the balance of armed force as upon the distribution of political popularity. Moses's state militia played a critical role in bringing about a Republican victory in the 1870 South Carolina state elections when it was able to discourage Democratic sympathizers from going to the polls while simultaneously preventing the Democratic party's paramilitary forces from intimidating black and other Republican voters. The state militia also prevented Moses's opponents from using judicial processes that they controlled against him. During his term as governor, Moses was named the "Robber Governor" by his foes and was often accused by Democrats of diverting public funds for his personal use—a charge that had some merit.[22] At one point, Moses was able to block his own arrest on corruption charges only by calling up four companies of black militia to guard his residence and office.[23]

Moses was not the only Jew who became prominent in South Carolina politics during Reconstruction. Two of South Carolina's most prominent black politicians of this same era, Francis L. Cardozo and Robert C. DeLarge, curiously enough were both the offspring of black mothers and Jewish fathers. Cardozo, the son of a Jewish economist and a free black woman, was educated at the University of Edinburgh, Scotland, and served as South Carolina secretary of state. DeLarge served as a state land commissioner and, with the vigorous assistance of Moses's militia, was elected to the U.S. House of Representatives in 1870. The House, however, refused to seat DeLarge, nominally because of charges of election fraud and voter intimidation brought by his opponents. As this example suggests, the political alliance between blacks and Jews that became so important in the United States during the mid-twentieth century has older and far more complex roots than is sometimes realized.[24]

Industrial Development

In addition to their activities in the area of public finance, German-Jewish bankers played a major role in promoting American industrial development during the post–Civil War era. The single most important aspect of industrial development in this period was the construction of railroads, which provided the nation with a unified continental market and thus served as a major spur to economic and industrial expansion. The U.S. government, of course, worked to promote railroad construction by giving enormous land grants to firms in exchange for the construction of rail lines.

Such land grants subsidized railroad construction. They did not, however, actually provide the capital needed to lay track and purchase equipment. This is where the role of private financiers was critical. Financiers would arrange to loan a railroad corporation the funds needed for construction and to begin operation in exchange for bonds secured by the value of the land grant that the road received from the federal government. Thus, private financiers were actually responsible for the government's success in promoting railroad construction by translating the initial land grant into the capital needed to actually build a rail line.[25] Jewish bankers were among the most important participants in this process.

Among the German-Jewish bankers active in railroad finance was Jacob Schiff. Schiff's clients came to include the Pennsylvania Railroad; the Chicago, Milwaukee and St. Paul; the Baltimore and Ohio; the Chesapeake and Ohio; the Denver and Rio Grande; the Great Northern; the Gulf, Mobile and Northern; the Illinois Central; the Kansas City Southern; the Norfolk and Western; the Missouri Pacific; the Southern Pacific; the Texas and Pacific; and the Union Pacific.

Schiff generally marketed these railroad securities in Europe, serving as a major conduit for European capital into the United States. Among Schiff's principal European banking partners was Sir Ernest Cassell, one of London's most prominent German-Jewish bankers.[26] Schiff and Cassell, working together, provided the capital for E. H. Harriman's reorganization and expansion of the Union Pacific Railroad in the 1890s. Schiff was also the chief financial backer for the expansion of the Pennsylvania Railroad during the same period.[27]

The Seligman family, often in close collaboration with non-Jewish industrialists and financiers, also played an important role in the construction and expansion of railroads. Joseph Seligman, working together with Jay Gould and Daniel Drew, was involved in the great struggle for control of the Erie Railroad in1868 that came to be known as the "Erie War." In the early 1870s, Seligman's firm invested heavily in railroad construction in the South and West and was the dominant factor in the consolidation of the Atlantic and Pacific and the Missouri Pacific, resulting in the construction of what became the St. Louis–San Francisco transcontinental railroad. During the same period, Seligman's firm helped to finance the construction of the K & T (known as the Katy) from Fort Riley, Kansas, to New Orleans. It also helped to finance the expansion of the New

Orleans, Mobile and Texas into a major interregional line and also helped to expand the Missouri, Kansas and Texas line.[28]

Imperialism

Like their British counterparts, late nineteenth-century American-Jewish financiers were proponents of imperialist programs and policies and participants in the American imperialist coalition of the period. As in the European case, the American Jews were often impelled to seek opportunities in more speculative areas than their Gentile colleagues. For example, Jewish financiers sometimes found that Gentile banking houses such as the powerful Morgan bank would allow them to participate only in the more speculative Western railroad investments, while reserving opportunities to invest in the securities of the safer Eastern roads for the Gentile banking community.[29]

For similar reasons, American Jews often found themselves with investments abroad—usually in Latin America—that could not be protected by local governments. This led them to turn to the government of the United States to protect their property. In the nineteenth century, the capacity of the American government to project military and political influence outside its own borders was quite limited in comparison to that of Britain or the other major European powers. Albeit on a relatively small scale, American-Jewish financiers were very eager to support policies, politicians, and institutions that could enhance the ability and willingness of the U.S. government to provide them with assistance if it was needed. By the same token, American politicians like Theodore Roosevelt and governmental institutions with a stake in a larger American role in the world found useful allies in the Jewish financiers.

One notable example of such a partnership is the relationship that developed between the Seligman bank and the U.S. navy during the 1870s. In the post–Civil War era, the navy department was chronically underfunded. Often, the navy could not meet its expenses or payroll obligations, particularly outside the United States. Through their London branch, the Seligmans extended credit to U.S. naval pay officers throughout the world. At one point, in 1877 according to Birmingham, the navy department had accumulated a debt of several hundred thousand dollars to the Seligmans—a debt it was unable to pay.[30] Nevertheless, the Seligmans were happy to continue to extend credit. The navy, in turn, was delighted to cooperate when the Seligmans needed help, as in the case of the Panama Canal.

Seligman and Company had become involved with the Panama

Canal project in 1880 when the French Panama Canal Company allowed Joseph Seligman to take charge of its initial stock issue. The Seligmans raised more than $100 million, virtually the entire estimated cost of building the canal. The Seligmans also undertook to mobilize American public opinion in support of the canal project and to gain the backing of the U.S. government for the undertaking. This latter task they accomplished by engaging a number of prominent former government officials, such as former Secretary of the Navy Richard Thompson, as lobbyists. The Seligmans had approached former President Grant with an offer of a $24,000 per year position as head of the Panama Canal Committee, but he turned them down.[31]

Unfortunately, the expense and difficulty of canal construction had been underestimated, and in 1885 the French Panama Canal Company collapsed with huge losses for investors in both America and Europe. Indeed, as was noted in Chapter 1, in France the involvement of a number of prominent Jewish financiers in the collapse of the Panama Canal Company played a role in sparking anti-Semitic sentiment. After the demise of the French endeavor, the U.S. government decided that it would promote the construction of a canal through Nicaragua. The Seligman family, however, strongly opposed the Nicaraguan route, since they had purchased a railroad and a great deal of land along the ill-fated Panama route and stood to suffer substantial losses if the canal's location was altered.

The Seligmans lobbied furiously on behalf of the original Panama route, working closely with Ohio Republican Senator Mark Hanna, and retaining a French journalist, Philippe Buneau-Varilla, as a publicist on behalf of the Panama Canal cause. Buneau-Varilla led a successful public relations and lobbying effort that eventually helped to persuade Congress to favor the Panama route over the Nicaraguan route. At one point, Buneau-Varilla was apparently able to convince a large segment of the public that a Nicaraguan canal would face constant threats from nearby volcanos. Unfortunately, however, after congressional approval was secured, one major new stumbling block appeared. The Isthmus of Panama was part of the nation of Colombia, and the Colombian government now refused to sign a treaty with the United States granting a right-of-way for new canal construction.

Buneau-Varilla and the Seligmans concluded that their only option was to induce Panama to secede from Colombia. The Seligmans made funds available to a group of Panamanians assembled by Buneau-Varilla. The latter then sat in an office at the Seligman bank and wrote a Panamanian declaration of independence as well as the new Panamanian constitution. Buneau-Varilla, a man of many talents, designed and hand-stitched a new Panamanian flag at James Seligman's summer home.

These preparations having been completed, the Seligmans turned to President Theodore Roosevelt to support the revolution they had arranged. Roosevelt was extremely eager to expand American influence in the Western hemisphere and favored both the canal project and the creation of a regime in Panama closely linked to the United States. Under the rubric of protecting American lives and property during a period of political unrest, Roosevelt dispatched American warships to Panama. American naval forces oversaw the surrender of the Colombians and the transfer of power to the new Panamanian government. After this victory, the Seligmans had Buneau-Varilla, nominally a French citizen, appointed Panama's first ambassador to the United States. Just as the Rothschilds had acquired the Suez Canal for Britain, the Seligmans had secured control of the Panama Canal for the United States.

What is, indeed, notable about the entire Panama affair is that Jewish financiers played a role in it similar to the one played so often by their British colleagues during this period. Jews helped to generate the financial means and political support for an imperialist enterprise. In this enterprise they were allied with the national executive and with governmental institutions like the U.S. navy that stood to gain from an enlargement of America's world role and military commitments. Their role in overseas finance had linked the interests of the Jews firmly to those of the state.

Corruption

The post–Civil War era was not only a period of corporate organization and reorganization but was also among the most corrupt and scandal-ridden in American history. Great fortunes were made and lost through stock and bond manipulations and what would today be called corporate mergers, buy-outs, and hostile acquisitions. Indeed, the Gilded Age bore some resemblance to the 1980s in the sense that huge quantities of capital imported from overseas as well as equally huge quantities of debt were used to finance a major reorganization and restructuring of the American economy. Inevitably, some of these dealings involved financial irregularities and fraud. Just as in the 1980s, often a small number of brokers and bankers with access to information about trades and deals used their "insider" data to make money at the expense of thousands of unwitting investors who were not privy to such information.

Their intimate ties to virtually every aspect of the finance, government, and politics of the Gilded Age meant that Jews were frequently associated with corruption and scandal. This was particularly true in the realms of industrial development and finance and the funding of the Reconstruction-era Southern state debt. As a result of their involvements in these areas, Jews came to be implicated in the great scandals and notorious financial manipulations of the latter half of the nineteenth century.

For example, as noted above, Joseph Seligman was closely allied with Daniel Drew, James Fisk, and Jay Gould in the infamous "Erie War" of 1868. Seligman served as the broker for Drew, Fisk, and Gould when they sold millions of dollars in Erie stock to Cornelius Vanderbilt, took short positions themselves, and then drove the price down.

Vanderbilt lost several million dollars as did thousands of other investors, many of whom had bought their Erie shares from Seligman and Company. The Erie Railroad came to be known as "The Scarlet Woman of Wall Street," and Gould was arrested and charged with fraud. Joseph Seligman put up Gould's bail of $20,000.[32] Subsequently, Seligman became involved in Gould's effort to corner the gold market, which led to the famous "Black Friday" crash that ruined thousands of investors, implicated President Grant, and led to a congressional investigation of Gould and Seligman.

Similarly, in the early 1890s, Jacob Schiff collaborated with E. H. Harriman in the latter's effort to wrest control of the Northern Pacific Railroad from J. P. Morgan and James Hill. With Schiff serving as his broker, Harriman bought millions of dollars in Northern Pacific shares, driving the price from under $100 per share to an incredible peak of more than $1000 per share. When the price of the Northern Pacific stock collapsed, the entire market crashed in the notorious "Black Thursday" panic that led to a nationwide economic depression.

In the same vein, Seligman and Company was involved with the "Panama scandal" that resulted from the collapse of the first Panama Canal project. During nine years of construction, the Panama Canal Company had issued some $400 million dollars in stock, selling much of it through Seligman's brokerage. The Panama Company's collapse ruined thousands of investors in America and in France who had been confident that a project directed by Ferdinand DeLessups, builder of the Suez Canal, and sponsored by the world's leading investment houses could not fail.

In the wake of the collapse, both the U.S. Congress and the French parliament organized investigations. In both countries, major Jewish financiers were implicated: Baron Jacques de Reinach in Paris, and Seligman in the United States. The American congressional investigating committee wanted to determine how so many shareholders lost so much money while the Seligmans and other brokers who sold the stock were able to escape without losing a penny.

The congressional committee also determined that Seligman and Company had used its contacts with important government officials to inflate popular confidence in the investment and had profited collaterally by obtaining—on an insider basis—lucrative procurement contracts and pocketing hefty fees from the Panama Company even while the corporation was on the verge of failure. In contemporary parlance, the Seligmans engaged in influence peddling, insider trading, and corporate asset stripping and looting—all at the expense of credulous investors.

As to the Reconstruction-era Southern state securities, the processes by which this debt was acquired and marketed were among the most corrupt in American history. Generally, the Southern state legislatures that authorized bond issues were staffed by elected officials with little or no administrative experience or understanding of public finance. Often, state bond issues were authorized in response to lobbying efforts or outright bribery on the part of the promoters of railroads or other internal improvements who had no intention of doing anything more than pocketing the proceeds.

For example, in Georgia during the early 1870s, the state legislature endorsed over $30 million in bonds for thirty-seven railroads that promised to lay track in the state. The president of three of these roads was a close friend of the state governor who, not surprisingly, worked tirelessly to obtain legislative approval for the securities. The proceeds from bonds worth several million dollars, marketed in Berlin and Frankfurt, simply disappeared, presumably into the pockets of state officials, financiers, and railroad promoters. Virtually no track was ever laid.[33]

Under the leadership of Franklin Moses and his cohorts the South Carolina state government was among the most corrupt of the period. During the Moses administration, more than $6 million in unauthorized, fraudulent state securities were issued and sold. The proceeds were widely assumed to have lined the pockets of state officials, though proof was never found. Moses also diverted hundreds of thousands of dollars in state funds for his own personal use, including the purchase and upkeep of the most elegant mansion in Columbia, the state capital.

In 1877, Democrats regained control of the South Carolina government in the wake of the departure of federal troops from the state. The new administration brought many former Republican officials to trial. At this point, Franklin Moses defected to the Democrats and testified against some of his former allies. During their trials, Moses was compelled to testify to some of his own misdeeds. For instance, Moses admitted that while governor he had taken money from an attorney to bribe one Jonathan J. Wright, a black justice of the South Carolina supreme court.[34]

Moses's one-time half-Jewish allies, Cardozo and DeLarge, were tried and found guilty of official fraud and corruption in connection with the sale of state lands. They were pardoned, however, as part of a larger settlement in which the national Republican administration granted pardons to some Democrats who had been found guilty of violations of federal election law in connection with the 1876 presidential election, in exchange for state pardons for Republican politicians who had been ousted in the wake of the termination of Reconstruction.[35]

Thus, as part of their intimate connection to the finances, politics, and society of the Gilded Age, Jews were also involved in many of the most visible and spectacular frauds of the post–Civil War period as well as in the economic dislocations and financial manipulations that characterized the era. This had important consequences. Because Jews had become identified with the worst excesses of the nineteenth-century industrialist order, it became a simple matter for the opponents of that regime to attack it by attacking the Jews.

Anti-Semitism in the Nineteenth Century

As indicated above, two sets of forces, both bitterly opposed to the economic transformations of the late nineteenth century, made use of anti-Semitic rhetoric and propaganda as one element in their attack upon the industrialist order. The first of these consisted of Western and Southern radical agrarians who, through the Populist movement, were engaged in a bitter struggle against the economic and political changes associated with American industrial development. The second comprised old-stock New England patricians, some associated with the Mugwumps, whose own economic and political importance had waned relative to the new, post–Civil War class of industrialists and financiers.

Populist Anti-Semitism

The issue of Populist anti-Semitism has occasioned considerable debate, much of which has less to do with the Populists than with interpretations of more contemporary political movements. During the 1950s, for example, social scientists and historians like Richard Hofstadter who almost reflexively saw mass popular movements as anti-democratic, sought to portray the Populist movement as a hotbed of nativism and intolerance. For Hofstadter, of course, the more genteel and upscale Progressives were the true heroes of nineteenth-century political reform.[36] Other historians, more friendly to the idea of popular protest and grass-roots movements in contemporary politics, were concerned to refute Hofstadter's charge and prove that the Populists were as tolerant as angels.[37]

Obviously not all Populists were anti-Semites, and, indeed, some may even have been philo-Semitic. Nevertheless, a constant theme of anti-Semitism is manifested in the writings and speeches of some of the major Populist leaders and intellectuals. One well-known example is William Hope Harvey's 1894 work, *Coin's Financial School,* which was one of the best-selling works of the ninteenth century.[38] The major thesis of the book was that the demonetization of silver— the Populist equivalent of original sin—was part of a plot by the Rothschilds and other Jews allied with the British to dominate the United States and, indeed, the entire world by obtaining a financial stranglehold.

Harvey also wrote the popular novel, *A Tale of Two Nations,* also published in 1894, which made much the same point. In this book, a British Jew named Baron Rothe (read Rothschild) sends his nephew Victor Rogasner (presumably August Belmont) to the United States to bring about its economic ruin. Rogasner finds the corrupt Grant administration to be a perfect vehicle for his plans. Making good use of the sly cunning for which members of his race are said to be noted, Rogasner has no difficulty manipulating and bribing members of Congress and other high government officials to support his nefarious schemes. Rogasner also hires corrupt economics professors to testify against bimetallism.

During the course of the story, it should perhaps go without saying, Rogasner falls in love with a fair-haired and pure American girl. He schemes to steal her from her own true love, a young and honest congressman from Nebraska who seems to bear some resemblance to William Jennings Bryan. The blond and virtuous heroine, of course, is appalled by the dark and slimy Rogasner and forthrightly declares him to be "repulsive to me."[39]

The most famous literary example of Populist anti-Semitic propaganda was Ignatius Donnelly's 1889 work, *Caesar's Column*.[40] Donnelly had served as the Populist lieutenant governor of Minnesota and was the author of the preamble to the 1892 national Populist platform. He was also the editor of two notable Populist newspapers, *The Anti-Monopolist* and *The Representative*. *Caesar's Column*, which sold more than 250,000 copies, is set in a mythical future and is an example of the same genre as Edward Bellamy's *Looking Backward*, that is, a book that tries to project some putative contemporary trend to its logical future conclusion in order to warn readers of the consequences of allowing present tendencies to continue.

The main character of Donnelly's work leaves a mythical Populist paradise in Uganda to visit New York exactly 100 years in the future. He discovers that the leadership of the United States has secretly fallen into the hands of a small group of greedy and fabulously wealthy financiers, most of whom are Jews. The leader of this secret Jewish cabal is one Jacob Isaacs, who calls himself Prince Cabano. The Jews and their allies have reduced the other people of the United States to poverty and slavery. The world, according to Donnelly, has become "semitized." Of course, when he is not busy ruling the world, Prince Cabano, like his slimy coreligionist Victor Rogasner, devotes himself to lusting after the virtuous, blond, Gentile maiden Estella Washington. Like her alter ego in *A Tale*, Estella finds Cabano "repulsive."

Anti-Semitic themes were also employed by Populist orators and politicians. Mary Lease, the so-called Kansas hell-raiser, often attacked the Cleveland administration as the agent of Jewish bankers. In Lease's fiery speeches, Jews were usually described as usurers, landlords, and bankers and often used to symbolize the inequity of the contemporary economic and political order—a regime that allowed Jewish parasites to prey upon farmers and such their life-blood.[41]

Similarly, William Stewart, a free-silver senator from Nebraska, asserted that the Rothschilds were embarked upon a plan to enslave the entire world to the rule of the "money power," and to that end were seeking to "concentrate wealth, build up aristocracy, and destroy Democracy in the United States."[42] In the same vein, Tom Watson asked rhetorically whether in his wildest dream Thomas Jefferson would have thought [that by 1892] "red-eyed Jewish millionaires would be the chiefs of his party," prostituting it to the vilest services of greed and monopoly?[43]

Hofstadter reports that by the time of the campaign of 1896, anti-Semitism had become, if not all-pervasive, at least common in the Populist movement. "One of the striking things about the Populist convention in St. Louis," wrote an Associated Press reporter cited by Hofstadter, "is the extraordinary hatred of the Jewish race. It is not possible to go into any hotel in the city without hearing the most better denunciation of the Jews." Later in the campaign, William Jennings Bryan was compelled to reassure Jewish Democrats in Chicago that the anti-Semitic rhetoric used by some Populists did not really represent an attack upon Jews as a race. Jews were, he said, attacked only because they symbolized greed and avarice.[44]

Patrician Anti-Semitism

The second group to launch an attack upon the economic and political transformations of the late nineteenth century consisted of members of the old-stock New England gentry. This American aristocracy found that its own economic and political fortunes had declined relative to those of the new class of industrialists and financiers. For the New England brahmins, the Jew served as a symbol of the greed and corruption of the new order. By assailing Jews, they attacked the industrialists, financiers, and railroad barons who were displacing them in the nation's political and economic life. This fear was expressed in a stream of anti-Semitic writings and speeches on the part of New England's leading public figures and intellectuals during the late nineteenth century.

One of the foremost examples is Henry Adams. Grandson of President John Quincy Adams, Henry sought to pursue a career of leadership and public service in the family tradition. He discovered, however, that his breeding, education, and background were irrelevant in the new world of big business, international finance, corruption, and money. The symbol of this materialistic society in which an Adams had no place was the Jew. For Adams, writes Barbara Solomon, Jewish was a synonym for greedy, materialistic, and avaricious, and Jew was interchangeable with the nouveau riche businessman, capitalist, or goldbug.[45]

The new industrial capitalist world order was, in Adams's mind, a thoroughly Jewish order. In his autobiographical work, *The Education of Henry Adams*, he writes about himself, "His world was dead. Not a Polish Jew fresh from Warsaw or Cracow—a furtive Yakoob or Ysaac still reeking of the ghetto, snarling a weird Yiddish to the officers of the customs—but had a keener instinct, an intenser energy and a freer hand than he—American of Americans."[46] Adams saw Jews everywhere and in control of business, politics, finance, and journalism. He longed for a cataclysmic collapse of the established order. "In [the present] society of Jews and brokers," he observed in 1893, "I have no place."[47]

These themes were echoed by other New England patricians, including Henry James who used Jewish characters to symbolize greed and the decline of society.[48] Similarly, Henry Adams's brother, Brooks, in this 1896 work, *The Law of Civilization and Decay*, demonstrated that throughout history Jews had used their money and financial acumen as instruments of exploitation, domination, and oppression. In the United States and Britain, productive industrial capitalism had been replaced by parasitic finance capitalism, symbolized by the Jewish usurer.[49] This became a common theme in the literary and scholarly works of the New England patricians and other upper-class intellectuals. The Jew was attacked as the representative of a materialistic society with no values or culture.

Immigration Restriction

From the patrician perspective, not only was the Jew a symbol of the corruption of America's new ruling class, but the Jew symbolized the decay of American values in another way as well. To the patricians, Jewish immigrants, along with other newcomers from Southern and Eastern Europe, represented a threat to American culture, society, and the Anglo-Saxon race. The uncouth and dirty Jewish immigrant was as much an emblem and product of the moral decay and avarice of the industrialist order as the slimy and repulsive Jewish capitalist. And, of course, the two were clearly linked. Was it not the avaricious manufacturers who, in their quest for cheap labor, had thrown America's borders open to hordes of filthy Yids? Opposition to immigration was as much an attack on business as on immigrants.

One major vehicle for this aspect of the patrician attack on the industrialist regime was the Immigration Restriction League. The League was founded in 1894 by a trio of New England bluebloods—Charles Warren, Robert Ward, and Prescott Farnsworth Hall—and a group of their Harvard classmates. The League quickly promoted the creation of affiliates throughout the nation, often making use of the Harvard alumni network and other organizations of transplanted New Englanders.[50]

The League's major focus was on the threat posed by the "newer" immigrants to America's institutions and way of life. As distinguished from the older immigrants of Anglo-Saxon or Teutonic stock, the newer immigrants were primarily from Southern and Eastern Europe and were Catholics and Jews. These new "degraded" immigrants were said to be responsible for crime, delinquency, drunkenness, and pauperism. To their fellow Americans, League spokesmen addressed the essential question. Did they "want this country to be peopled by British, German and Scandinavian stock, historically free, energetic, progressive, or by Slav, Latin, and Asiatic races, historically down-trodden, atavistic and stagnant?"[51]

Among the League's most important intellectual spokesmen was Edward Ross, one of the pioneers of American sociology. In his widely read 1914 work, *The Old World and the New*, Ross explains the importance of protecting Anglo-Saxon Americanism against pollution through immigration. As "beaten members of beaten breeds" came to America, the "immigrant blood" of races morally inferior to the races of Northern Europe was polluting "American blood" with the end result being "race suicide."[52] In his chapter on the "East European Hebrews" Ross observes that "Jews rarely lay hands to basic production," that in college "Jewish students always want their grades changed," and that Jewish businessmen are "slippery." It is interesting that Ross's attack on Jews and other immigrants was presented as part of his more general assault on business values in the United States. Like other restrictionists, Ross blamed the flow of undesirable immigrants into the country on "our captains of industry."[53]

In Congress, the forces of restriction were led by Senator Henry Cabot Lodge of Massachusetts. In 1896, Lodge sponsored legislation that would require all persons seeking admission into the United States to be literate in the language of the country from which they sought to emigrate. This provision was designed to keep out many of the often illiterate Southern and Eastern European immigrants and especially the Jews who were usually literate in Yiddish or Hebrew rather than the language of their nominal country of origin. This bill passed both houses of Congress in 1896 but was vetoed by President Cleveland.

After McKinley took office in 1897, the issue was revived and continued to be emphasized for the ensuing decade. However, the lobby forces of business and manufacturing, such as the Chamber of Commerce of the United States and the National Association of Manufacturers, who favored unrestricted immigration in order to ensure a steady source of cheap labor, opposed restriction. In addition, groups speaking for the newer immigrants and their descendants, with the Jews taking the lead, organized the National Liberal Immigration League to fight for the continuation of an open door policy.

A Populist-Patrician Alliance?

The initial support for immigration restriction was provided mainly by the political spokesmen of the Northeastern upper classes. However, the vague outlines of an alliance began to develop around the issue of immigration—and on opposition to the industrialist order more generally—between the Brahmins and the political representatives of the South and rural West. Indeed, after the turn of the century, the leaders of the restrictionist movement in Congress were Senators Edward "Cotton Ed" Smith of South Carolina, Oscar Underwood of Alabama, and F. M. Simmons of North Carolina.

Support for immigration restriction in the far West was related mainly to prejudice against the Chinese and Japanese who had entered the region in large numbers to work on the railroad and as farm laborers. In the South, however, support for immigration restriction was not primarily an expression of hostility to local foreigners. Relatively few immigrants settled in the South and hardly any in the rural South where support for restriction was greatest.

Instead, Smith, Tom Watson, and other rural Southern politicians, like their counterparts among the New England patricians, saw immigrants—Catholics and Jews in particular—as blatant examples of the evils of the new industrialist order. This regime had come to dominate the Northeast and was now encroaching into such Southern cities as Atlanta where factories, often owned or managed by Jews, were being developed. Watson wrote, "The scum of creation has been dumped upon us. Some of our principal cities are more foreign than American." The blame for this fell directly upon the industrialist class, "the manufacturers and bankers," who "wanted cheap labor and did not care how much harm to our future might be a consequence of their heartless policy."[54]

To the political spokesmen of the rural South, an attack upon immigration and undesirable foreigners who threatened the Southern way of life was a means of attacking the entire industrialist regime. After the turn of the century, the leadership of the anti-immigration movement passed from Lodge to men like Smith and Watson, and the chief bastions of support for immigration restriction became the rural South and West, though from time to time organized labor also supported restriction on the theory that immigration drove down wage rates.

For a brief moment at the turn of the century, what might have seemed to be an improbable alliance between agrarian radicals and patricians, an American coalition of the top and bottom, was a possibility. The two groups were divided by an enormous cultural chasm but, nevertheless, shared a common hatred for the new capitalist order and the forces that it was bringing to power. In 1896, it should be recalled, William Jennings Bryan's presidential candidacy was supported by some members of the New England gentry including Henry Adams. Like the Populists, the New England gentry saw the gold standard as a symbol of the victory of finance capitalism and the business classes they detested.[55] Though the gentry had disdain for rabble rousers, they were willing to swallow their contempt to support a fellow enemy of industrial capitalism. In this respect, the behavior of some members of the New England gentry was not so different from the conduct of the European aristocrats during the same time period who held their own noses and supported their countries' Drumonts and Stoeckers.

The moment when such an alliance was even remotely possible, however, was a very brief one. In response to patrician anti-Semitism, leaders of the new industrial order had already begun in the 1880s to move to rid themselves of the Jews and make a place for their patrician foes. Once the patricians had a stake in the new regime, their interest in its failings diminished.

As to the Populists, agrarian forces continued to make use of anti-Semitic appeals into the early twentieth century. The Populist cause, however, suffered a devastating defeat at the hands of Northeastern business in the critical election of 1896. After that time, agrarian radicalism was no longer a threat to the industrialist regime at the national level. Anti-Semitism became mainly a Southern instrument of regional defense against capitalist encroachment rather than a weapon in a national struggle against the industrialist order.

Social Discrimination and Elite Formation

During the late nineteenth century, the new business classes simultaneously co-opted their patrician foes and rid themselves of their former Jewish allies. This feat was accomplished through the creation or reconstitution of social institutions that effectively linked the interests of the old privileged strata with those of the new moneyed classes. These new or reconstituted institutions were designed to be *judenrein* and to serve as the social bases for a new, united, Anglo-Saxon ruling class.

The earliest glimmerings of this process of elite formation and institution building could, in retrospect, already be seen during the 1870s, but the process began in earnest in the late 1880s and was fully in place by the end of the First World War. Members of the nation's old-stock patrician stratum had charged that the newly rich businessmen and financiers who were displacing them were greedy, unprincipled, uncouth, and, indeed, little better than the Jews with whom they associated. The business classes responded by offering the patricians a share of their wealth and a renewed sense of importance in exchange for being granted the social acceptance and status they they coveted.

To cement this relationship, a set of institutions was established that brought together money and social standing. These included private boarding schools, college preparatory schools, summer resorts, country clubs, college fraternities, and private clubs. The new business stratum financed these institutions while the old elite operated them and used them to confer status and social prestige upon the groups that paid for them. One stratum gained prestige while the other acquired the power to confer prestige.

For example, the Groton School was founded in 1884 by Endicott Peabody to rear young gentlemen in the tradition of the British public school and, according to Digby Baltzell, to protect them from the increasing heterogeneity of the public school system.[56] At the same time, other New England boarding schools such as the Taft School, the Hotchkiss School, St. George's School, and the Choate School were founded while others such as Deerfield, Exeter, and Andover were expanded during this period. These schools enrolled and mixed the sons of the new and old rich from all across the nation, teaching them a common set of values and helping to create a national ruling class. In most instances, Jews were excluded or admitted in very small numbers under informal but rigid quota systems.

Exclusion of the Jews was an important part of this process of elite formation and was part of the price that the new moneyed classes had to pay for an alliance with the patricians. Between the 1880s and the first two decades of the twentieth century, Jews were systematically excluded from the resorts, clubs, boarding schools, and universities that were the institutional base of the new national elite.

One of the earliest and best-publicized incidents was the refusal in 1877 of the Grand Union Hotel in Saratoga Springs, New York, to admit Joseph Seligman as a guest. This incident generated wide-spread publicity because it was so unusual. Jews retaliated by purchasing or building a number of hotels in Saratoga Springs. Soon, however, resort hotels that presumed to cater to an elite clientele, or even merely to give that impression, openly advertised that they admitted Gentiles only. Within a few years, separate systems of resort communities for Jews and Gentiles had developed in most areas of the country.[57]

As to clubs, by the 1890s most elite business and social clubs refused to accept Jewish members even when, as was sometimes the case, prominent Jews had been among the founders of the clubs. Thus, for example, Theodore Seligman was blackballed from New York's Union League Club because he was a Jew even though his father, Jesse, had been one of the founding members. Similarly, during the Civil War, Joseph Gratz was president of the Philadelphia Club and several other Jews were members. After the 1890s, however, no Jews were admitted as members. Jews responded by establishing their own clubs and, soon, separate systems of "exclusive" clubs developed across the nation.[58]

In the case of universities, the more fashionable private clubs and fraternities, around which the social life of many schools was organized, began to exclude Jews in the 1890s. After 1900 few Jews were, according to Higham, elected to the Princeton clubs or to the fraternities at Yale. The literary and gymnastic societies at Columbia excluded Jews as did the exclusive boardinghouses and "final clubs" at Harvard. Jews responded by forming their own clubs and fraternities. The first Jewish Greek-letter society, Zeta Beta Tau, was established at City College of New York in 1903 and at Columbia in 1904. By the 1920s, there were twenty-two national Jewish Greek-letter fraternities and three sororities, with 401 chapters and nearly 25,000 members at some 114 universities.[59]

More important, around the time of the First World War a system of Jewish quotas for university and professional school admission was instituted—first at the elite East Coast schools and later at lesser institutions that, like their counterparts among resort hotels, sought to acquire an image of exclusivity by aping the practices of their betters. Informal and unpublicized quotas dated from the early 1900s. By the end of the war, however, university administrators made no secret of their concerns about "excessive" Jewish enrollments.[60]

Meeting at Princeton in May 1918, the Association of New England Deans, including representatives of Bowdoin, Tufts, Brown,

M.I.T., and Yale, held lengthy discussions about the Jewish problem. The following year, Columbia, led by President Nicholas Murray Butler, introduced new admissions procedures designed to reduce the number of Jews in its classes. The new application process required a psychological test designed to measure character and included a form that asked for religious affiliation and father's name and birthplace. It also required a photograph. The percentage of Jews at Columbia was quickly cut in half.[61] Other universities soon followed suit.

At Harvard, President Lowell in 1922 openly called for a reduction in the number of Jews. This created a controversy on campus and among the alumni, and the president's policies were formally rescinded. However, new admissions processes were quietly introduced that accomplished the same objective.[62] By the late 1920s, only Chicago, Cornell, Brown, and Penn among the elite schools remained relatively open to Jews. Even in these institutions, the schools of law and medicine maintained anti-Jewish quotas.[63]

This process of elite formation also entailed the creation of new beliefs and worldviews. Every ruling class endeavors to generate ideologies that justify its privileged status. The new American elite was no exception. The ideology that it developed to justify or rationalize the marriage of old and new money, and to explain the exclusion of Jews and other non-Protestants from its ranks, was a doctrine of Anglo-Saxon supremacy.

Social theorists like Louis Hartz have asserted that America's dominant ideology was always a Lockian liberalism in which status was achieved through individual effort rather than ascribed on the basis of background and breeding.[64] The implications of Lockianism, however, were seldom accepted by Americans in a pure or undiluted form. At the turn of the century, the intellectual defenders and spokesmen of the emerging American ruling stratum sought to blend liberalism with racism to demonstrate that a true elite class was marked both by success and breeding.

These authors and philosophers, who included eugenicists like the zoologist Charles Davenport, social Darwinists like M.I.T. President Francis Walker, and practitioners of the new "social science" disciplines like Edward A. Ross, argued that this combination of traits was particularly notable among Anglo-Saxons. Indeed, the moral sense of the Anglo-Saxons was scientifically shown by Ross, Davenport, and the others to lie at the very top of the evolutionary tree.[65]

While even Jews might be able to make money, only Anglo-Saxons, as Houston Stewart Chamberlain proved in his influential 1900 work, *Foundations of the 19th Century*, also understood the importance of character, loyalty, and leadership.[66] Similarly, Madison Grant was able to demonstrate in his 1916 classic, *The Passing of the Great Race,* that membership in an elite class ultimately depended upon possession of the appropriate racial background. "Environment," that is, talent and achievement, was by itself not enough. Grant was especially concerned to prove that Jews could not be members of a true aristocracy.[67]

The widespread acceptance of this view explains why wealthy turn-of-the-century Americans became so obsessed with genealogy. Between 1883 and 1900, they formed the Sons of the Revolution, the Colonial Dames, the Daughters of the American Revolution, and a host of other societies, and invested heavily in genealogical research. Wealth and personal achievement were no longer sufficient to confer social status. Since a proper Anglo-Saxon background was now also necessary in America, as in Germany half a century later, the *Sippenforscher* held the key to membership in the elite social stratum.[68]

Thus, Americans may have been Lockians to the extent that they believed in individualism and success through hard work and self-help. However, at the turn of the century, their liberalism came to be tempered as it related to the Jew with the notion that Jewish success was the result of craft, cunning, dishonesty, and cheating. This certainly provided sufficient intellectual justification for the exclusion of Jews from elite circles—an exclusion largely accomplished by the First World War.

The exclusion of the Jews made anti-Semitism less useful as an instrument for attacking the industrialist order. Moreover, as they jettisoned the Jews and linked themselves, instead, to the patricians, the industrialists provided the latter with a stake in the regime.

After the turn of the century, the major set of forces that continued to use anti-Semitism as a political weapon were based in the rural South and Middle West rather than the Northeast. These forces were too weak to oppose industrial capitalism at the national level. Indeed, the nativism and anti-Semitism of agrarian forces made it virtually impossible for them to unite with the only other potential opponent of industrialism—organized labor—which had a sizable foreign-born membership and Jewish leadership.

However, while they might be weak at the national level, agrarian forces, especially in the South, were still capable of mounting a regional defense against the intrusion of industrial capitalism. During this period, as witnessed by the Scopes case, Southerners sought to prevent the ideas and worldview of the industrial North from penetrating their region and fought in Congress to maintain their racial purity by restricting immigration.

In the early years of the twentieth century, Jews, including many of Northern or even foreign origin, played a prominent role in Southern industrial and commercial development. This meant that anti-Semitism could play a useful role in the rural South's program of regional defense against capitalism. It is for this reason that Southern nativist and anti-Semitic agitation increased after the turn of the century when the Populist cause had been defeated nationally. Rural Southerners were now engaged in a struggle for control over their own bastions against the encroaching forces of industrial capitalism. And, in this battle at home, they scored a great victory in the case of Leo Frank.

The Case of Leo Frank

Leo Frank was a Northern Jew, raised in Brooklyn and educated at Cornell University. In 1907, he moved to Atlanta where he became the part owner and superintendent of his uncle's National Pencil Factory and a prominent member of Atlanta Jewish society. The turn of the century was a period of industrial and urban development in the South, and Atlanta was at the forefront of both trends. The city's population had grown rapidly as rural white tenant farmers left the countryside to search for work in the cotton mills and other factories that were being built by both Northern and Southern industrialists, including Jews.

Jews had occupied an accepted place in the "Old South." They were typically merchants, tradesmen, and professionals and, in a pattern not so different from the one existing in Central Europe in the eighteenth and early nineteenth centuries, were seen as a useful middle class by the Southern aristocracy. In the late nineteenth century, however, the economic place of Jews in the South began to change as Jews participated eagerly in the development of an industrial economy.

This change in the role of Jews was especially notable in Atlanta where they were major factors in manufacturing, banking, railroads, and wholesaling. The Fulton Bag and Cotton Mill owned by Jacob Elsas and the Southern Agricultural Works owned by Sigmond Landauer were two of the largest factories in Atlanta. Other Jewish companies manufactured strawhats, whiskey, cottonseed oil, paper bags, and furniture. Aaron Haas, a prominent German Jewish entrepreneur, was president of the Atlanta and Florida Railroad and the Atlanta City Street Railway, while his cousin Jacob was president of two banks. Some of Atlanta's Jewish entrepreneurs were natives, others were German Jewish immigrants, while still others, like Frank, were transplanted Northerners who had moved South looking for economic opportunity.[69]

The result of Atlanta's economic transformation was that large numbers of native Protestant whites were employed in menial jobs by industrialists among whom Jews were a prominent and visible segment. To make matters worse, many of the workers in question were women. It was already an affront to the manhood of rural white Southerners to be forced to allow their women to work in factories where it was feared that they would be subjected to what now would be called sexual harassment by their employers. This resentment and fear was even greater when those employers were Jews. Two decades of anti-Semitic propaganda had depicted Jews as sexual perverts who lusted after virtuous Anglo-Saxon maidens. To poor whites, Jews symbolized the worst evils of an industrial system that subjected them to poverty and forced them to send their women to work in factories where they were at the mercy of crazed Jewish sex fiends.[70]

The place of Atlanta's Jews as exemplars of oppressive capitalism and exploitation was both exploited and enhanced by the Populist campaigns of the turn of the century. Atlanta's Jewish business community was strongly opposed to Populism and, especially, to Populist economic theories. Prominent Jewish businessmen like M. L. Adler, owner of the Atlanta Paper Company, furniture manufacturer Otto Schwalb, as well as Joseph Hirsch, Harry Silverman, Jacob Haas, and Oscar Pappenheimer were active and visible opponents of Populism.[71]

In their turn, Populists made use of anti-Semitic images to attack their opponents. The major Populist newspaper in Georgia, former Populist vice-presidential candidate Tom Watson's *People's Party Paper*, avoided anti-Semitic appeals during the 1896 Populist campaign, in part to avoid offending the Jewish merchants whose advertisements were one of its major revenue sources. However, the Democratic *Atlanta Constitution* was in the hands of prosilver Democrats during this period and did not hesitate to use anti-Semitic stereotypes to highlight its economic theories. An 1895 *Constitution* cartoon depicted President Grover Cleveland as a pawnshop proprietor pawning the United States to Britain while a New York Jewish banker named "Ickelheimer" swept the floor of the shop.[72]

A parade float designed to promote the free silver cause also made use of the Ickelheimer character who was depicted as a stooped and hook-nosed creature. A *Constitution* editorial suggested that the issue of free silver was a question of "money against patriotism; the flag against the three balls." Atlanta readers, knowing that virtually all the city's pawnbrokers were Jews, understood this as a thinly veiled anti-Semitic reference, and the Jewish press protested vehemently.[73]

It was against this backdrop that the Frank case became a national cause célèbre in the decades before the First World War. In 1913, Frank was accused of murdering Mary Phagan, a fourteen-year-old employee of the pencil company, whose body was found in the basement of the factory. At first, suspicion fell on Newt Lee, the factory's black watchman. The evidence against Lee, however, proved flimsy. Gradually, suspicion began to center on Frank. Some circumstantial evidence potentially linked Frank to the crime. More important, however, were the anti-Semitic stereotypes of the period.

To those seeking revenge for the murder of "Little Mary Phagan," Frank epitomized the licentious Jew, eager to take advantage of the pure young Christian maidens in his employ. In his articles on the trial, Tom Watson referred to Frank as a "lascivious pervert" with "bulging satyr eyes . . . protruding fearfully sensual lips; and also the animal jaw." The suspicion that Frank sought to take advantage of the girls in his employ was fueled when the proprietor of a local bordello charged that Frank was a regular customer who enjoyed "perverted" sex. After a short trial and less than four hours of jury deliberation, Frank was found guilty and sentenced to death.[74]

After the conviction, Jewish groups in Atlanta mobilized the support of national Jewish leaders such as Louis Marshall and Albert Lasker to seek a new trial for Frank. On the other side, however, was former Populist leader Tom Watson. He became involved in the Frank case mainly because in March 1914 the *Atlanta Journal*, which generally expressed the views of Watson's mortal political foe, U.S. Senator Hoke Smith, urged that Frank be given a new trial. Watson responded in his paper, *The Jeffersonian*, with an anti-Frank editorial charging that Smith had been accepting money from Frank's wealthy friends.

The response among Watson's readers to his attack upon Frank was so enthusiastic that Watson stepped up his campaign. What began as an effort to embarrass a local political opponent evolved into a full-dress effort to mount still one more campaign against the alien industrial regime that had routed Watson and his allies at the turn of the century. To Watson, the anti-Frank campaign became another opportunity to mobilize his poor rural and urban constituents against the moneyed classes and their political servants. That

Leo Frank was a Jew—a Jew with bulging satyr eyes, to boot—and a Northerner made him a perfect symbol of the corruption and oppression of the regime that dominated the nation and now was tightening its grip upon the South. He was portrayed as a capitalist and college graduate from the North, brought to the South to exploit the labor of the wives and daughters of ruined farmers. Now, they claimed, he was seeking to use his money and connections to escape punishment for having murdered a Southern girl who resisted his perverse advances. What could be a more perfect symbol and rallying point than what Watson called "a typical young libertine Jew."[75]

Through the year 1914, Frank's defenders pressed their appeals through the Georgia courts which, ultimately, rejected them. The pro-Frank forces turned to a campaign to rally public opinion on his behalf. Hundreds of newspapers throughout the country urged that Frank's death sentence be commuted to life imprisonment. A petition campaign was mounted that ultimately produced more than one million signatures. Prominent non-Jews spoke out on Frank's behalf. These included the president of the University of Chicago, nine governors, seven senators, many congressmen, and six state legislatures.

At the same time, Watson's anti-Frank campaign was succeeding beyond Watson's wildest dreams. The circulation of his newspaper tripled, and in response to its call anti-commutation rallies were held throughout the state. Mass meetings were scheduled in Atlanta almost every day during the month of June 1914 as the Georgia prison commission met to consider what recommendation to make to the governor. Watson's attacks repeatedly focused on the wealth and connections of Frank's supporters. A conspiracy of "Big Money" was at work seeking to corrupt the state's courts, its governor, and its newspapers to free a rich "Sodomite." "Frank belongs to the Jewish aristocracy and it was determined by the rich Jews that no aristocrat of their race should die for the death of a working-class gentile."[76]

After careful deliberation, Georgia Governor John Slaton concluded that Frank was probably not guilty of Mary Phagan's murder and commuted his sentence to life imprisonment. After this decision, Slaton found his life in danger. A mob, armed with dynamite, attacked the governor's residence and was beaten back only after a pitched battle with the state militia. Slaton left the state and did not return until after the First World War. As for Frank, within eight weeks of the commutation order and his transfer to a state prison farm, he was seized by a group of men calling themselves the Knights of Mary Phagan and hung from an oak tree near Marietta, Georgia.

The anti-Frank campaign failed to revive Populism as a national political movement, though it did succeed as a weapon of regional defense. The leaders of the anti-Frank forces enhanced their grip on political power. For example, Tom Watson's political career was revived, and he was elected to the Senate in 1920. There he became a leader of the immigration restriction movement.

On the other hand, development of the political power of the forces of the "new South" was retarded. In Atlanta and other Southern cities, political and business alliances between Jews and native-stock Southerners were disrupted as it became disreputable to have too close an association with Jews. As Steven Hertzberg notes, in Atlanta, itself, in the wake of the Frank affair, social discrimination against Jews increased, "Jew money" became an issue in local politics, and the once-vigorous Jewish business community virtually withdrew from political life.[77] This weakened the coalition supporting political and social change in the South and retarded the region's political development.

Dating from the Frank affair, moreover, Jews came to identify the South as a bastion of anti-Semitism and radical nativism. When opportunities emerged in later decades to ally themselves with forces seeking to bring about a transformation of the Southern political system, Jews were only too happy to do so. In the meantime, however, the forces of the rural South had succeeded in using anti-Semitism as a weapon of regional defense, holding off the forces of Northern industrialism.

Jews and Progressivism

The political system that had emerged in the United States at the turn of the century was one that deprived Jews of access to economic and political power and to social standing. Not surprisingly, Jews were attracted to political movements that opposed that regime. Working-class Jews espoused socialism. Many middle- and upper-class Jews, on the other hand, supported Progressivism. The Progressives were a heterogeneous group of politicians that included such diverse individuals as Robert LaFollette of Wisconsin, Hiram Johnson of California, Albert Cummins of Iowa, William U'Ren of Oregon, Woodrow Wilson of New Jersey, and Theodore Roosevelt of New York, tied together by a network of organizations such as the National Municipal League and publications such as the *National Municipal Review*.

As Martin Shefter has noted, Progressives were united less by ideology than by a common place in the political system. In the wake of the election of 1896, the great majority of states and the national government, as well, came to be governed by one-party systems. The Progressive movement linked politicians who found their careers blocked by the leadership of the dominant party, with groups and forces that did not enjoy the favor of or access to the locally dominant party—shippers in states where that party was tied to a railroad, firms that sold in national markets in cities where the party machine was tied to businesses that sold in local markets, and so forth.[78]

The ideology and the program that bound the Progressive movement together, Shefter observes, were formulated by intellectuals and professionals who argued that governments dominated by party machines were corrupt and irrational. These should, the Progressives argued, be replaced by governments that listened directly to the voice of the people and paid heed to the dictates of science. Thus, Progressives fought for the elimination of patronage practices and the introduction of a merit-based civil service in its stead, the substitution of primary elections for party conventions, the introduction of nonpartisan municipal government, and for a variety of other reforms that would weaken political party machines. In addition, middle-class Progressives sought to create institutions such as advisory commissions, legislative reference bureaus, and municipal research bureaus that would provide the professional and managerial classes with direct access to the government.[79]

Progressives also sought to strengthen the autonomy and power of bureaucratic agencies, to introduce principles of personnel administration to executive agencies, to introduce scientific management techniques in governmental departments, and to construct a state with the capacity to intervene more actively in the nation's economy and society.

Because it not only attacked a regime that excluded them but also advocated the principles of merit, rule by experts, and careers open to talent, and sought the creation of a powerful state that could enforce these norms, Jews supported the Progressive movement. In turn, Progressives in power relied upon the talents and energies of Jews. Jewish journalists supported Progressive causes. Often Jews served as links between Progressive politicians and working-class voters. Moreover, because Progressives constantly sought to identify theories that would justify their efforts to change the nation's institutions, politics, and policies, they were forced to look for talented advisors and to seek the support of intellectuals who were disaffected from the established political and social order. This meant that almost inevitably Progressives would come to rely heavily upon the intellectual assistance of Jews.

Thus, Theodore Roosevelt became the first president since Grant to offer a cabinet position to a Jew. Roosevelt appointed Oscar Straus to serve as his secretary of commerce and labor. President Woodrow Wilson relied upon Bernard Baruch and, especially, upon Louis Brandeis, who became his closest economic advisor. Brandeis's career epitomized the history of the relationship between Jews and Progressivism.

Before Jews were expelled from the nation's political and social elite, Brandeis had been an important corporate attorney, an associate of the Northeast's most powerful industrialists, and a member of the most exclusive clubs. By the turn of the century, however, Brandeis discovered that he and his wife were no longer welcome in their old circles. This helped spur his conversion to the cause of reform—and, eventually, of Zionism.[80]

Brandeis, more than anyone else, was responsible for translating Wilson's pledge of a New Freedom into concrete policies. Brandeis played a decisive role in planning Wilson's economic program, and particularly in formulating the Federal Reserve and Federal Trade Commission bills.[81] Wilson rewarded Brandeis with a Supreme Court appointment which was confirmed by the Senate after a long and bitter confirmation battle. Thus, during the Progressive era, a rather typical alliance began to emerge between Jews and state builders. This Progressive-Jewish alliance, however, was a victim of World War I and the great Red Scare.

The Red Scare

During the nineteenth century, the identification of Jews with industrialism made it possible for the opponents of the industrialist order to use anti-Semitism to attack it. However, the rulers of the industrialist regime had successfully defended themselves against this tactic by casting off their Jewish allies, co-opting the New England patricians, and making anti-Semitism irrelevant as a weapon against the industrialist regime, at least at the national level.

In the twentieth century, the political role of anti-Semitism was transformed. Rather than serve as a weapon against capitalism, anti-Semitism became a weapon against liberalism and Progressive reform. At the turn of the century, Jews came to be identified with socialism and communism. The rapacious Jewish banker was transmuted into the menacing Jewish Red.

Jewish immigrants from Eastern Europe had often brought their Socialist and Communist ties to the United States with them, and at the turn of the century Jews constituted a major fraction of the leadership of the American Socialist and Communist movements. In addition, Jews such as Sidney Hillman and David Dubinsky were prominent leaders of left-wing labor unions. Moreover, urban immigrant Jewish voters, along with other immigrants, became part of the electoral constituency for liberal and Socialist candidates and a segment of the popular base of support for reform in the areas of labor, social welfare, and regulatory policy at the state and municipal levels.

Beginning prior to the First World War, and culminating in the postwar "Red Scare," the association of Jews with radicalism allowed conservative forces to use anti-Semitism to attack not only the Socialist and Communist movements, but also the labor movement and liberal reform as well. Groups such as the American Protective League charged that labor agitators and strike leaders were typically "Russian Jews with Americanized names," who should be driven from the country.[82]

Similarly, opponents of liberal reform in the early twentieth century sought to associate reform and reformers with Jewish Bolshevism. In New York, for example, between 1900 and the beginning of the First World War, such Jewish politicians as State Representative Aaron J. Levy played major roles in the struggle for the creation of public utilities commissions, banking, securities and insurance regulation, workers' safety legislation, the recognition of labor unions, and various forms of social welfare legislation.[83] Opponents of these measures often sought to discredit them by depicting them as the work of Jewish radicals and other foreigners that should be opposed by loyal Americans.

This use of anti-Semitic appeals culminated in the great "Red Scare" of 1919–1920. The Red Scare was, in many respects, the closest parallel in American history to Tsarist anti-Semitism, that is, an officially sponsored effort by an agency of the executive branch of the United States government to use anti-Semitism to attack its own Socialist opponents. In the aftermath of World War I and the Bolshevik seizure of power in Russia, Attorney General A. Mitchell Palmer led a series of raids on Communists and other presumed subversives in the United States. Several hundred were arrested, and 250 socialists and anarchists, including Emma Goldman, deported to Russia.[84] Other raids followed. Palmer and his allies noted that the majority of the "Reds" were immigrants. Indeed, as Palmer noted, a great many were Jews, living on New York's East Side.

Palmer asserted that another 60,000 agitators of the "Trozky" type could be found on the streets of New York's East Side where, it was said, "Trozky" himself had once lived as "a disreputable alien." Palmer's allies circulated data purporting to prove that of the top Bolshevik leaders all but Lenin were Jews, many of whom had lived in New York before leaving for Russia to overthrow the Tsar.[85]

After several months, the Red Scare died down. Major business leaders, who had initially supported Palmer as an antidote to labor agitation, now felt that the point had been made and called for a restoration of order.[86] The business community was never anxious to encourage unnecessary rabble-rousing. Palmer, himself, was discredited when Bolshevik uprisings he had predicted failed to materialize. Newspapers then began to treat him as something of a buffoon, and the "fighting Quaker's" political ambitions were ended. The Red Scare, however, had a significant impact upon American politics and upon the place of Jews, in particular. First, in the wake of the Red Scare, the "national origins" immigration quota system was introduced in 1921, greatly limiting immigration from Southern and Eastern Europe and severely reducing the number of Jewish immigrants able to enter the United States.

Moreover, the Red Scare undermined the coalition between Jews and non-Jewish Progressives that had begun to develop during the Roosevelt and Wilson administrations. In the wake of the Red Scare, native-stock Progressives and such Progressive leaders as Hazen Pingree and Hiram Johnson disassociated themselves from organized labor and the urban working class which, in many states, had provided the popular and electoral base for Progressive reform. While they did not support or even condone the anti-Bolshevik crusade, native-stock Progressives had no desire to be tarred by the same brush as their immigrant and Jewish cohorts.

In state after state, the Progressive coalition broke apart in the wake of the conservative campaign against Jewish and other immigrant radicals. Though Jews continued to support Progressives, as John Buenker has observed, the enthusiasm of the native-stock middle class for social and economic reform waned after 1920, when members of this stratum became nervous about too close an association with urban immigrants and organized labor.[87] The role this played in the disruption of turn-of-the-century liberal Progressivism was, perhaps, one of the greatest political victories for anti-Semitism in American political history—separating old and new stock liberals until the New Deal.

In the decade between the end of the Red Scare and the beginning of the New Deal, anti-Semitic activity in the United States was most prominent among native-stock Protestants in rural areas of the South and Midwest—the former bastions of Populist strength. These regions provided the audiences for Henry Ford's anti-Semitic *Dearborn Independent* and the most fertile recruiting ground for the Ku Klux Klan and other nativist groups. Here, anti-Semitism still served as a weapon of regional defense against the regime and values that had conquered the remainder of the United States at the end of the previous century, and Ford's readers could still be stirred by his attacks upon "international Jew financiers" and the "money changers of Wall Street."

During the 1920s, this provincial anti-Semitism had little national political significance. At most, it reminded native-stock Americans of the undesirability of entering into political alliances with Jews and reinforced the pattern of social discrimination against Jews that had been devised in earlier decades. Indeed, during the decade of the 1920s, Jews probably faced the most severe and systematic pattern of discrimination and exclusion that they have ever faced in the United States. Access to higher education was severely restricted, with some top universities and professional schools limiting Jews to no more than 3% or 4% of their entering classes. Employment discrimination was the norm with major corporations, law firms, and universities declining to offer positions to Jews. Housing discrimination was commonplace, and so forth.

The continuation of anti-Semitic agitation, political isolation, and social discrimination, however, would make Jews extremely eager to cooperate with any government willing to promise them protection from anti-Semitic attacks, freedom from discrimination, and greater political and economic opportunity. Just such a regime came to power in the United States in 1933.

3 Jews and the American Liberal State: From New Deal to New Politics

J ews entered the 1920s handicapped by political isolation and social ostracism. During the succeeding half century, however, Jews became politically powerful and won full access to social institutions, such as the elite universities, that had systematically excluded them at the turn of the century. Indeed, during the 1990s, individuals of Jewish origin were serving as presidents of schools that had been among the most restrictive, including Columbia, Dartmouth, and Princeton. Moreover, Jews came to comprise large segments of the faculties—to say nothing of the student bodies—of the same distinguished law and medical schools that once had turned away all but a handful of Jewish applicants.

To achieve the status and win the opportunities that they currently enjoy, Jews relied heavily upon the assistance of the national government and the governments of several of the major states. Beginning in the 1930s, Jews were able to forge alliances with prominent politicians and major political forces at the state and federal levels and to become important members of national and state governing coalitions organized by the Democratic party.

These alliances permitted Jews to use the power of the national and state governments to combat threats to their religious freedom; to further their educational, employment, and housing opportunities; to protect themselves from attacks by anti-Semitic groups; to influence U.S. foreign policy in order to bring about the creation of a Jewish state in Palestine; and generally to enhance their influence and status in American society. During the 1960s and 1970s, the importance of Jews in the Democratic coalition increased. Moreover, as the reach and power of the American national government expanded, first, during the New Deal era and, again, with the social service and civil rights programs of the 1960s, the access Jews enjoyed to the national regime enabled them to use it to break down most barriers to their full participation in American life.

Jews and the State: Opportunity, Protection, and Status

First, in the areas of education and employment opportunity, Jewish groups made substantial use of both the national and state governments to end discrimination and provide Jews with access to educational and job opportunities from which they had long been excluded. In 1944, several major Jewish organizations, including the American Jewish Committee, the American Jewish Congress, and the Anti-Defamation League (ADL), joined together with a number of smaller groups to form the National Jewish Community Relations Advisory Council (CRC) to combat discrimination against Jews in employment, education, and housing.

The CRC was instrumental in securing the enactment of legislation prohibiting discrimination in employment in a large number of states during the late 1940s and early 1950s. Once a statute was enacted, Jewish agencies monitored compliance and threatened to bring legal action against firms that continued to engage in discriminatory practices. Such corporations as the American Telephone and Telegraph Company, Consolidated Edison, Pacific Gas & Electric, and major New York City law firms that had been bastions of discrimination against Jews were compelled to open their doors to Jewish job applicants.

During the 1960s, the American Jewish Committee enlisted the support of the federal government in its campaign against employment discrimination. A 1965 executive order, prompted by the committee's efforts, prohibited firms holding federal contracts from discriminating against Jews in employment. In 1966, this order was extended to banks handling federal funds. With the advent of the Medicare program, this policy was extended to insurance companies serving as Medicare carriers.

In the 1940s, both the AJC and the ADL launched major efforts to combat discrimination against Jews in college and professional school admissions. At the turn of the century, as noted in Chapter 2, most major American colleges and universities imposed Jewish quotas, drastically limiting the percentage of Jews admitted to undergraduate and professional programs. The exclusion of Jews from major universities was an outgrowth of the consolidation of the Protestant "Establishment" at the turn of the century as well as a response to the growing number of children of recent Jewish immigrants seeking admission, especially to universities in the Northeast.

As a result of discriminatory admissions policies, Jewish enrollments declined sharply in the early years of the twentieth century, particularly in the most prestigious colleges such as Harvard and Yale and in the top medical and law schools. For example, at the beginning of the century, nearly half the students enrolled in Columbia

University's College of Physicians and Surgeons were Jews. By the beginning of World War II, less than 7% of Columbia's medical students were Jews. Similarly, before the First World War, 40% of the students enrolled in Cornell University's School of Medicine were Jews. By the Second World War, less than 4% of Cornell's medical students were Jews. During the same period, Jewish enrollments at Harvard's medical school fell from just under 30% of the student body to just over 4%. The discriminatory admissions practices of medical and law schools were among the factors prompting many ambitious Jewish students to seek admission to less desirable and, hence, more readily available positions in dental, pharmacy, and accounting schools.

During the 1940s and 1950s, Jewish organizations began to use the threat of legal action to compel universities to end overt discrimination against blacks and Jews in their admissions policies. In 1945, for example, Columbia University altered its restrictive admissions procedures when the American Jewish Congress's Commission on Law and Social Action (CLSA), initiated a legal challenge to Columbia's tax-exempt status.[1] Other universities, including Yale, moved to preclude similar suits by modifying their procedures as well.[2] In mounting an attack upon discriminatory admissions practices, Jewish organizations found it useful to link themselves to blacks. The number of blacks seeking admission to elite universities in the 1940s was very small. By speaking on behalf of blacks as well as Jews, however, Jewish groups were able to present themselves as fighting for the abstract and quintessential American principles of fair play and equal justice rather than the selfish interests of Jews alone. This would not be the last time that Jewish organizations found that helping blacks could serve their own interests as well.[3]

The CLSA and other Jewish groups also were active in securing the enactment of state laws, such as New York's 1948 Quinn-Oliffe Act prohibiting colleges from discriminating against any applicant on the basis of race, religion, creed, color, or natural origin. In New York, moreover, Jewish groups played a major role in persuading Governor Thomas Dewey to establish the commission whose work led to the creation and consolidation of New York's state university system in 1948.

Jewish organizations in New York at that time despaired of ever completely ending discrimination against Jews in private college admissions. New York City's Jewish residents had, for decades, sent their children to schools in the city's public college system. Indeed, many of the nation's most distinguished contemporary Jewish scientists, physicians, attorneys, and university professors earned their undergraduate degrees at the City College of New York (CCNY) because they could not hope to break through the barriers confronting Jewish applicants to private universities. After the Second World War, however, large numbers of New York's Jewish families moved to the Long Island suburbs, losing access to the city college system. As a result, Jews fought for the creation of a public university that would provide educational opportunities for Jewish students on a statewide basis.

At the national level, Jewish organizations induced President Truman to create a number of panels to investigate discrimination in employment and education. These panels issued reports that identified widespread bias in university admissions. The President's Commission on Higher Education recommended that university applications eliminate all questions pertaining to race, religion, and national origin—questions used primarily to identify Jewish applicants. Similarly, the President's Committee on Civil Rights attacked Jewish quotas in university admissions. During the postwar period, colleges and universities were beginning to compete for and rely heavily upon federal funding, especially to pay for staff and equipment needed to remain competitive in the physical sciences. As a result, they could not afford to ignore such federal guidelines.

Jewish organizations also lobbied vigorously for state legislation prohibiting discrimination in housing. In 1948, the American Jewish Congress and American Jewish Committee submitted friends of the court briefs to the United States Supreme Court in the case of *Shelley v. Kramer*, urging that restrictive covenants in housing be declared unconstitutional.[4] In these endeavors to end discrimination in housing and employment, as in their campaign against restrictions on access to higher education, Jews very often joined forces with blacks on the theory that they could be useful allies in the struggle against bigotry. Gains achieved on behalf of one, Jewish organizations reasoned, would serve the interests of both, while allowing Jews to project an image of unselfish pursuit of the public good.

In the realm of religious freedom, Jews were a major element of the coalition opposed to school prayer and other forms of public exercise of religion. The American Jewish Congress, together with the American Jewish Committee and the Anti-Defamation League, joined with the American Civil Liberties Union and a Protestant group—"Protestants and Other Americans United for Separation of Church and State"—to oppose school prayer in the federal courts.

Fearing an anti-Semitic backlash, the three Jewish organizations were very anxious to diminish the public visibility of Jews in the opposition to school prayer and other forms of religious exercise. The American Jewish Committee, for example, insisted that the ACLU find both a non-Jewish plaintiff and non-Jewish attorney for its ultimately successful attack on a New York state law providing for released time from school for religious instruction.

The ACLU complied with the AJC's wishes. Ironically, it was generally assumed that plaintiff Tessim Zorach and attorney Kenneth Greenawalt—both Gentiles—in the 1952 case of *Zorach v. Clausen* were Jews.[5] Similarly, for the 1962 case of *Engel v. Vitale*, challenging the constitutionality of New York's nondenominational school prayer, the New York Civil Liberties Union (NYCLU) insisted that both the plaintiff and lead attorney be non-Jews. As a result, the case was assigned to William Butler, who happened to be the only non-Jew on the NYCLU lawyer's committee.[6]

As to protection from anti-Semitic attack, as early as the 1930s, Jewish defense organizations such as the ADL began to secure the cooperation of federal and state law enforcement agencies to collect information on anti-Semitic groups and activities. In recent years, the ADL has often worked in cooperation with the Southern Poverty Law Center's (SPLC) Klanwatch program to maintain extensive surveillance of the Ku Klux Klan and other neo-Nazi or racist groups. Information collected has been shared with law enforcement agencies and also used as the basis for civil litigation designed to undermine racist and anti-Semitic groups by forcing them to pay large damage claims.[7]

In a well-publicized 1987 case, the SPLC brought suit against the United Klans of America (UKA), one of the nation's three major KKK factions, charging that the UKA, as a corporate entity, was liable in the death of Michael Donald, a nineteen-year-old black student who had been murdered by klansmen in 1981. A jury awarded the dead youth's mother $7 million in damages, forcing the UKA to surrender to her the deed to its national headquarters building in Tuscaloosa, Alabama. By establishing the principle that the parent organization could be held financially responsible in civil court for the violent acts of its members, the SPLC created a potent weapon to be used against violent racist and anti-Semitic organizations.

In 1989, the SPLC and the ADL joined to file a civil suit against three neo-Nazi "skinheads" who had murdered an Ethiopian refugee in Portland, Oregon, in 1988. The suit charged that the three had acted at the behest of a neo-Nazi group called White Aryan Resistance (WAR). In 1990, a jury awarded a multimillion-dollar judgment against the murderers and Tom and John Metzger, the leaders of WAR. In 1991, the ADL and the AJC were among the groups that fought for passage of the federal Hate Crimes Statistics Act designed to increase the attention that police forces devote to crimes that involve racial or religious antagonism. Both the ADL and AJC have been heavily involved in teaching local police forces about their responsibilities under the act.

Beginning in 1948, American Jews also were able to use their access to the federal government to exercise a substantial measure of influence over American foreign policy. During World War II, American Jews had been reluctant to attempt to intercede with the Roosevelt administration to even attempt to save the Jews of Europe from destruction at the hands of the Germans. After the war, some American Jewish groups sought a revision of America's restrictive immigration laws to permit European Jewish refugees to enter the United States. This effort, however, was unsuccessful. Both the Displaced Persons Act of 1948 and the McCarran-Walters Act of 1952 continued the "national-origins" quota system that had been American policy since the Immigration Act of 1924. This system favored immigrants from Northern and Western Europe and effectively held Jewish immigration to a trickle. Though Jewish groups had lobbied for it, the Displaced Persons Act of 1948 was decidedly unfavorable to Jewish refugees. It gave preference to refugees from the Baltic states swallowed by the Soviet Union, to Eastern and Central Europeans of German ancestry, and to agricultural workers. Few Jews qualified for admission under any of these categories.

This failure was more than offset, however, by the great triumph of American Jewish organizations during the postwar period—the creation of the State of Israel. American Jewish groups succeeded in securing the support of the Truman administration for the creation of a Jewish state. This came despite the opposition of large segments of the British government and the U.S. state and defense departments which feared that American support for a Jewish state would jeopardize American security interests in the Middle East as well as America's relationship with the Arab oil producers.

From the perspective of pro-Zionist Jewish groups, the creation of Israel was the ultimate step in preventing another Holocaust—the creation of the Jews' own state. But even non-Zionist groups like the American Jewish Conference saw a relationship between the issue of Israel and the problem of protection. Israel could absorb the

Jewish refugees whose possible arrival in the United States was seen as a potential impetus for anti-Semitism. Subsequently, Israel became the central focus for the efforts of American Jewish groups at communal mobilization. Over the ensuing decades, American Jews were able to induce the U.S. government to provide the Jewish state with billions of dollars in American military and economic assistance.

Finally, the benefits Jews demand for access to government becomes especially evident when we see the extent to which Jews have relied upon the state and the public economy to achieve positions of influence and status in American society. Jews are, as a group, wealthier and better educated than virtually all other segments of American society, and, as noted earlier, Jews have risen to positions of leadership throughout American society. Nevertheless, Jews who have achieved positions of prominence in the United States have most often done so in the public economy of government agencies, universities, foundations, law firms, and public interest groups as well as the mass media that is so closely associated with these institutions.

According to one recent national survey comparing Protestants, Catholics, Jews, and blacks who have attained some measure of prominence in the United States, Protestants tend to derive their positions mainly from activities in the private sector and Catholics from trade union leadership. Jews, on the other hand, have depended primarily upon the media, foundations and public interest groups, and appointive governmental posts to achieve positions in the American political and social elite.[8]

Jews are only 3% of the nation's population and comprise 11% of what this study defines as the nation's elite. However, Jews constitute more than 25% of the elite journalists and publishers, more than 17% of the leaders of important voluntary and public interest organizations, and more than 15% of the top ranking civil servants. The business sector, by contrast, appears to be solidly controlled by white Protestants, who constitute more than 80% of the corporate leaders. Fewer than 7% of the top executives and managers of American corporations are Jews. In short, Jews have relied heavily upon the public or quasi-public spheres rather than the private sector as their route to power and status in American society.

The prominence of Jews in the public sector and their resulting capacity to use the national government to combat discrimination and secure economic opportunity dates from the time of the New Deal. During the Roosevelt era, the regime's needs and the capacity of Jews to serve them gave Jews significant and enduring access to the American government.

Jews and State-Building: The New Deal

As we saw earlier, Jews had played significant roles in American government during the Gilded Age and, again, in the Progressive era but were unable to sustain their influence when they and the regimes with which they were associated came under attack. Beginning in the 1930s, however, Jews were able to achieve a lasting position of power and prominence as members of a state-building and governing coalition that emerged in the United States in the wake of the Great Depression. During the New Deal era, Jews provided the administration of Franklin D. Roosevelt with a vitally important pool of talent and expertise. Consistent with the centuries-old pattern of the relationship between Jews and the state, Roosevelt and his successors reciprocated by offering the Jews protection and opportunity in exchange for their services.

When he came to power in 1933, Roosevelt and the Democratic party that he led were opposed by much of the nation's established elite. As a result, Jewish attorneys, economists, statisticians, and other talented professionals became critical sources of leadership and expertise for the Roosevelt administration. Jewish labor leaders, most notably Sidney Hillman, president of the Amalgamated Clothing Workers, played an important role in Roosevelt's political campaigns.[9] More than 15% of Roosevelt's top-level appointees were Jews—at a time when Jews constituted barely 3 percent of the nation's populace and were the objects of considerable popular antipathy.[10] The majority of Jewish appointees were given positions in the new agencies created by the White House to administer New Deal programs. In these agencies, Jews came to constitute a large and highly visible group. The term "New Deal" itself was coined by one of Roosevelt's Jewish aides, Samuel Rosenman.[11] For their part, Jews found the Roosevelt administration and New Deal programs to be a major route to power, status, and employment in a society that otherwise subjected them to severe discrimination in virtually every occupational realm.

A number of Jews achieved positions of considerable influence in the Roosevelt administration. Harvard law professor, Felix Frankfurter, whom Roosevelt appointed to the Supreme Court in 1939, was a key Roosevelt adviser and consultant. Frankfurter played a central role in formulating New Deal programs and in channeling large numbers of bright young Jewish lawyers to Washington to work in New Deal agencies and programs. These came to be called "Frankfurter's happy hot dogs."[12]

Among the most important of these individuals was Benjamin Cohen. Cohen, advised by Frankfurter, was instrumental in writing major pieces of New Deal legislation including the Securities Act of 1933, the Securities and Exchange Act of 1934, the Public Utility Holding Act of 1935, the Federal Communications Act, the TVA Act, the Wagner Act, and the Minimum Wage Act. Other Jews who played significant roles in the Roosevelt administration included Supreme Court Justice Louis Brandeis who advised the administration on ways of securing Supreme Court approval for its legislative enactments; Treasury Secretary Henry Morgenthau, Jr.; and a host of others such as Abe Fortas who joined the SEC; Isador Lubin who became head of the Bureau of Labor Statistics and Roosevelt's chief economic advisor; Charles Wyzanski in the Department of Labor; and White House special assistant, David Niles.

Jews were especially prominent in the Department of the Interior where Nathan Margold served as department solicitor, Abe Fortas served first as director of the Division of Manpower and later as undersecretary, Saul K. Padover as assistant to the secretary, and Michael Straus as director of the War Resources Council. Also in Interior, Felix Cohen was the architect of New Deal policy toward Native Americans, emphasizing tribal sovereignty and cultural pluralism.

Jews, in particular Jewish lawyers, were also prominent in the Department of Labor, the Justice Department, the Securities and Exchange Commission where Jerome Frank served as chairman, the Tennessee Valley Authority chaired by David Lilienthal, the U.S. Housing Authority administered by Nathan Straus, the National Labor Relations Board, the Social Security Administration, and the Agricultural Adjustment Administration.

For Jewish professionals, lawyers in particular, New Deal agencies were a critically important source of employment and a vitally important route to professional status and successful careers.[13] Jews faced significant discrimination in the private sector and previously had few career options in the public sector. Talented Jews were able to more than hold their own against Protestants in college, graduate school, and professional school but found that academic success did not give them access to jobs and high-status careers. Nowhere in the country would major law firms hire Jews except under the most extraordinary circumstances. Law school faculties generally also refused to hire Jews. Service with the Roosevelt administration gave

status and, ultimately, power to bright Jewish professionals who had
few other options. Roosevelt, for his part, was happy to take full
advantage of this pool of underemployed talent to develop ideas and
progress and to staff his agencies.

More generally, Jews were strong supporters of Roosevelt's efforts
to institute administrative and governmental reforms during the New
Deal era and to expand the power of the national state. Roosevelt
was anxious to increase and centralize the power of the national
government and to that end sought to establish institutions that
would link the administration to a mass constituency and enable it
to assert its control over the entire governmental structure.[14] Jews
strongly favored these aims and played important roles in bringing
them about.

The first of these goals was achieved by the National Labor Relations Act, which established procedures for organizing workers into
unions that would be staunch supporters of the Democratic administration, and by the Social Security Act which established a bureaucracy to provide benefits to Americans in times of need. Jewish labor
leaders like Sidney Hillman played major roles in molding the
unions into effective political forces. In 1943, Hillman organized the
CIO's political action committee, America's first PAC, to strengthen
labor's capacity to act on the president's behalf. The CIO PAC created
an elaborate political machinery based on the CIO unions, city and
state industrial union councils, and any independent or AFL unions
willing to cooperate.[15]

The CIO PAC played a major role in the 1944 campaign, engaging
in voter registration, propaganda, and get-out-the-vote efforts. Hillman worked closely with the president in these endeavors, especially
in efforts to oust conservative Democrats and replace them with liberal allies of the Roosevelt administration. Thus, the CIO PAC helped
to defeat three members of HUAC in the 1944 Democratic primaries:
Martin Dies of Texas, Joseph Costello of California, and Joseph
Starnes of Alabama. The CIO PAC also helped to defeat a number of
other conservative Democrats.

Jews also played major roles in the organization and administration of the Social Security system. Under amendments to the Social
Security Act enacted in 1939, the Social Security Board required
states to establish merit systems covering the employees who administered its program at the state and local levels. This requirement was
policed by a Division of State Merit Systems, and led to the creation
of the first civil service systems in most states of the union. In this
way, the framers of the act sought to assure that control of the pro-

gram would not be seized by whatever political forces happened to be dominant locally. New Dealers wanted the flow of these new social security benefits to be controlled from the center, and the political advantages of the program to accrue to the national Democratic administration that enacted it.

Jews welcomed this because of their growing influence at the "center" and because since the Progressive era they had strongly favored the adoption of merit systems. The creation of a modern personnel system based upon competitive examinations and educational requirements was likely to require the recruitment of civil servants with technical proficiency and education and would, thus, skew the distribution of public jobs to the advantage of Jewish professionals working in the public sector—teachers, social workers, and the like.

The second of the purposes mentioned above—the creation of a set of institutions that would enable the administration to extend its control over the nation's policy-making and administrative apparatus—was served by the Executive Reorganization Act of 1937. Through this act Roosevelt sought, though ultimately with only partial success, to expand the White House staff, extend the merit system, replace the Civil Service Commission with a single personnel director appointed by the persident, create a central planning agency in the Executive Office, and place all administrative agencies including the independent regulatory commissions under one of the cabinet departments. These reforms, as Martin Shefter has observed, were designed to provide the administration with the institutional capacity to control the initiation, coordination, and implementation of public policy in the United States.[16] Jews had reason to support these reforms as well, since their influence in the Roosevelt administration gave them a stake in the expansion of its power.

At the state and local levels, Jews also allied themselves with Roosevelt and played important roles in his efforts to oust incumbent Democratic leaders hostile to the national administration. In New York, for example, Jewish liberals organized through third-party organizations and reform clubs such as the American Labor party and later the Democratic reform movement. Reformers allied with the White House attacked the patronage system in an effort to dry up the resources upon which local party leaders relied. Reformers also challenged the legitimacy of the party organizations their opponents led, accusing them of "bossism." Jews and other New Deal liberals sought in these ways to undermine the incumbent party leaders who opposed the administration and to gain power at the local level.

In these endeavors, liberals were not only serving the administration's interests, they were serving their own as well. To the extent that Jews and other middle-class liberals could use the support of the national administration to destroy traditional local patronage machines and replace them with modern, issue-oriented parties, they could also hope to enhance their own importance in the process of policy formulation and implementation at the state and local levels.

Candidates who appeal for votes by promising to enact new programs and to develop new policies, as Shefter observes, need the advice of technocrats, mainly middle-class professionals and administrators who can be the most fertile sources of ideas for new public policies. Presidential or mayoral "task forces" such as the President's Committee on Income Security, which drafted the Social Security Act, accord far more influence to these groups than had the traditional mechanisms of policy formation in the United States, especially at the state and local levels, which were controlled by machine politicians less interested in new ideas than in dispensing patronage and favors to blocs of voters and financial supporters.[17]

As a result of all these factors, the New Deal regime provided Jews with numerous opportunities and advantages, and by the end of Roosevelt's first term in office most Jews had given the president and his party their allegiance. To this day, Jews largely remain in the Democratic camp as voters, activists, and financial contributors—a point to which we shall return below.

THE ANTI-NAZI COALITION

During the late 1930s, Jews came to serve the Roosevelt administration in still another way. Jews became vitally important allies of the administration in its struggle against isolationism and pro-Axis sentiment in the years preceding World War II. Roosevelt and the American Jewish community had a common set of enemies—right-wing, pro-German, and isolationist organizations. The Roosevelt administration opposed these groups because of their opposition to American help for England. Jews, of course, opposed them because they were anti-Semitic and supported the cause of Nazi Germany. The struggle against these forces cemented the relationship between American Jews and the Roosevelt administration. Jews came to see the president and his party as their only reliable defense against Nazism at home and abroad.

Curiously enough, the struggle against Nazi Germany and its allies in the United States also united Jews and the "Eastern establishment" that had made itself *judenrein* only a few decades earlier.

Much as it disdained association with Jews, the Eastern Protestant establishment was, on the basis of education, economic interest, and often family connections, strongly Anglophilic and found in the Jewish community virtually the only reliable American allies for the British cause. Indeed, Jews and upper-class, Northeastern Protestants were the two groups in American society that most vehemently opposed Germany and supported England at a time when large segments of the American public, including Americans of German, Italian, Irish, and Scandinavian descent, either supported Germany, opposed England, or were against any form of American intervention in European affairs.

Jews and members of the Eastern establishment united during the late 1930s to create the "Century Group," which worked vigorously for American intervention against Nazi Germany. After the defeat of France in 1940, the Century Group called for the United States to declare war against Germany without waiting to be attacked. Jewish members of this group included financier James Warburg; film producer Walter Wanger; and Harold Guinzburg, president of the Viking Press. Well-known establishment members of the organization included the prominent manufacturer Ward Cheney, the journalist Joseph Alsop, the diplomat Frank Polk, and prominent attorneys and public servants Dean Acheson and Allen W. Dulles.[18]

Subsequently, Jews such as Warburg, Guinzburg, Hollywood producers Jack and Harry Warner, labor leader Abe Rosenfield, and New York restauranteur Mac Kriendler (owner of "21") were active in the "Fight for Freedom Committee," a group chaired by Episcopal Bishop Henry Hobson, whose membership included such establishment figures as Allen Dulles, Grenville Clark, Sinclair Weeks, and Walter White. In the years preceding World War II, Fight for Freedom organized a nationwide effort—with the tacit support of the White House—to mobilize public opinion against Germany and in support of Britain. Fight for Freedom worked vigorously to discredit isolationists and pro-German groups. Most of Fight for Freedom's major donors were either Jews or members of the Eastern Protestant establishment.[19]

The interventionist alliance between Jews and the Eastern establishment was evident in Roosevelt's appointment of Henry Stimson as secretary of war in 1940. Stimson, a Republican and pillar of the establishment was a partner in an elite Wall Street law firm once headed by Elihu Root. He had served as secretary of war under President Taft and secretary of state under Herbert Hoover. Though Stimson opposed Roosevelt's domestic program and had voted against him in both 1932 and 1936, he strongly supported an interventionist foreign policy and believed that American security required the defeat of the Axis. Stimson had not been among those initially considered for a cabinet post after Roosevelt's 1940 electoral victory. Roosevelt and Stimson, however, were brought together by Justice Felix Frankfurter for a luncheon discussion of foreign policy. After this meeting, Frankfurter lobbied strongly for Stimson's selection as to the War Department post and ultimately prevailed upon the president to make the appointment.[20]

A pattern of close cooperation between Jewish organizations and national security agencies also developed during the years before the war. During the 1930s, the Anti-Defamation League engaged in an active and extensive program of surveillance directed against pro-German and isolationist groups, organizations and prominent individuals. The ADL monitored the activities of such organizations as the German-American Bund, the isolationist America First Committee, the anti-Semitic National Economic Council, and such prominent isolationists as Charles Lindbergh, General Robert Wood of Sears, Montana Senator Burton Wheeler, North Dakota Senator Gerald Nye, Mississippi Senator Theodore Bilbo, North Carolina Senator Robert Reynolds, New York Representative Hamilton Fish, and many others. The ADL also monitored the activities of such overtly pro-Nazi or anti-Semitic politicians as Gerald L. K. Smith, Gerald Winrod, Laurence Dennis, and Father Charles Coughlin.

The ADL often employed investigative agents who secretly penetrated isolationist and anti-Semitic organizations and collected potentially damaging or incriminating information. One ADL agent, Marjorie Lane, became an active and trusted member of a number of isolationist and anti-Semitic groups, including Women for the USA, Women United, We, and Mothers Mobilize for America. The ADL's opponents engaged in their own espionage activities. On one occasion, an ADL investigator married a young woman after a whirlwind courtship. At the end of his first day at work after their honeymoon, the agent found that his new wife had disappeared along with all his files. Within a few days, the files surfaced in the offices of Senator Burton Wheeler.[21]

Information secured by the ADL was often turned over to federal agencies such as the FBI and the Immigration Bureau for possible criminal action. The ADL also worked closely with such sympathetic newspaper columnists and broadcasters as Walter Winchell and Drew Pearson. Winchell and Pearson used their columns to publicize and attack the activities of isolationist and pro-Nazi groups and politicians, relying heavily upon the information supplied to them by ADL investigators. For example, an ADL agent who had worked his way into Mississippi Senator Theodore Bilbo's inner circle provided a flow of embarrassing information on the senator's conduct and contacts for Winchell's Sunday radio exposes and Pearson's national column.[22]

The American Jewish Committee conducted its own surveillance of the activities of anti-Semitic groups and individuals. These were directed by George Mintzer, a former U.S. district attorney. Detectives working for the AJC infiltrated anti-Semitic groups and over a period of five years compiled a card index listing fifty thousand individuals who had some association with these organizations. This index was frequently used by the FBI and army and navy intelligence offices.[23]

On one occasion, an AJC investigator was able to "obtain" the files of a German agent, calling himself Baron von Stein, apparently sent to the United States by the gestapo to bring about a greater degree of cooperation among the various pro-Nazi groups operating in the United States. While in the United States, the baron made contact with Royal Gulden, leader of "The Order of 76"; William Dudley Pelley, leader of the Silver Shirts; George Deatheridge, head of the Knights of the White Camelia; and a number of others including well-known anti-Semites James True, Robert Edmondson, and Representative Louis T. McFadden of Pennsylvania who made a viciously anti-Semitic speech on the floor of the House not long after conferring with von Stein. Von Stein's files were given to the FBI, but the baron had already fled the country.[24]

The activities of pro-German organizations, the German-American Bund, in particular, were also attacked by New York Representative Samuel Dickstein. The Dickstein Resolution, adopted in 1934, called for a congressional investigation of all groups in the United States with ties to Nazi Germany. The House created a committee co-chaired by Dickstein and John McCormack of Massachusetts to investigate "un-American activities." The committee sought to harass and intimidate Bundists and other pro-German groups. In the 1940s, under the leadership of Martin Dies, HUAC began to turn its attention, instead, to investigating pro-Communist groups and organizations.

In addition, Jewish filmmakers, columnists, and radio personalities were only too happy to cooperate with the administration's anti-Nazi and pro-British interventionism. During the late 1930s, for example, when Roosevelt was engaged in bitter struggles with isolationist, pro-German, and anti-British forces in the public and in Congress, Hollywood cooperated with the White House by producing films depicting the evils of the Nazi regime, presenting Nazi Germany as a threat to the United States, and suggesting that a pro-German fifth column was at work inside the United States to undermine the nation's will to resist the Nazis.

For example, in the 1938 Warner Brothers release, *Confessions of a Nazi Spy,* starring Edward G. Robinson, Nazi Germany is depicted as intent on world domination and presenting a clear and present danger to the United States. Robinson, in the role of an FBI agent, asserts that through espionage and subversion Germany has already embarked on a war against the United States. At the end of this film, the audience is warned that continued isolationism will leave the United States and its way of life vulnerable to German attack from within and without. This was, of course, precisely the message that the Roosevelt administration sought to convey to the American public.

By 1940, Hollywood studies were producing a number of feature films and film shorts promoting American rearmament and attacking Germany. The Warners offered to make any film short on the need for military preparedness free of charge. At the administration's request, MGM produced a film on foreign and defense policy entitled *Eyes of the Navy,* which dramatically presented the importance of a strong national defense and activist foreign policy. The White House showed its gratitude to Hollywood by ordering the Justice Department to settle, on terms favorable to the studios, an antitrust suit it had brought against the major film producers in 1938. Roosevelt also intervened to secure a reduced sentence for Joseph Schenck, head of Twentieth Century Fox, who had been convicted of income tax evasion.[25]

Anti-Semitism and the "Jew Deal"

Their importance to the New Deal regime made Jews the objects of severe anti-Semitic attacks during the 1930s. The economic hardships and social dislocations occasioned by the Great Depression were already conducive to the growth of nativism, and enemies of the regime quickly saw anti-Semitism as a useful instrument through which to unite FDR's various opponents and to undermine confidence in the government. Foes of the New Deal, especially of its social programs, sought to discredit the administration by variously charging that Roosevelt was a tool of Jewish Communists, Jewish bankers, or sometimes both.

In upper-class circles, the New Deal was commonly called the "Jew Deal" and Roosevelt described as the descendent of a Dutch Jewish family—the Rosenvelts. Frank Buxton, editor of the *Boston Herald*, wrote in 1934: "Substantial men sympathized with the anti-Semitism. I was amazed at the intensity with which highly intelligent men argued that the Jews were controlling the President."[26] This view was echoed by the editors of *Fortune* the following year who stated that "Jew-baiting hysteria in anti–New Deal circles was common."[27]

Many upper-class opponents of the administration were reluctant to be publicly associated with unseemly anti-Semitic rabble-rousing. Some were quite willing to condone anti-Semitic attacks on the administration, however, and even to contribute to political groups such as the Liberty League that, in turn, provided funding and support to organizations that were not too squeamish to make use of anti-Semitic appeals to attack the White House. The latter included Robert Edward Edmondson's Edmondson's Economic Service, whose weekly newsletter, the *Economic Bulletin*, described the New Deal as the "Communist Jew Deal," directed by the "Frankfurter-Brandeis-Baruch-Morgenthau Monopoly."[28]

While most upper-class opponents of the regime were reluctant to be publicly associated with overt anti-Semitism, a number of more radical political figures were not at all hesitant to use anti-Semitic propaganda to appeal to working-class and lower-middle-class audiences. Among the most active radical opponents of the administration were Father Charles Coughlin, William Pelley, and Gerald Winrod. During the mid-1930s, Coughlin told millions of listeners to his weekly radio braodcasts from Detroit that the New Deal was controlled by Jews. William Dudley Pelley was the founder of the Silver Shirts, a neo-Nazi organization that sought to mobilize anti-Semitic sentiment. Pelley charged that Roosevelt and his top aides were Jews who had now taken almost complete control of the nation. Gerald Winrod, founder of the Defenders of the Christian Faith, published a monthly magazine, *The Defender*, with a circulation of more than 100,000 copies. Winrod charged that the Roosevelt administration was dominated by Felix Frankfurter and his staff of Jewish lawyers.

During the late 1930s, isolationist and pro-German forces sought to use anti-Semitic appeals to discredit the administration's efforts to pursue a more activist and pro-British foreign policy and to enhance

American military preparedness. In his *Economic Bulletin*, Edmondson wrote that Roosevelt was seeking to push the United States into war on behalf of Jewish financial interests. He charged further that the press, radio, and motion pictures, all controlled by Jews, were flooding the nation with propaganda designed to involve the country in the war. "The only people who want war," he wrote, were "the Jews."[29] This was a common theme of isolationist propaganda during the 1930s. An anonymously authored popular tune of 1939 proclaimed:

> O haven't you heard the news?
> We're at war to save the Jews
> For a hundred years they pressed our pants
> Now we must die for them in France
> So we sing the Doughboy Blues.[30]

Major isolationist groups such as the America First Committee publicly disavowed anti-Semitism but accepted financial contributions from anti-Semites and cooperated with anti-Semitic journalists. Even the most prominent isolationists and anti-interventionists were willing to make use of anti-Semitic appeals to attempt to discredit the Roosevelt administration's foreign policy which they characterized as the work of Jews foisted upon the nation by Jewish propagandists. For example, aviation hero Charles A. Lindbergh, Jr., an admirer of Nazi Germany, warned in a 1940 speech: "Instead of agitating for war the Jewish groups in this country should be opposing it in every possible way, for they will be among the first to feel its consequences . . . A few farsighted Jewish people realize this and stand opposed to intervention. But the majority still do not. The greatest danger to this country lies in their large ownership and influence in our motion pictures, our press, our radio, and our government."[31] In a later speech, Lindbergh declared, "The three most important groups who have been pressing this country to war are the British, the Jewish and the Roosevelt administration."[32]

Isolationist Senator Hiram Johnson of California wrote to his son that the struggle between isolationists and interventionists found "all the Jews on one side, wildly enthusiastic for the President, and willing to fight to the last American, both Germany and Italy." On the other side were those who "are thinking in terms of our country and that alone." "This," Johnson went on to say, "is the basis of the struggle here, and I don't know but what somebody ought to say it openly, but everybody is afraid of offending the Jews."[33]

Similarly, Joseph P. Kennedy, former U.S. ambassador to Great Britain and outspoken proponent of American appeasement of Nazi Germany, warned American Jews to halt their support for American intervention on the side of Britain. In 1940, Kennedy met with a number of Jewish film producers and strongly urged them to stop producing anti-Nazi films. Kennedy suggested to the Jewish producers that they learn from the experience of their brethren in Europe to avoid behavior that might offend their non-Jewish neighbors.[34]

In the same vein, isolationist Senator Burton Wheeler, chairman of the Senate Interstate Commerce Committee, appointed a subcommittee to investigate efforts by the movie industry to lead America into the war by inflaming opinion against Germany. The first witness called by the subcommittee in its hearings was Wheeler's close ally, isolationist Senator Gerald Nye of North Dakota. Nye castigated the producers of anti-German propaganda films, whom he described as a small group of foreign-born Jews who "came to our land and took citizenship here" while "entertaining violent animosities toward certain causes abroad."[35]

These assaults made American Jews feel even more dependent upon, and more supportive of the Roosevelt White House. For its part, the administration was leery of being too closely identified with Jews. Jewish advisors often were asked to keep a low profile. Moreover, the administration sought to distance itself from specifically Jewish causes—such as the plight of Jews under German rule. However, Jews were sufficiently important to the Roosevelt regime—there was, after all, a sense in which the New Deal *was* a Jew Deal—that it could not follow the example of the Gilded Age industrialists and simply jettison its Jewish problem. Thus, during the 1930s, foes of the Roosevelt administration were able to continue to make use of anti-Semitism to mobilize opposition against the president and his policies. Anti-Semitism became a major political force in America during the 1930s but ultimately, of course, was defeated by Jews and their political allies.

The Failure of Anti-Semitism in the 1930s

During the 1930s, opponents of the Roosevelt administration sought to make use of the relationship between the White House and the Jews to energize and unite upper- and lower-class opponents of the New Deal. And, at both the top and bottom of the social scale, there were audiences receptive to anti-Semitic appeals. Some American businessmen and industrialists, fiercely opposed to New Deal domestic programs, were at least willing to toy with the idea of an American equivalent of Hitler or Mussolini to replace the hated President Rosenvelt.

Thus, for example, when notorious anti-Semite and rabble-rouser Gerald L. K. Smith organized his "Committee of One Million" in 1936 to save the nation from Jews, Communists, and the New Deal, his largest financial contributors included William Bell, president of American Cyanamid; Lewis Brown, president of the Johns-Manville Company; James Noe, former governor of Louisiana and a millionaire from the oil business and radio broadcasting; the automaker Horace Dodge; and the Pew family of the Sun Oil Company. To win the support of these wealthy donors, Smith dropped his former populist emphasis on "sharing the wealth" and, instead, emphasized his opposition to Jewish New Deal schemes that, in his view, would result in the nationalization of business.[36]

Similarly, during the 1930s, the Boston banker Alexander Lincoln organized a group called the "Sentinels of the Republic" to battle the "Jewish threat" to America. The Sentinels, in turn, received funding to fight against Social Security and other New Deal programs from the Liberty League, an organization established by the captains of American industry including General Motors President Alfred Sloan.[37] Liberty League support for the Sentinels was withdrawn when the relationship between America's most eminent and respectable businessmen and a fanatical anti-Semitic group was made public. Sloan and the others claimed that they had no idea of the Sentinels' true character when they agreed to provide the group with financial backing. However, prominent members of the Liberty League were involved with a number of other anti-Semitic opponents of the Roosevelt administration as well. For example, Liberty Leaguer Henry B. Joy, former president of the Packard Motor Company and a director of the U.S. Chamber of Commerce, was a major financial supporter of Howland Spencer, an author of widely circulated anti-Semitic tracts charging that Roosevelt was a pawn of his Jewish advisors—Frankfurter, Morgenthau, and Cohen.[38]

At the same time, a sizable popular audience was ready to respond favorably to anti-Semitic propaganda. Nativism, as we saw earlier, had been a factor in the politics of the rural South and Midwest since the turn of the century. The rural Midwest and South had provided the audience for Henry Ford's anti-Semitic editorials in his newspaper, the *Dearborn Independent*, in the 1920s. During the 1930s, leaders of agrarian protest movements such as the Farmer's Holiday Association, which had become disenchanted with New Deal farm policies, echoed the familiar charge that Roosevelt was a traitor and the New Deal a "Jew Deal."[39]

In a similar vein, throughout the country, Americans of German descent were a credulous audience for the anti-Semitic propaganda of the German-American Bund which called upon them to support the Vaterland against the pro-British and anti-German schemes of Roosevelt and his Jewish cabal. Americans of Irish descent, who had reason to be anti-British and, hence, favorably disposed toward Germany and against the Jews, were the core of Father Charles Coughlin's enormous radio audience and formed the nucleus of support for his "Christian Front." After breaking with Roosevelt in 1934, Coughlin often made use of anti-Semitic themes to attack the president. For example, Coughlin frequently asserted that Bernard Baruch was the real president of the United States and that Baruch, in turn, was a tool of the international Jewish bankers who had organized an anti-Christian conspiracy to lead America into war.

Moreover, in America as in Europe, millions of ordinary individuals found themselves in desperate circumstances during the 1930s and were willing to listen to politicians who claimed both to understand their problems and to have a ready cure—a cure that seemed to work quite well in Germany. This made anti-Semitism a powerful and effective weapon of mass mobilization. More than one hundred anti-Semitic organizations were founded between 1933 and 1941 and, according to a *Fortune* survey, roughly a half-million Americans at least occasionally attended anti-Semitic rallies or meetings during this period.[40] Coughlin's newsletter, *Social Justice,* at its peak had a circulation of more than a million copies a month.[41]

Whatever its political potential, however, anti-Semitism was decisively defeated in America during the New Deal era. First, despite the efforts of politicians like Gerald L. K. Smith and the flirtation of some major industrialists with anti-Semitic forces, a European-style, anti-Semitic coalition of the top and bottom did not emerge in the United States during the 1930s.

Such a coalition, a latent possibility in 1896, was manifestly possible in 1936, when at least some businessmen were desperate enough to use any means to stop the New Deal. By 1937–38, however, a powerful conservative coalition of Republicans and Southern Democrats had formed in Congress and blocked the further expansion of New Deal domestic programs. At the same time that business's fear of expropriation diminished, moreover, the economy began to slowly revive, in part as the result of the beginnings of increased defense spending.

As noted earlier, anti-Semitism can be a useful instrument for uniting upper- and lower-class forces because it can mobilize the latter without overtly threatening the former. Nevertheless, the upper classes generally distrust and fear politicians who endeavor to excite the masses. Persons of substance and property will usually consider allying themselves with rabble-rousers and risk the emergence of a politics of mass mobilization that can potentially sweep them away along with everything else, only if they are desperate. After 1937, upper-class opponents of the New Deal simply were not desperate enough to countenance large-scale rabble-rousing and popular mobilization.

In addition, a large segment of the American upper class was Anglophilic while anti-Semitic forces were almost always pro-German. As the German threat to Britain increased during the 1930s, members of the Eastern establishment were thrown into an alliance with Jews and compelled to oppose anti-Semitic forces even when they were personally less than sympathetic to their Jewish allies. Thus, for example, as noted above, Jews and members of the Protestant establishment were united in the pro–British Fight for Freedom Committee which, as it sought to undermine pro-German and isolationist forces, was compelled also to attack anti-Semitic groups.

In one notable case, Fight for Freedom discovered that New York Congressman Hamilton Fish, a prominent isolationist, was allowing William Pelley, leader of the rabidly anti-Semitic, Silver Shirts, to distribute anti-Jewish literature under his congressional frank. Fight for Freedom was able to bring about a federal investigation of the relationship between Fish's office and anti-Semitic groups that helped to undermine the influence of several anti-Semites who were lodged in Fish's congressional office, and resulted in a perjury indictment for Fish's secretary.[42]

In the absence of reliable support for anti-Semitic movements at the top of American society, radical anti-Semites at the bottom were completely vulnerable to governmental investigations and prosecutions. Without backing in some segment of the elite, anti-Semitic groups could not count upon the news media or foundations or other powerful institutions to step forward to defend their liberties against the heavy hand of the government. As a result, federal and state investigators were free to devote a great deal of energy and attention to the tax records and finances of politicians who sought to use anti-Semitic appeals to attack the Roosevelt administration. Given sufficient scrutiny, defects can be found in most tax and financial records. Hence, it should not be surprising that a large number of anti-Semitic politicians were discovered to have committed financial or personal transgressions of one sort or another and packed off to jail. For example, Fritz Kuhn, leader of the German-American Bund, was convicted of forgery and larceny after a painstaking federal and state investigation of his handling of the Bund's finances which he— and probably most of his followers—had conceived to be indistin-guishable from his own.[43]

With the Japanese attack on Pearl Harbor and America's entry into World War II, anti-Semitic activity was temporarily discredited through its association with the national enemy. The Roosevelt ad-ministration was then freed to take even more decisive action against anti-Semitic, pro-German forces in the United States. These were, for the most part, destroyed through indictments, arrests, and, in some cases, deportations.

Thus, with the top of a potential coalition of the top and bottom unavailable and the association of anti-Semitism with the German enemy in wartime, American Jews were able to survive the anti-Semitic assault launched against them during the 1930s. Ultimately, of course, the failure of anti-Semitism in the 1930s reflected the fact that the regime constructed by Jews and their allies during this period was able to lift the country out of depression, and to mobilize military and police forces with the capacity to crush its enemies at home and abroad. Anti-Semitism failed in America during the 1930s because the New Deal regime, unlike the Weimar regime or the Third French Republic or Trianon Hungary, was strong enough to defend its Jew-ish constituents and defeat their—and its—political antagonists. This success, however, did not bring an end to efforts by forces opposed to the Democratic New Deal order to use anti-Semitism against it.

The Postwar Period

After World War II, opponents of the liberal Democratic postwar regime moved to revive anti-Semitism as a political weapon. Postwar investigations of Communist influence in the United States often focused on institutions in which Jews played prominent roles. Though this is often called the period of McCarthyism, Senator Jo-seph McCarthy generally attacked institutions and organizations dominated by Eastern-establishment WASPs. In general, the McCar-thyites represented Midwestern Republicans. Their major animus was directed toward their establishment rivals within the Republican party—rivals who, in their view, had betrayed Republicanism by cooperating with the New Deal. Because in the public's mind, at least, the upper-class, high Episcopalian foes of the Midwesterners could not plausibly be identified with Jews, the McCarthyites had no particular use for anti-Semitism as a political weapon. Indeed, several of McCarthy's most important aides, such as Roy Cohen and David Schine, were themselves Jews.

On the other hand, the House Un-American Activities Committee (HUAC), originally established to investigate Nazis, was controlled for all but a brief period by conservative and Southern Democrats who used the committee to attack their foes in the liberal and labor union wings of the Democratic party by identifying them with communism. Since these political forces *were* associated with Jews, HUAC probes, unlike those associated with McCarthy, *did* come to involve an element of anti-Semitism.

For example, during HUAC's probe of Communist infiltration of the motion picture industry, Mississippi Congressman John Rankin took great delight in unmasking the Jewish identities of Hollywood personalities identified with the liberal "Committee for the First Amendment" that had circulated a petition attacking HUAC. One signature on the petition was June Havoc. "We found out," said Rankin, "that her real name is June Hovick." Another one was Danny Kaye and, "we found ut that his real name is David Kaminsky." "Another one is Eddie Cantor and his real name is Edward Iskowitz." "There is one who calls himself Edward G. Robinson. His real name is Emmanuel Goldenberg." "There is another one out here who calls hismelf Melvyn Douglas, whose real name is Melvyn Hesselberg." Some Jewish producers and screen writers, who had cooperated enthusiastically with the Roosevelt administration's efforts to produce anti-nazi films in the late 1930s, were now declared by HUAC probers to have been "prematurely anti-Fascist" and, hence, possibly Communists.[44]

Jews responded to these attacks in part by distancing themselves from Communists or anyone with leftist sympathies and disciplining Communists and leftists in their own ranks. For example, in response to HUAC investigations of Communist infiltration of Hollywood, the Jewish film producers fired and blacklisted writers, actors, and producers with known leftist sympathies. The American Jewish Committee, when asked for help, refused to intervene on behalf of the blacklisted movie people. Indeed, the AJC was busy purging left-leaning groups, such as the Jewish People's Fraternal Order, from the CRC.

The most notable instance of this effort by Jews to demonstrate their loyalty and 100% Americanism was the 1950 Rosenberg case. Julius and Ethel Rosenberg had been accused of betraying American atom bomb secrets to the Soviet Union. Jewish organizations feared that this espionage case would greatly intensify anti-Semitism by underlining the relationship between Jews and communism. These organizations pressured the Truman administration, which also feared leaving itself open to attack for its links to Jews, to involve Jews in the Rosenberg Prosecution.

Both the presiding judge and the prosecutor named to the case were Jews. After the guilty verdict and death penalties were handed down, and a storm of protest ensued, Jewish organizations, most notably the American Jewish Committee, propagandized extensively in support of the verdicts and in favor of the death penalty. They sought, thereby, to demonstrate that Jews were staunchly anti-Communist. For example, a July 1950 memo prepared by an AJC staffer for Executive Director John Slawson after the arrest of the Rosenbergs was entitled, "Public Relations Effects of Jewish Atom Spies." The memo read:

Considerable concern has been expressed over public disclosures of spy activites by Jews and people with Jewish-sounding names. The present situation is regarded as being potentially more dangerous than the situation which obtained during World War II . . . The main reason for concern is the belief that the non-Jewish public may generalize from these activities and impute to the Jews as a group treasonable motives and activities . . . We miss yet another bet in the use of our investigative staff. During recent years we infiltrated into rightist organizations to explore them, etc. Why can't we do this with communist organizations, also using our knowledge to scare off Jews? Because it seems likely that the AJC will undertake some propaganda campaign in connection with these problems I should like to make some constructive suggestions along propaganda lines.[45]

The memo goes on to suggest that the AJC work to promote news stories showing how Communist efforts to infiltrate American institutions were thwarted by such Jews as labor leader David Dubinsky and U.S. attorney Irving Saypol, stories demonstrating Israeli support for the United States in the United Nations and the Israeli government's suppression of domestic Communists, stories about the Soviet government's oppression of Jews and attacks on Israel and Zionism, and stories reporting Soviet efforts to recruit spies from among Communist party members and other left-leaning Americans (this latter to be published in the Jewish press as a warning to Jews). The obvious aim of this effort was to demonstrate to Americans that

Jews were as staunchly anti-Communist as any of their neighbors while, at the same time, warning Jews not to associate with Communist organizations.

Subsequently, AJC staff member, Rabbi S. Andhill Fineberg, authored a book entitled *The Rosenberg Case: Fact and Fiction,* which supported virtually every aspect of the government's handling of the case and exposed alleged Communist infiltration of one of the major organizations backing the Rosenbergs—The Committee to Secure Justice in the Rosenberg Case.[46] Other Jewish organizations and organizations in which Jews were influential, such as the ACLU, took a similar posture.

For example, during the late 1940s and early 1950s the ACLU took great pains to assert that no free-speech issues were involved in the conviction of individuals for teaching or advocating communism. After studying the transcript of the Rosenberg trial, ACLU board member Osmond Fraenkel became convinced that the Rosenberg's constitutional rights had been violated in the course of the trial. However, when Fraenkel raised this issue with the Board, it voted 18–4 in favor of a resolution denying that the case raised any civil liberties questions.[47] By so doing, the ACLU board affirmed the fairness of the trial in the face of worldwide criticism of the government's handling of the case.

In addition, long-time ACLU counsel Morris Ernst contacted the FBI offering to join the Rosenberg defense camp as a covert FBI informant. According to Ernst's FBI contact, L. B. Nichols, "Ernst stated he would be interested [in involving himself in the Rosenberg case] on only one ground, namely that he could make some contribution . . . he is convinced that if Rosenberg breaks and tells all he knows this would be a terrific story and probably would be most helpful to the Bureau."[48]

The cooperation of Jewish groups with the prosecution and execution of the Rosenbergs and other Jews accused of spying for the USSR was the price Jews felt they had to pay for continued access to the political establishment. During the 1930s, Jews had built a relationship with the Democratic regime. In the 1940s and 1950s, this relationship was used by right-wing forces to attack the liberal Democratic order. These forces sought to undermine Democratic liberals by demonstrating that they were unable to deal effectively with the menace of communism even in their own camp. Since Jews were prominently associated with the liberal regime and, in the public mind, were easily linked to communism, exposing and attacking

Jewish Communists in government and in the media represented a very useful way of connecting liberalism with communism.

It was in response to this threat, seen by Jewish groups as posing a severe danger to the Jewish community, that Jewish organizations made a determined effort to disassociate Jews from left-wing groups and causes and, hence, to reduce the plausibility of efforts by conservative forces to tie Jews to the Red menace.

During the 1950s and early 1960s, the threat from the right was largely defeated by a renewal of the prewar alliance of Jews and establishment Protestants. As noted above, segments of the Eastern Protestant establishment were also under attack in the postwar period, nominally for having been too tolerant of the Communist threat. Senator Joseph McCarthy had charged that members of the Protestant elite had betrayed the country by engaging in, or at least condoning, Communist activities. McCarthy's targets included such pillars of the WASP establishment as Secretary of State Dean Acheson. McCarthy characterized the distinguished secretary as the leader of the treasonous "Acheson Gang" which had sheltered Alger Hiss and was involved in the sellout of American interests at Yalta.

After Eisenhower's victory in the 1952 presidential election, the WASP establishment closed ranks against McCarthy and its other right-wing opponents and sought allies that would help it to destroy its foes' political power. Jews and members of the WASP establishment had been allied in the period preceding the Second World War because they faced common antagonists. This situation was now repeated. Using the institutions in which one or both groups were influential—the media, the foundations, the universities, the courts, and public interest groups—Protestant and Jewish opponents of the anti-Communist crusaders joined forces to charge them with violating civil liberties and "chilling" free speech.

Major news organizations such as CBS, an institution owned by Jews and staffed by WASPs such as Edward R. Murrow, whose March 1954 "See It Now" broadcast was instrumental in discrediting McCarthy, played an important role. The ACLU, whose executive board was an alliance of Jews and WASPs, began to vigorously defend the victims of HUAC and the Hollywood blacklists as well as individuals prosecuted for refusing to take loyalty oaths. The Ford Foundation, an establishment bastion, created the Fund for the Republic which sponsored books and articles defending civil liberties and made awards to individuals who had fought against the anti-Communist crusaders.[49]

Together with their allies, Jews also organized efforts to deprive anti-Semites of access to the media. This effort began during the late 1940s and continued into the 1950s. For example, during this period, the American Jewish Committee developed a strategy it called "dynamic silence" to combat the activities of Gerald L. K. Smith.[50] Working together, officials of the American Jewish Committee, the American Jewish Congress, and the ADL would approach the publishers of major newspapers and owners of radio stations in cities where Smith had scheduled appearances to ask that Smith be given no coverage whatsoever. If newspapers and radio stations failed to cooperate on a voluntary basis, Jewish organizations were usually able to secure their compliance by threatening boycotts by Jewish advertisers. This strategy of dynamic silence was extremely effective in suppressing Smith and other right-wing anti-Semites.

In other instances, Jews attacked their antagonists more directly. Before the war, Jewish and pro-Roosevelt newspaper and radio commentators had often been able to discredit right-wing politicians by securing and publicizing information about their illicit financial or sexual activities. The damaging disclosure became an important weapon for Jews in the 1940s and 1950s as well. For example, in 1948, columnist Drew Pearson who had worked closely with the ADL during the 1930s, revealed in his nationally syndicated column that J. Parnell Thomas, chairman of the House Un-American Activities Committee, had been billing the U.S. treasury for nonexistent committee employees and pocketing the cash. Thomas was closely aligned with Gerald L. K. Smith and various forces on the anti-Semitic right, and had been a major figure in the investigations of Jewish Communists in the movie industry. Indeed, Thomas had been instrumental in securing the contempt of Congress convictions of ten Hollywood screenwriters (the Hollywood ten) in 1947.

On the basis of Pearson's revelations, Thomas was called before a grand jury and indicted for conspiracy to defraud the government. He pleaded no contest and was sentenced to serve an eighteen-month term in the federal prison in Danbury, Connecticut. Ironically, Thomas's coinmates at Danbury included several of the Hollywood screenwriters who had been convicted of contempt of Congress after refusing to answer questions put to them by Thomas's committee.[51]

The ultimate result of all these efforts was the defeat of the anti-Communist right and a diminution of Jews' fear that they would be labeled as "Communists." Now that Jews were linked with the Eastern establishment on this question, the two together were powerful enough to declare that any efforts to mark Jews as Communists "smacked of McCarthyism" and automatically should be seen as beyond the pale of the politically permissible.

From the late 1950s, conservative anti-Communists who sought to maintain a modicum of respectability, particularly among Northeastern WASPs, carefully avoided the least hint of anti-Semitism in their literature and broadcasts. William Buckley is an important example. This victory over the anti-Communists and, especially, relegation of the charge that Jews were Communists, to the outermost fringes of American politics, made it possible for Jews to take a leading role in the great liberal offensive that began during the 1960s.

Jews and the Liberal Resurgence

The Democrats' return to power in 1961 initiated another great state-building period in American history. During the administrations of John Kennedy and Lyndon Johnson, a coalition of Jews and liberal Protestants and a smaller number of liberal Catholics within the Democratic party sought both to increase their power inside the federal government and to expand the power of the federal government vis-à-vis the states and local governments. Alliance with blacks on a platform of civil rights was the critical instrument that served both these purposes. Enfranchising blacks while discrediting Southern and conservative forces as ricists increased the power of liberal forces at the federal level. At the same time, civil rights and, later, Great Society programs served to increase the federal government's power vis-à-vis the states and other jurisdictions.

Since its creation in the 1930s, one of the major accommodations underlying the New Deal Democratic coalition had involved civil rights. Southern votes were crucial to the Democratic party's fortunes, and therefore Franklin Roosevelt avoided challenging the Southern caste system. The emergence of a vigorous black civil rights movement in the 1950s and 1960s made it impossible to ignore the issue of race any longer. Northern Democratic liberals were sympathetic to the plight of blacks and, at the same time, found in the issue of civil rights a means of discrediting their opponents within the Democratic party—initially Southern conservatives and subsequently working-class ethnics in the North.

For Jews and other middle-class liberals, support for civil rights was not only a moral commitment but also an important political tactic. By allying themselves with blacks, enfranchising black voters, and delegitimating Southern white state and local governments, Jews and other liberals hoped to undermine the power of the same forces that had accused them of disloyalty, and had subjected them to anti-

Communist witch hunts during the previous two decades. For Jews, additionally, gains achieved on behalf of blacks in terms of equality of opportunity also promised to serve their own interest in eliminating discrimination. Jews, moreover, had been suspicious of conservative Southerners at least since the 1920 Leo Frank case and were only too happy to help reduce their influence in American politics.

Subsequently, as the civil rights movement initiated its Northern campaign, middle-class liberals seized the opportunity to attack and weaken their political rivals in the North as well. Liberals charged the Northern Democratic party's coalition of machine politicians and labor leaders with racism, worked to deny them representation at Democratic national conventions, and sought to cut off their access to federal patronage. In this way, liberals used the civil rights movement to attempt to enhance their influence over the Democratic party in the North at the same time that the power of the Southern conservatives was being eroded.

Jews served as major financiers and strategists for the civil rights movement. Jews served as well as the key liaisons between the civil rights movement and the government during both the Kennedy and Johnson eras. Jewish groups, organized through the National Jewish Community Relations Advisory Council, had long worked closely with blacks in efforts to eliminate housing and employment discrimination from the 1950s and after.

Jewish organizations also worked closely with civil rights groups during the 1960s in their struggles on behalf of voting rights and for the desegregation of public facilities and accommodations. Jewish contributors provided a substantial share of the funding for such civil rights groups as the NAACP and CORE. Jewish attorneys were at the forefront of the legal offensive against the American apartheid system. Stanley Levinson, a longtime official and fund-raiser for the American Jewish Congress, became Martin Luther King's chief aide and advisor, having previously served as a major fund-raiser for Bayard Rustin. Harry Wachtel was a major legal advisor and fund-raiser for the SCLC. Levison and Wachtel were often called King's twin Jewish lawyers. Jack Greenberg, head of the NAACP Legal Defense Fund was the most important single civil rights lawyer in the United States. Jews comprised a large segment—perhaps one-third of the whites who participated in civil rights marches and protests in the South during the 1960s.[52]

A mix of considerations also underlay liberal support for the urban programs of the Kennedy and Johnson periods. As a number of scholars have noted, the major urban programs of the New Frontier and Great Society were drafted on the initiative of task forces created by the White House rather than in response to demands from the black slum dwellers who were their presumed beneficiaries.[53] The members of these task forces were typically academics, foundation officials, senior civil servants, representatives of professional associations, and the like. For their part, Presidents Kennedy and Johnson were receptive to proposals for policy and social reform that could strengthen their support within the important middle-class liberal segment of the party's national constituency.

Middle-class liberals exercised considerably less influence on the local level. In many large cities after World War II, a stable accommodation had been achieved among party politicians, businessmen, union leaders, newspaper publishers, middle-income homeowners, and the ethnic working classes. These forces allied around a program of urban renewal in the Central Business District for the business community and construction unions, low taxes for homeowners, and secure jobs in the municipal civil service for the lower-middle class and upwardly mobile members of the working class.[54]

Upper-middle-class liberals sought to use their access to the Kennedy and Johnson administrations to circumvent these local accommodations and to increase their influence over municipal government agencies. The presidential task forces that drafted New Frontier and Great Society legislation argued that municipal bureaucracies did not command the resources, the talent, or the initiative that was needed to solve what was defined as the "urban crisis." To deal with this problem they proposed to extend federal grants-in-aid to local governments to support "innovative" programs.[55]

To obtain these federal grants, cities often established independent agencies under the control of the local counterparts of the officials in Washington who dispensed this money. Alternatively, they had existing municipal departments contract with consulting firms or hire administrators who understood the outlook or knew the vocabulary of the dispensers of federal grants. The "grantsmen" who were most successful in obtaining federal funds, as Shefter observes, naturally were those whose educational backgrounds, social origins, and institutional affiliations were similar to the federal grant givers, and who proposed to spend federal moneys for purposes their Washington counterparts favored. In this way, the federal grant-in-aid programs initiated by the Kennedy and Johnson administrations allowed upper-middle-class professionals and their political allies to make use of their access to the White House to extend their influence over the policies, programs, and hiring practices of municipal agencies. Federal grants-in-aid to state and local governments expanded dramatically during the 1960s and 1970s.[56]

Blacks were important allies in the liberals' battle to win control of these agencies. Liberals denounced municipal bureaucracies as "insensitive" and "unresponsive" to the needs of the black community. Blacks had strong reasons to join this attack. The mechanisms of community participation that were attached to Great Society programs gave them channels through which to influence the way municipal departments distributed their benefits and allowed them to obtain access to the patronage that was directly controlled by federally funded community action agencies, model cities boards, neighborhood service centers, and community development corporations. These mechanisms of community participation, furthermore, legitimized federal intervention in local affairs and provided an institutional framework through which blacks could be organized to provide local political support for new programs.[57]

Jews played a leading role in these efforts. Though Kennedy was a Catholic, his background and aspirations led him to look mainly toward the Eastern Protestant establishment for administrators and advisors. Thus, his cabinet included men like Douglas Dillon and other pillars of the financial community. Kennedy, however, also saw himself as a reformer and innovator who would bring new programs and policies—indeed, a "new frontier"—to America. For this purpose, the Eastern establishment was not an ideal source of expertise. To identify new programs, ideas, and policies, Kennedy turned to a pool of talent that was not fully "established" and, hence, was prepared to cooperate with reform and innovation—the Jews.

Jews figured prominently among Kennedy's staffers, speech writers, and "idea men." Thus, for example, immediately after his election, Kennedy created a number of task forces to develop new ideas and initiatives in domestic and foreign policy. A number of Jews, including Paul Samuelson, E. M. Bernstein, and Robert Nathan played important roles in these groups. In the area of housing policy, Milton Semer and Morton Schussheim played important roles. Later, Arthur Goldberg served as secretary of labor before being appointed to the Supreme Court. Wilbur Cohen and Abraham Ribicoff both served as secretaries of what was then called HEW (Health, Education, and Welfare). Richard Goodwin and Myer Feldman served as White House special assistants. Goodwin had been a law clerk for Felix Frankfurter and was responsible for Kennedy's Alliance for Progress speech. Walt Rostow served as a major foreign policy advisor. Arthur Schlesinger became White House resident intellectual and historian of Camelot. Adam Walinsky became Robert Kennedy's closest advisor, and Adam Yarmolinsky became Sargent Shriver's chief aide.

Jews continued to play major roles in the Johnson administration after Kennedy's assassination. Abe Fortas was Johnson's closest advisor and continued in that capacity even after his appointment to the Supreme Court. Walter Rostow was Johnson's National Security assistant. Johnson was eager to innovate and make his mark, and Jews were the idea men for Johnson as they had been for Kennedy. Adam Yarmolinsky, for example, was one of the architects of Johnson's "Great Society" programs, particularly Legal Services and the Job Corps. Francis Keppel and Wilbur Cohen were among the architects of the Elementary and Secondary Education Act of 1965. Large numbers of Jewish academics and intellectuals served on the task forces and study commissions that worked to develop Great Society programs. For example, the planning sessions leading up to the 1966 White House Conference on Civil Rights, were dominated by Jewish intellectuals such as Urie Bronfenbrenner, Herbert Gans, Nathan Glazer, Frank Riesman, Charles Silberman, and Marvin Wolfgang.

The Vietnam War and the New Politics Movement

In the late 1960s, Jews and other liberals broke with President Johnson over the Vietnam War. Liberals were genuinely outraged by what they saw as the senseless carnage of Vietnam. At the same time, however, just as the struggle for civil rights and the domestic programs of the New Frontier and Great Society had involved a mix of motives, so too did liberal opposition to the Vietnam War. In the early stages of the Vietnam conflict, Johnson sought, as much as possible, to limit increases in military spending in order to avoid draining resources from the domestic programs of the Great Society. Johnson's desire to minimize the diversion of resources from his domestic programs to the war is one reason that American policy in Vietnam was characterized by gradual escalation rather than a massive military effort from the beginning.

As time went on, however, the war began to drain enormous resources away from domestic social programs. Moreover, conservative forces in Congress that bitterly opposed Great Society initiatives increasingly were able to demand and receive domestic concessions from the White House in exhange for their support of its policies in Vietnam. Thus, from the prospective of liberals, including members of Johnson's own cabinet like John Gardner, HEW secretary, and Willard Wirtz, labor secretary, the Vietnam War was undermining the programs and institutions to which they were committed and that represented their own base of power while strengthening the hand of their political opponents.[58]

With the possible exception of blacks, Jews had a greater stake than any other element of the liberal coalition in domestic institutions, programs, and expenditures. Jews, more than members of most other groups, had risen to positions of power and prominence through their roles in the public and quasi-public institutions of the domestic state—municipal social service agencies, universities, think tanks, and public interest law firms as well as federal and state agencies. These institutions were, in turn, dependent upon high levels of domestic social spending which were now threatened by the Vietnam War. As a result, Jews were far more likely than members of other groups to oppose the war. One national survey taken in 1967 indicated that 48% of the nation's Jews were against the war as compared to only 16% of the Protestants and 27% of the Catholics surveyed.[59] At the time this was seen as a reflection of some naturally "dovish" tendency on the part of Jews. It is worth recalling, however, that barely a quarter century earlier Jews were among the nation's most vehement "hawks."

During the last two years of the Johnson administration and continuing after the election of Richard Nixon, liberal forces mobilized an all-out effort to end the war. Jews played a very noteworthy role in this endeavor. A number of Jewish student radicals such as Mark Rudd, Abbie Hoffman, Jerry Rubin, and the leaders of the violent "Weatherman" faction of the Students for a Democratic Society became well-known organizers of antiwar protest activities in the late 1960s and early 1970s. Interestingly, however, many of the most prominent Jewish leaders of the antiwar movement were not students but, rather, young government officials or congressional staffers who had both a moral commitment to, and a political stake in, the domestic programs and initiatives that were being strangled by the war. Among the many examples of such individuals are Daniel Ellsberg, Richard Goodwin, Adam Walinsky, Frank Mankiewicz, Gar Alperovitz, and Arthur Waskow.

Through the antiwar movement, these and many other liberal Democrats sought to end the massive diversion of funds away from domestic programs while also increasing their own influence within the Democratic party and expanding their power nationally. Within a relatively short period of time, opponents of the war were able to attack and discredit conservative Democrats and Republicans alike for having led the nation into the quagmire of Vietnam, while rallying support for their own causes, especially among young people. Liberal opposition compelled the Nixon administration to negotiate an end to the war early in the president's second term.

With the Republicans in control of the White House, however, the domestic state continued to be subjected to enormous pressure. President Nixon appointed conservatives to positions of power in domestic agencies, sought to reorganize domestic agencies in ways that would reduce liberals' influence over them, and impounded funds that congressional liberals appropriated for domestic social purposes. The administration also sought to attack the quasi-public components of the domestic state through such means as attempting to use the Internal Revenue Service to investigate the tax exempt status of liberal foundations. These actions set the stage for the great conflict that led to Nixon's ouster from office.

With their special stake in domestic programs and spending, a number of Jews played important roles in mobilizing opposition against the Nixon administration. Indeed, the testimony of White House counsel John Dean, during the congressional Watergate hearings, revealed that Jews constituted more than one-third of the major critics of the administration who occupied positions on Nixon's now-famous "enemies list." Jews on the list included Edward Guttman, Howard Stein, Allard Lowenstein, Morton Halperin, Daniel Schorr, and Leonard Bernstein.[60]

The White House was so well aware of the prominence of Jews and Jewish organizations among its opponents that it was suspicious even of Jewish Republicans. For example, according to congressional testimony, in 1971 a Republican activist named Lawrence Goldberg was being considered for a role in the "Jewish section" of the Committee for the Reelection of the President (CRP). White House security chief John Caulfield, however, learned that Goldberg was also actively involved with the Anti-Defamation League. Caulfield sent a memorandum to John Dean, pointing out Goldberg's ADL membership as well as his extensive connections to other Jewish organizations. This background, according to Caulfield's memo, raised a substantial question of loyalty to the president.[61]

In their battles with the Nixon administration, forces defending the domestic state were able to rely upon the support of another major institution in which Jews played key roles—the mass media. During the 1960s, the media that had been created by Jewish entrepreneurs—the national television networks—had become increasingly important in American journalism. Largely for commercial reasons, the networks had expanded their news and public affairs coverage and had come to play a major, if not dominant, role in American politics.

In the 1930s and 1940s, and even as recently as the 1950s, the national news media were generally conceived to be a conservative force in national politics. During the Vietnam War, however, the networks, along with elite newspapers—in which, as it happened, Jews also had significant influence, most significantly the *New York Times* and the *Washington Post*—discovered that there was a substantial middle- and upper-middle class audience for investigative reporting and critical coverage of administration policies. These segments of the media were able to enhance their own power, status, and autonomy in American politics by abandoning their traditionally respectful coverage of the White House and turning to a posture of criticism and opposition. Journalists could count upon their liberal audience to come to their defence when they came under presidential attack.[62]

In alliance with middle- and upper-middle-class liberals, segments of the print and broadcast media—institutions that had been subservient to the presidency since the days of Franklin D. Roosevelt— became powerful and independent forces in American politics. The benefits that the media derive from this alliance, rather than some inherent ideological bias, explain why the press seems so often to oppose conservative national administrations.

This alliance between segments of the media and liberal forces played an important role in the great struggle that eventually drove Nixon from office. The Watergate scandals, of course, began with revelations in the *Washington Post.* Over the next two years, the administration was battered by a series of additional revelations published in the *New York Times* and broadcast by the three networks. The *Times* also published the secret Pentagon Papers, which helped to discredit the government's policies in Vietnam.

Thus, during the 1960s and 1970s, as a result of a convergence of interests rather than design, the elite media became firmly linked to the liberal political camp. Subsequently, these media gave their support to a new set of institutions and organizations, calling themselves "public interest" groups, that sought to enhance the political power of liberal forces in the United States. The alliance between the media and the public interest movement became an important force in American politics during the 1970s. Their influence in both the media and public interest groups greatly enhanced the prominence of Jews in the Democratic party and the American governmental process.

The Public Interest Movement

In the wake of Nixon's resignation, Jews were prominent among the political activists who worked to solidify liberal control over the Democratic party as well as to strengthen and expand the domestic state to which liberal Democrats were so closely tied. The mechanism through which both these goals were to be achieved was through the activities of the host of "public interest" groups established to promote the goals of the "new politics"—environmentalism, consumerism, feminism, and so forth. During the 1970s, nearly two hundred public interest groups were established, and nearly one hundred public interest law firms were organized to protect them. In addition, major liberal funding agencies such as the Ford Foundation provided these groups with tens of millions of dollars in support. The elite media generally supported these groups and, indeed, virtually never questioned their claim to speak for the "public interest."

The public interest movement, as usual, served a mix of purposes. On the one hand, liberals strongly supported such goals as affirmative action, equal rights for women, protection for the environment, and consumer safety. At the same time, through the public interest movement, liberal forces hoped to win control of the Democratic party (and through it the government), to reorder national priorities to increase the flow of funds into agencies and programs that they controlled and that served their constituents, and to expand the federal government's penetration of society. To this end, liberals developed a domestic agenda consisting of political reform, affirmative action, diminution of military spending, and expansion of the government's regulatory efforts. Jews played major roles in all these endeavors; they served as leaders of the public interest movement and, through it, substantially enhanced their influence in the American political process.

First, during the 1970s, liberal political forces brought about substantial changes in the structure and practices of the Democratic party that strengthened the role of issue-oriented middle-class activists and public interest groups at the expense of traditional party cadres and organizations. The party reforms enacted following the defeat of antiwar candidates at the 1968 Democratic National Convention were the most comprehensive since those of the Progressive Era. Chief among them were rules requiring that delegations to future national conventions be composed of blacks, women, and youths in a "reasonable relationship to their presence in the population of the state"; rules encouraging states to select convention delegations through

primary elections or open caucus procedures; and regulations discouraging the slate-making efforts of party organizations. Groups
such as Common Cause also sponsored a number of reforms in the
area of campaign finance: public subsidies to candidates, limitations
on individual contributions, and public disclosure of the names of
contributors.[63]

Through these reforms liberals weakened the position of their major competitors for influence within the Democratic camp—urban
ethnic politicians, labor, and business leaders—and enhanced the
importance of middle-class activists and racial minorities. Beyond
this, the political reforms of the 1970s all but destroyed what remained of state and local party organizations. This left the Democrats
more fully dependent upon networks of liberal activists, public interest groups controlled by liberals, and segments of the elite media
which, since the Vietnam War, had been linked to liberal political
forces and sympathetic to liberal causes.[64] In addition, the reforms of
the 1970s left the Democratic party's presidential nominating process
more fully under the influence of networks of liberal activists including wealthy liberal contributors—a group in which Jews figure very
prominently.

In addition to party reform, liberal Democrats sought to secure a
number of major changes in governmental and bureaucratic organization that, whatever their other virtues, again served the interests
of middle-class liberal professionals. To begin with, they sought to
modify the public personnel system built around competitive examinations and a career civil service by advocating various mechanisms
of affirmative action, and the delegation of many public tasks to
nongovernmental institutions whose employees were not career civil
servants.

In contrast to the New Deal, which had drawn support from a
mioddle class and upwardly mobile working class whose members,
Jews in particular, could expect to secure civil service jobs through
competitive examinations, Democratic liberals in the 1960s and
1970s sought to win the support of blacks who were effectively excluded from public jobs by such examinations, and from members
of an upper-middle class that no longer had much interest in moving
slowly up the ladder in career civil service systems. Blacks would
benefit from affirmative action programs, while upper-middle-class
professionals stood to gain if public responsibilities were delegated
and public moneys allocated to the institutions with which they were
affiliated, such as nonprofit social service agencies, legal service clin-
ics, public interest law firms, and the like.[65] Ultimately, of course,

affirmative action posed some threat to the immediate interests even of upper-middle-class liberals, but eventually most were willing to bear the costs in order to maintain their alliance with blacks.

In the 1970s, liberals also launched a full-scale attack upon the national security establishment. They strongly disapproved of the purposes for which American military power was being used and argued that the funds spent on weapons could better be used to meet pressing domestic needs. Of course, such a reordering of national priorities would direct the flow of federal funds toward the agencies of the domestic state over which liberals exercised influence, and away from the political forces they now opposed.

Opponents of American military and national security policy began to sharply criticize practices that previously had aroused little journalistic attention or public opposition: the Pentagon's tolerance of cost overruns in weapons procurement contracts, the public relations campaigns and lobbying efforts of the Pentagon, the hiring of retired military officers by defense contractors, the failure of Congress to monitor the activities of the CIA and other intelligence agencies. Liberals sought to subject the "military-industrial complex" to stricter external control and to limit the role it had come to play in the nation's life during the Cold War years.

The post-Vietnam attack on the national security sector was quite successful, and defense spending as a percentage of GNP dropped sharply through the 1970s. Especially after the 1979 Soviet invasion of Afghanistan, however, conservative Republicans were able to charge that their opponents had dangerously weakened the nation's defenses and in this way to rally support for a major military buildup. This provided the Republicans with an opportunity to cultivate support in regions of the country and among interests in the business community with a stake in defense spending.[66]

Finally, the 1970s witnessed a major expansion of the regulatory activities of the federal government initiated primarily by liberal forces in Congress and in the Democratic party. Consumer advocates, environmentalists, and their supporters in Congress asserted that existing regulatory agencies had been captured by business and proposed major reforms that promised to better protect the public and the environment while at the same time enhancing their own political influence.

Thus, consumer advocates and environmentalists undertook to alter the procedures and practices that led regulatory agencies to serve business rather than broader public interests. These included the interchange of personnel between agencies and the interests they regulated; the cocoon of minimum rates, entry restrictions, public subsidies, and tax benefits that had been placed around one sector of the economy after another; and the mutually beneficial relationships that had developed among executive agencies, congressional committees, and private interests. Such groups as Common Cause, the Nader organization, and the Natural Resources Defense Council attempted to put an end to these practices and increase their own influence in the regulatory process by sponsoring sunshine laws, subjecting regulatory agencies to close judicial supervision, and by providing for the representation of public interest groups in the administrative process.[67]

In addition, consumer and environmental activists insisted that it was imperative that the federal government undertake major new programs to deal with such problems as air and water pollution, product safety, and health hazards associated with food and drugs. Between 1966 and 1976 they were able to secure the enactment of a number of important new regulatory statutes, greatly expanding the federal government's role in the economy. In contrast to the typical New Deal regulatory program that encompassed a single industrial sector, such as trucking or airlines, the "new regulation" of the 1960s and 1970s affected firms throughout the economy. To administer these programs, Congress created a number of new federal regulatory agencies such as the Environmental Protection Agency, the Consumer Product Safety Commission, and the Occupational Health and Safety Administration. These agencies and the congressional committees that oversee and protect them subsequently became major liberal Democratic bastions and greatly expanded liberal Democratic influence over the domestic economy.

After their break with the Johnson administration and defeats in the 1968 and 1972 presidential elections, liberal Democrats lost the access they previously had enjoyed to the presidency. Consequently, they opposed reforms—such as those proposed by the Ash Council in 1970, or the ones President Nixon sought to implement by fiat in 1973—that would have increased presidential control over the executive branch. Instead, liberal Democrats sought to reduce the powers of the presidency and to increase the influence within the administrative process of the institutions with which they were allied or to which they enjoyed access.

Thus, liberal Democrats sought to subject the bureaucracy to increased public scrutiny, and to influence its behavior through investigative reporting and Naderite exposes, because they enjoyed access to the national news media. Throughout the 1970s and 1980s, the media cooperated with liberal forces in attacking programs and administrators that liberals opposed. During the Reagan presidency, for example, the national media helped to attack EPA administrator Ann Burford Gorsuch and Attorney General Edwin Meese when these individuals became embroiled in conflicts with liberal groups. Subsequently, of course, the media played a major role in the Iran-contra affair that nearly drove Reagan from office.

Similarly, civil rights, environmental, and consumer groups attempted to subject the bureaucracy to tighter supervision by the courts because they commanded considerable legal talent, and because the federal judiciary in the 1960s and 1970s loosened requirements for standing, considerably narrowed the scope of the doctrine of political questions, and enriched the range of remedies it was prepared to consider in class action suits. And, after decades of seeking to limit the powers of Congress, liberal Democrats beginning in the late 1960s sought to expand Congress's power over the administration—especially in the areas of budgeting, investigations, and executive privilege—because of the access they enjoyed to that body.[68]

For a large number of Jews, leadership roles in the public interest movement represented an opportunity to move from a peripheral, albeit important role to a central place in the American political process. During the 1930s and, again, in the early 1960s, Jews had served as advisors, political operatives, congressional staffers, "idea men," and powers behind the throne. In the late 1960s and early 1970s, as noted above, Jews rose to political prominence in the anti–Vietnam War movement. From the 1970s onward, Jews led or were influential in most, though not all, of the political reform, feminist, consumer rights, gay rights, environmentalist and other public interest groups and related foundations, study groups, and think tanks that came to dominate the Democratic party during the 1970s and continue to be the leading forces within that party today.

At the present time, Jews play important roles in a diverse group of such liberal political and public interest organizations as Environmental Action, Center for Democratic Renewal, Center for Policy Alternatives, National Association of Working Women, Women's Legal Defense Fund, Center for Biomedical Ethics, Center for Science in the Public Interest, Food Research and Action Center, Common Cause, People for the American Way, Mental Health Law Project, National Organization for Women, Clean Water Action, U.S. Public Interest Research Group, National Women's Law Center, Center for Law and Social Policy, Children's Defense Fund, Public Citizen, Save Our Security, National Coalition against the Misuse of Pesticides,

Advocacy Institute, Citizens against PACs, Congress Watch, National Women's Caucus, Alliance for Justice, Institute for Policy Studies, and hundreds of others.

Jewish liberals who found these organizations just a bit too progressive played important roles in organizing and financing political groups whose agendas—while still decidedly liberal—were at least somewhat closer to the ideological center. The most significant of these was, of course, the Democratic Leadership Council (DLC), which played such an important role in Bill Clinton's 1992 presidential victory. The DLC's think tank, the Progressive Policy Institute (PPI), helped to shape the Democratic party's 1992 platform and policy agenda.

The political reforms of the 1970s gave these organizations and issue-oriented liberal activists, more generally, a greatly enhanced voice in the Democratic party's presidential nominating process and in the nation's policy-making and administrative processes as well. Jews had always been *the* most active of liberal activists—willing to invest incredible time, energy, and money in politics—and were, thus, particular beneficiaries of the Democratic party reforms adopted in the 1970s.[69]

In addition to the Democratic presidential nominating process, public interest groups and liberal activists became extremely important in the national congressional electoral arena. While American presidential races have become media contests, candidates in congressional races continue to rely upon volunteers and activists to register and mobilize voters. Tens of thousands of political activists affiliated with local governments, public interest groups, nonprofit organizations, and the quasi-public institutions of the domestic state form the backbone of the Democratic party's congressional campaign efforts. These individuals have a stake in the domestic expenditures and programs championed by the Democrats and have become the political army which, more than anything else, has allowed the Democrats to control Congress despite Republican victories in presidential elections.

Because of the Democratic party's continuing hold on Congress and on most of the bureaucracies of the domestic state, the influence of liberal Democratic groups waned but by no means disappeared in the wake of the Republicans' capture of the White House after 1980. During the Reagan and Bush presidencies, the Republicans were able to thwart the development of new domestic programs. Despite their various efforts, however, the Republicans were never able to shut off the flow of federal funds into the existing complex of institutions that comprise the domestic state or, indeed, either to destroy or win control of many of its agencies.

These organizations and institutions, in alliance with Congress and the national media, form a permanent government, providing the Democrats with a continuing ability to administer programs and influence the nation's policies even when they do not control the White House. Institutions linked to the domestic state, moreover, serve as the base from which liberal Democrats launch their congressional and presidential bids. For example, in 1992, many of the key staffers and policy advisors who organized Bill Clinton's successful presidential campaign were drawn from or had backgrounds associated with such public or quasi-public institutions. These include major universities and colleges (Robert Reich from Harvard, Stanley Greenberg from Yale, and Derek Shearer from Occidental), think tanks and public interest groups (Al From, former executive director of the DLC, Rob Shapiro from the PPI, and David Wilhelm of Citizens for Tax Justice), public programs (Micky Kantor, a former aid in the War on Poverty and a board member of the Legal Services Corporation), politically active Washington law firms (Samuel Berger, a member of the law firm of Hogan and Hartson and a former director of the State Department's policy planning staff), and liberal consulting firms (Ira Magaziner).[70] A number of these individuals subsequently were appointed to prominent positions in the Clinton administration.

It is through their political activism, their willingness to make major financial commitments to the Democrats, and the leadership role that they play in this complex of agencies and organizations and, in turn, in the Democratic party—a political institution that both supports and is supported by the domestic state—that Jews have come to play a major role in electoral politics and policy-making in the United States. In short, in little more than a half-century, through their participation in a great state-building endeavor—the construction of the American domestic state—Jews were able to move from social ostracism and political isolation to established positions of considerable power in America's governmental apparatus and political processes.

Indeed, by the 1980s, Jews had come to be such political insiders at the national level that local-level Jewish political activism focused in such arenas as school board and city council elections—once areas in which Jews were very involved—had all but disappeared. Some Jewish leaders began to express concern that Jews were abandoning grass-roots politics to their political opponents.[71]

Jewish Liberalism

This historic background, and the continuing relationship between Jews and the national government, help to explain one of the most notable characteristics of Jews in American politics—their strong adherence to liberalism and the Democratic party as loyal voters, leading activists, and major financial contributors. Jewish liberalism is sometimes ascribed to the inherently humanistic character of Jewish values and traditions.[72] However, this explanation seems a bit fanciful since, as we saw in Chapter 1, in some political settings Jews have managed to overcome their humanistic scruples enough to organize and operate rather ruthless agencies of coercion and terror.

Like the politics of the Catholic church which, during the course of European history, was often liberal where Catholics were in the minority but could be reactionary where Catholics were in the majority, the politics of Jews varies with objective conditions. Jews have, at various times and in various places, been Republicans, monarchists, Communists, and Fascists as well as liberals. In the United States, Jews became liberal Democrats during the 1930s because in the face of social discrimination they found protection and opportunity as members of a political coalition organized by the Democrats around a liberal social and economic agenda.

This coalition greatly expanded the American domestic state, providing Jews with opportunities not fully available to them in the private corporate sector. As we saw earlier, over the subsequent decades Jews gained access to and positions of prominence in the public or quasi-public economy of government agencies, helping professions, private foundations, think tanks, and universities much more fully and rapidly than to the private corporate economy. This reinforced Jews' stake in the liberal ideologies that justify the role played by these institutions and in the Democratic party that serves as the public economy's political champion.

The liberal Democratic coalition also promoted and, to some extent, continues to promote principles of civil rights that serve the interests of Jews. Democratic civil rights policies have worked to Jews' advantage in a direct way by outlawing forms of discrimination that affected Jews as well as blacks. Equally important, these policies have served to expand the reach and power of the federal government (an institution in which Jews exercised a great deal of influence) relative to the private sector and subnational jurisdictions (where Jews' influence was less).

Finally, membership in the liberal Democratic coalition has provided Jews with access to and favorable treatment from important social institutions that had formerly excluded them. For example, participation in this coalition has given Jews full access to the nation's elite universities. This originated during the civil rights era when Jews and liberal Protestants began to work closely together on behalf of the cause of equal opportunity for blacks. One area in which Jews and Protestants cooperated closely in the early days of the civil rights struggle was in the effort to open universities to blacks. Jewish leaders calculated that opening universities to blacks necessarily meant opening them more fully to Jews as well. Indeed, as an outgrowth of the civil rights effort, liberal Protestants strove to unlock the doors of a number of the most exclusive schools to Jews as well as to blacks.

At Yale, for example, President A. Whitney Griswald together with Provost (later President) Kingman Brewster and Chaplain William Sloan Coffin worked to open the admissions process, positions on the faculty and in the senior administrative ranks to talented Jews in the early 1960s.[73] Subsequently, liberal Protestants also benefited from this relationship. Their alliance with Jews helped liberal Protestants free a number of elite universities from subservience to their business-dominated alumni boards and gave them access to the financial support of the federal government and some foundations in the expanding grants economy where Jews had considerable influence. Yale is a notable example of just this process.[74]

In a similar vein, participation in the liberal Democratic coalition meant that Jews now would receive privileged treatment in the media. While it is not true that Jews control the American news media, Jews and the liberal political coalition of which they are members are closely tied to some of the nation's major organs of news and opinion. Beginning in the 1960s, these media declared anti-Semitic expression to be extremist and un-American and, at least for a time, banished it from mainstream political discourse.

The benefits they have derived from membership in the liberal Democratic condition, as well as some lingering sense that Democrats are simply more friendly to Jews than are Republicans, explain why Jews continue to support liberalism and the Democrats even though, as has often been observed, Jews' financial status might seem to suggest that many should be Republicans.

As Democrats, Jews play a leadership role in a powerful national political coalition. Membership in the Democratic coalition allows Jews to exercise considerable political influence and has provided them with access to important social institutions. Moreover, it is the

Democratic party that defends the institutions that are part of or depend upon the public economy, such as universities, in which Jews have a major stake. Jews remain liberal Democrats despite their contemporary economic status and even though their affiliation may require them, at times, to support positions that run counter to their short-term class or communal interests, as in the recent case of job quotas. This is primarily because liberal Democracy has protected them from their enemies and has been the source of their power and place in American society.

This becomes apparent if Jewish liberalism is closely examined. First, Jews are Democrats more than they are liberals. Jews differ much more from other whites in their *voting behavior* and political activity than in their *attitudes*. In terms of voting and party identification, Jews support the Democrats by a four-to-one margin. In 1988, for example, 70% of all Jewish voters supported Dukakis and more than 80% supported Democratic congressional candidates. In 1992, 78% of all Jewish voters backed Clinton.

On many attitudinal measures, however, Jews are not substantially different from other whites. Jews, to be sure, do disagree strongly with other whites on such issues as church-state relations and on social issues where their own marginal or minority status gives Jews a stake in cultural pluralism and protection for behavior that the majority regards as deviant or nonconformist. However, they do not differ substantially from other whites on most standard policy questions.

In one recent survey, for example, 74% of all Jewish respondents compared with 73% of the other white respondents opposed abolition of the death penalty. In the same survey, hiring preferences for blacks were supported by only 27% of the Jewish respondents and 30% of the non-Jewish white respondents. Similarly, 77% of the Jewish respondents and 74% of the other white respondents agreed that government programs such as welfare have had many bad effects on their putative beneficiaries.[75]

Where Jews do differ markedly from other whites is in terms of their support for the Democratic party and the liberal groups and institutions that form the organizational backbone of the liberal political camp and, thus, of Jewish power in American politics. For example, 61% of the Jews as contrasted with only 37% of other whites surveyed identify with the Democratic party. Similarly, 33% of the Jewish respondents but only 14% of the non-Jewish white respondents report a favorable opinion of the ACLU. In a similar vein, 51%

of the Jews surveyed, as opposed to only 28% of the non-Jews, have a favorable impression of the National Organization for Women (NOW), another major group in the liberal camp. Thus, when it comes to support for liberal organizations, Jews differ quite markedly from the remainder of the white population.

It is interesting that Jews also differ from other whites in terms of their support for domestic spending. While only 25% of the non-Jewish white respondents surveyed were against reducing government spending on domestic programs, domestic cuts were opposed by 43% of the Jewish respondents. In effect, Jews are significantly more likely than other whites to oppose cutting domestic expenditures despite the fact that Jews are apparently just as dubious as other white respondents about the programs upon which the money is spent. Indeed, Jewish opposition to domestic spending cuts was as marked as that of blacks—44% of all black respondents were opposed—the group *most* dependent upon federal domestic spending.[76]

This helps to underscore the institutional, as opposed to attitudinal, character of Jewish liberalism. Jews are, as a group, more dependent upon the domestic state than are other whites and, hence, are more likely to support domestic state spending despite their own apparent doubts about the validity of some of the purposes for which the funds are employed.

Thus, in short, the data suggest that Jews are supporters of the Democratic party, liberal organizations, and the domestic state more than they are adherents of liberalism as an ideology. Jewish liberalism is more an *institutional* than an *attitudinal* phenomenon. It is associated more with Jews' political linkages and involvements than with their underlying attitudes. This is, of course, one reason for the failure of Republican efforts during the 1980s to convince Jews to change their political affiliations. Jews' affiliations are based more upon long-term institutional stakes than malleable attitudes and opinions.

The Anti-Semitic Reaction

Like the state-building endeavors of the New Deal era, those of the 1960s and 1970s precipitated a conservative reaction. The conservatism of the 1980s, however, made virtually no use of anti-Semitic appeals. This despite the prominence of Jews in the liberal camp and the importance of Christian evangelicism in the conservative movement during the 1980s. Not until the early 1990s and the

"America First" campaign of syndicated columnist and television personality Pat Buchanan did an element of overt anti-Semitism surface among conservatives.

Objections to the political influence and activities of Jews were voiced much earlier and more distinctly, however, by Jews' erstwhile allies—blacks and the liberal left. As noted earlier, a number of black leaders, including Louis Farrakhan and one-time Democratic presidential candidate Jesse Jackson, have periodically made anti-Semitic comments that other black politicians have been reluctant to disavow. At the same time, some forces on the liberal left made use of anti-Israel or anti-Zionist appeals to attack American national security policy long before Pat Buchanan appropriated this position. Chapter 4 discusses why anti-Semitism became visible among Jews' putative allies on the left, most notably among blacks, before it became a factor among Jews' nominal foes on the political right.

4 Blacks and Jews: Anti-Semitism and Interdependence

A nti-Semitic propaganda and organized anti-Jewish activities are most frequently employed by political forces that oppose a regime with which Jews are associated. Occasionally, however, groups that are nominally aligned with Jews may, in effect, turn against them. As shown in Chapter 1, this sometimes occurs when a regime to which Jews are linked, such as Trianon Hungary, comes under attack, and putative allies of the Jews feel compelled to throw them to the wolves in order to save themselves.

In other cases, however, the very success of a regime linked to Jews may make it possible for the Jews' allies to dispense with them. In the USSR, for example, it was only after Communist rule was firmly established that non-Jewish Bolsheviks were secure enough to seek to expand their own power in the governmental process by purging Jews from positions of leadership in both the Communist party and the Soviet state. Thus, in addition to functioning as an instrument through which its external adversaries attack a regime in which Jews participate, anti-Semitism can also emerge as a weapon in factional struggles between Jews and their nominal political allies. In the United States, as discussed below, the development of an anti-Semitic politics within some segments of the African-American populace and political leadership over the past two decades represents another variation on this general theme.

From Cooperation to Conflict

During the 1950s and 1960s, Jews and African Americans were closely allied in the civil rights movement, and, indeed, Jews played a prominent role in the leadership of most, if not all, of the major civil rights organizations. As noted earlier, Stanley Levinson, a Jewish attorney, was Dr. Martin Luther King's chief advisor. Kivie Kaplan, a retired Jewish businessman from Boston, served as president of the National Association for the Advancement of Colored People (NAACP) and was, as well, one of Dr. King's major fund-raisers and financial contributors. Marvin Rich, another Jewish attorney, was the chief fund-raiser and key speech writer for James Farmer, head of the Congress of Racial Equality (CORE). Rich was later succeeded by yet another Jewish attorney, Alan Gartner. Attorney Jack Greenberg headed the NAACP Legal Defense Fund after former Supreme Court Justice, Thurgood Marshall, was named to the Second Circuit Court of Appeals by President Lyndon Johnson.

More than half the white lawyers who made their services available to civil rights demonstrators in the South were Jews. Between half and three-quarters of the contributors to civil rights organizations—including the Student Non-Violent Coordinating Committee (SNCC), CORE, and Dr. King's Southern Christian Leadership Conference (SCLC)—were Jews. More than half the white freedom riders were Jews. Almost two-thirds of the whites who went into the South during the Freedom Summer of 1964 were Jews including, of course, Michael Schwerner and Andrew Goodman who, along with their black colleague James Chaney, were murdered by racist thugs in Mississippi.[1]

Jewish intellectuals and the journals of opinion that they controlled, including *Commentary*, spoke out forcefully on issues of civil rights. Jewish organizations such as the American Jewish Committee, the American Jewish Congress, and the Anti-Defamation League provided financial, legal, and organizational support for civil rights groups.

In the civil rights struggle, Jewish morality and Jewish interests pointed in the same direction. Morality dictated that Jews support the efforts of African Americans to free themselves from the apartheid system. To a generation of liberal Jews this was a supreme moral imperative. At the same time, however, many Jews and Jewish organizations, in particular, also recognized that they had an interest in supporting the civil rights movement. First, the goal of a society in which discrimination based on race was outlawed served the interests of Jews as much as—perhaps even more than—blacks. In the absence of discriminatory legislation and practices in such areas as education and employment, Jews had every reason to believe that they could compete successfully and rise to the very top of American society. By supporting African Americans in the cause of civil rights, Jews were eliminating the barriers that stood in their own way as well.[2]

Moreover, the political forces that the civil rights movement was attacking were forces in American society that were also enemies of the Jews. Jews were aligned with the liberal, New Deal wing of the Democratic party, and the civil rights movement attacked and sought to discredit the conservative Southern wing of the party—a group that had been associated with the anti-Communist and anti-Semitic campaigns of the 1950s. Through participation in the civil rights movement, Jews were striking a blow against their own foes in the Democratic coalition as much as against the enemies of blacks.

Despite this record of past cooperation, relations between African Americans and Jews have deteriorated significantly in recent years. Contemporary poll data consistently suggest that levels of anti-Semitic sentiment are higher within the black community than within virtually any other group in the American populace, and have been rising steadily over the past twenty years.[3] Moreover, African-American politicians and intellectuals have been far more willing than their white counterparts to voice anti-Jewish views and, often, to accuse Jews of conspiring against blacks.

Thus, for example, in a recent speech to students at Michigan State University, the black Muslim leader, Minister Louis Farrakhan, told Jews in the audience, "You suck the blood of the black community, and you feel we have no right now to say something about it."[4] In a similar vein, Steve Cokely, a former Chicago mayoral aide, claimed that Jewish doctors were responsible for injecting black babies with the AIDS virus.[5] Also manifesting a fear of Jewish racist cabals, CCNY Professor and former Black Studies Department Chairman Leonard Jeffries has often asserted that the university is run by a clandestine Jewish conspiracy.[6]

In another recent manifestation of anti-Semitism, mobs of young African Americans surged through the Crown Heights section of Brooklyn, New York, attacking Jews, in response to a traffic accident in which a Hasidic Jewish motorist inadvertently struck and killed a black child. A number of New York's more militant black politicians openly condoned the rioting, as well as the subsequent murder of an Australian Jew visiting the area, as justifiable revenge for the initial traffic fatality.

In general, efforts to explain black anti-Semitism focus upon three factors: first, the historic importance of Protestant fundamentalism and concomitant religious prejudice in the black community; second, the frictions and resentments that developed between blacks and Jews when the latter were major merchants and landlords in African-American neighborhoods; and, third, black anger over Jewish opposition to affirmative action.

While these explanations may have some merit, each is problematic in one way or another. First, as to religious prejudice, the spiritual message taught in fundamentalist churches is, at the very least, ambiguous. In obedience to the words of the scripture, Jews could be spurned as Christ killers or, with equal fidelity to the text of the Bible, extolled as God's chosen people. Which of these possibilities becomes manifest is mainly a matter of interpretation and emphasis and appears, often, to vary with political rather than spiritual factors.

In recent years, for example, white Protestant fundamentalists—a historically anti-Semitic group—seem to have discovered a portion of the holy writ that calls upon the faithful to give their fervent adulation, if not to all Jews, then at least to right-wing Israeli politicians. Similarly, in the not so distant past, black ministers emphasized the similarities between the African American and Jewish experiences—for example, the parallels between black history and the biblical Book of Exodus. During the heyday of the civil rights movement, black ministers had no difficulty allying themselves with Jews—at times allowing them to speak from their pulpits. To interpret black anti-Semitism as chiefly a result of the African-American religious experience, one would have to explain why this same background was conducive to philo-Semitism during some periods of time and anti-Semitism during others. Moreover, poll data indicate that anti-Semitic sentiment is greatest among urban, upper-income, college-educated blacks—precisely those least associated with religious fundamentalism.

Second, as to the role of Jews as merchants and landlords in the black community, this would seem to be a matter of declining importance. Jewish merchants and landlords were a major presence in black urban neighborhoods through the 1950s, but have today been replaced by Koreans, Arab Americans, West Indians, and others. As Glenn Loury has noted, "[T]he structural, economic basis for tension between the groups has diminished substantially from what it was twenty years ago—inner city merchants and landlords are no longer mainly Jews."[7] If the black reaction to Jewish slumlords and greedy shopkeepers is the chief explanation for black anti-Semitism, why should black anti-Semitism increase just when the Jewish presence in the ghetto has diminished?

Finally, Jewish opposition to affirmative action programs also seems to be an inadequate explanation. While many Jews do oppose such programs, poll data suggest that Jews, as a group, are more likely than any other segment of the white population to support affirmative action—this despite the fact that affirmative action and racial quotas pose a special threat to Jews, who are the most over-represented group in university and professional school admissions as well as in the most desirable professional positions.

During the late 1970s, to be sure, major Jewish organizations did fight against affirmative action programs. The American Jewish Committee, the American Jewish Congress and the Anti-Defamation League all opposed racial quotas. All three organizations, in fact, became involved in the famous DeFunis case. In this case, a white student, Marco DeFunis, who had been denied admission to the University of Washington law school, brought suit claiming that he had been a victim of reverse discrimination because affirmative action quotas allowed admission to the school to blacks with weaker qualifications than his own. In recent years, however, most Jewish organizations have softened their positions on affirmative action. While all nominally oppose "quotas," both the American Jewish Committee and American Jewish Congress now support "goals" and "timetables" which, in actuality, are little more than euphemisms for racial quotas.

At any rate, religious tradition, the role of Jews in the ghetto and Jewish opposition to affirmative action at most help to explain why there was a potential for anti-Semitism in the black community. They do not explain how this latent potential came to be realized. To put it another way, these factors may explain why African Americans do not like Jews but not how this dislike came to be mobilized into American politics. The emergence of an anti-Semitic politics—as opposed to anti-Semitic sentiment—among African Americans can, as shown below, primarily be understood in terms of the efforts of some black politicians to take advantage of a new set of opportunities that presented themselves during and after the 1970s.

Civil Rights and the Great Society: The Consequences of Success

Ironically, just as a necessary condition for Stalinist anti-Semitism was the success of the Bolshevik revolution, the political backdrop for contemporary black anti-Semitism was the success of the earlier black-Jewish alliance in the civil rights movement and in Lyndon Johnson's Great Society. The civil rights movement led to the enfranchisement of millions of black voters. The Great Society resulted in the construction or expansion of major domestic social programs and agencies which presently provide a multitude of services to the African-American community.

As a result of these two developments, the Democratic party came to be both electorally and institutionally dependent upon blacks. First, blacks came to account for nearly one-fourth of the votes cast for Democratic candidates in national elections and one-third or more of the votes received by Democrats in statewide races in a number of Southern states. Not only do the overwhelming proportion of African-American voters support the Democrats, but the civil rights policies with which the Democrats were associated drove sizable numbers of whites from the party, making it all the more dependent upon the support of blacks.

Second, and even more important, the Democratic party became institutionally dependent upon the educational, social, health-care, and other programs created initially by Roosevelt's New Deal and augmented and expanded by Johnson's Great Society. With the demise of traditional party machines, these programs and the agencies that administer them have become the institutional bastions of the national Democratic party. Federal domestic programs and agencies are typically staffed by Democrats and defended by Democrats in Congress. By permitting Democrats in Washington to establish ties with groups and forces throughout the nation, these agencies and programs, in effect, link the Democratic party to its national political base. Moreover, the domestic agencies in which the party is entrenched provide congressional Democrats with administrative capabilities that endure even when, as has come often to be the case, the Republicans control the presidency.

These agencies and programs upon which the Democratic party is now so dependent are, to a considerable extent, justified and legitimated in political debate under the rubric of the need to help African Americans (as well as members of other minorities) deal with poverty and racism and achieve full access to American society. As was noted in chapter 3, the programs of the Great Society were, for the most part, not created in response to demands from their nominal beneficiaries. Rather, Great Society agencies and programs were established at the behest of professional reformers, public policy intellectuals (policy "wonks" as they are known today), and spokespersons for service providers such as educators and mental health professionals. This has, in fact, been one of the great differences between the American and European welfare states. The European welfare state rests fairly securely on a broad base of support created by the organized recipients of services (the working-class and Social Democratic parties). The American welfare state, by contrast, teeters more precariously on a narrow base of support provided by the organized providers of services.

These groups, in effect, offered to provide a set of intellectual and professional services and identified groups of recipients whose needs could be said to justify the expenditure of billions of tax dollars for the construction and maintenance of the institutions needed to provide these services on a continuing basis. To a considerable extent, Great Society programs were promoted and explained to the public in terms of the distress of inner-city blacks. And, in subsequent decades, the needs of blacks have continued to provide the principal justification for virtually all social welfare programs and institutions with the exception of Social Security.

Liberal Democrats seek to characterize African Americans as victims of poverty and racism who are entitled not only to existing benefit programs but are badly in need of expanded federal efforts to protect them from discrimination, alleviate their poverty, provide them with educational opportunities, and generally help them achieve their proper place in American life. For the very reason that African Americans play such an important role in the legitimation of the American welfare state, conservative opponents of many domestic welfare programs seek to undermine their legitimacy by castigating blacks as a group in need of policing and supervision—to deal with their alleged criminality, drug abuse, and immorality—rather than additional social welfare benefits.

The positions taken by both liberals and conservatives, as always, reflect a mix of principle and interest. Liberal Democrats regard measures to provide for the needs of the poor—especially urban blacks—as matters of morality and social justice. At the same time, however, such measures also increase the flow of public funds into institutions controlled by liberal forces. Conservatives, for their part, are often guilty of more than a little racism. However, this is also consistent with their interest in shutting off the flow of funds into agencies and institutions controlled by their liberal Democratic foes.

Black Anti-Semitism

The growing electoral and institutional importance of African Americans to the Democratic party made anti-Semitism both useful and possible as a political tactic for some black politicians. First, as early as the late 1960s, the increased electoral weight of African Americans in the Democratic coalition encouraged black politicians to seek more influence within the Democratic party, greater access both for themselves and their constituents to the public and quasi-public institutions linked to the Democrats, and a larger share of the public expenditures controlled by the Democrats.

Very often these endeavors led to struggles between blacks and other groups in the Democratic coalition. Given the especially impor-

tant role played by Jews in the institutions of the domestic state—
federal agencies, municipal service bureaucracies, universities, and
the like—it was virtually a given that animosities would develop
between African Americans and Jews. Both groups were subject to
discrimination (albeit to different degrees) in the private sector and,
hence, especially dependent upon the public and quasi-public economies for opportunity and status. In effect, the new ambitions of African Americans inevitably put them into conflict with the established
interests of Jews. In these conflicts, anti-Semitic rhetoric sometimes
serves as a weapon through which blacks can intimidate their Jewish
rivals and supplant them in public positions and as the beneficiaries
of public funds. Occasionally, moreover, a posture of anti-Semitism
can help African-American politicians develop useful alliances with
some non-Jewish whites.

Second, the growing importance of blacks within the Democratic
party in the wake of the civil rights movement encouraged the emergence of several cohorts of ambitious young African-American politicians and new political forces, who were eager to supplant existing
black notables and assume positions of leadership within the black
community. A number of younger black politicians found anti-
Semitic rhetoric to be a weapon that could be usefully wielded
against the black establishment.[8] In a variety of different contexts,
insurgent forces within the African-American community charged
that incumbent leaders were the paid puppets of whites—of Jews,
in particular. Precisely because established black leaders *had* worked
closely with Jews in the civil rights movement, and often *were* dependent upon Jewish funding, they were quite vulnerable to this charge.

Finally, the importance of African Americans as a source of justification and legitimacy for social service institutions and domestic
social expenditures in the United States places limits upon the capacity of liberal white Democrats, Jews in particular, to respond to anti-
Semitic rhetoric and activities on the part of blacks. All liberal Democrats, but Jews especially, have a substantial stake in the American
welfare state. Jews played major roles in its creation and continue
to play important parts in its administration. Jews not only staff
domestic social agencies but are, as we saw in the previous chapter,
extremely active in the public interest groups, think tanks, consulting
firms, and universities that develop the domestic state's policies and
are funded by its grants.

Given this stake, Jews cannot afford to engage in or tolerate political tactics or public rhetoric that seriously threaten to discredit blacks.
This is one of the major reasons that Jewish racism, often expressed

privately, seldom manifests itself publicly. African Americans are simply too important to the legitimacy of the American domestic state. If Jews engage in attacks on blacks, or permit doubts to be raised about the merits of their political claims, then Jews are, in effect, undermining a major moral prop supporting the institutions from which they, themselves, derive enormous benefits and through which they exercise considerable power.

For this reason, black politicians usually have considerable leeway to indulge in anti-Semitic rhetoric and activities. Of course, Louis Farrakhan is frequently condemned for his rather intemperate statements. However, it would be deemed insensitive, to say the least, to demand that Jesse Jackson be barred from holding public office for his record of anti-Semitic slurs. The media—especially the elite media in which Jewish publisher, editors, and journalists play important roles—generally treat Jackson with considerable respect.

Indeed, the same liberal media that will denounce a white politician, especially a conservative white politician like Pat Buchanan who expresses antipathy for Jews, will usually greet anti-Semitic comments by black politicians with calls for understanding and dialogue. In a similar vein, the usually liberal and, often, Jewish faculties and administrations of elite colleges and universities quite properly regard racist expression by whites as a very serious offense. A number of major universities, such as Wisconsin and Michigan, sought to adopt so-called hate-speech codes to protect black and other minority students from racially offensive remarks. Anti-Semitic activities on the part of African-American student organizations and the speakers they bring to campus, on the other hand, are virtually always tolerated or, at most, will prompt university officials to deliver homilies on the importance of multicultural awareness and racial tolerance.

Thus, their institutional importance to Jews, and the liberal coalition more generally, gives black politicians the freedom to engage in anti-Semitic activities or, at least, to indulge in anti-Semitic rhetoric. At the same time, appeals to anti-Semitic sentiment can help black politicians intimidate their Jewish rivals, provide a number of advantages in the internal politics of the black community, and allow some black politicians to forge potentially advantageous alliances outside the black community.

Intimidation

As to the first of these, intimidation, in a number of institutional contexts African Americans and Jews have been pitted against one another in competition for jobs, access to education, and control of public institutions and funds. In these contexts, anti-Semitic appeals on the part of black leaders have served the function of intimidating Jews and compelling them to yield to black demands. This has been especially true in urban service bureaucracies and in universities where blacks are seeking positions presently held by Jews.

While African Americans also compete with members of other ethnic groups in similar contexts, because of their history and culture Jews seem more vulnerable to intimidation than some others. Blacks, for example, have not sought to drive the Irish from their municipal strongholds in New York City through a politics of intimidation. Similarly, intimidation usually does not force Italians from their neighborhoods.

Jews, however, appear to be more defenseless in the face of this tactic. Journalist Joseph Epstein, discussing Chicago, observed that blue-collar and working-class white ethnics in Chicago typically put up violent resistance to efforts by blacks to move into their neighborhoods. Jews, however, neither threaten nor abide violence. Usually, they attempt integration and, when it fails, simply move on—an option more readily available to Jews than to less affluent groups.[9] The Chicago case is typical.

In the New York City school system, for example, since the 1940s when they displaced the Irish who had previously controlled the schools, an overwhelming proportion of the teachers, principals, and administrators have been Jews. During the 1960s, as the children in the school system came, increasingly, to be black or members of other minority groups, African Americans began to challenge Jews for teaching and administrative positions.

In their struggles against the Jews, organizations of black teachers and their allies made frequent use of anti-Semitic slogans, pamphlets, and epithets designed to frighten and intimidate Jewish teachers and principals and to encourage them to give up their positions—often in poor black neighborhoods where they already felt threatened and vulnerable. As early as the 1960s, groups like the Afro-American Teacher's Association, an organization formed in 1964 to represent black teachers in Brooklyn, asserted, "We are witnessing today in New York City a phenomenon that spells death for the minds and souls of our black children. It is the systematic coming of age of the Jews who dominate and control the educational bureaucracy of the New York public school system . . . In short, our children are being mentally poisoned."[10] At the same time, individuals like Robert "Sonny" Carson, head of the Brooklyn chapter of CORE, frightened and intimidated Jewish teachers and principals by visiting their schools or school board meetings accompanied by a phalanx of tough-looking bodyguards.

Matters in New York came to a head during the Ocean Hill–Brownsville school controversy which has been described, in great detail, by Jonathan Kaufman, Diane Ravitch, and others.[11] In 1967, the Ford Foundation had issued a document which came to be known as the Bundy Report, proposing that the New York school system be broken into neighborhood districts supervised by elected community school boards. The Bundy Report predicted that decentralization would give local parents more of a sense of control and more of a stake in their schools. In particular, it was thought that this would contribute to the education of poor, black children.

On an experimental basis, three school districts were created to test the merits of decentralization. One of these was located in Ocean Hill–Brownsville, a predominantly black and poor area in Brooklyn. In the summer of 1967, with financial assistance from the Ford Foundation, a local school board was established and the Reverend C. Herbert Oliver, a prominent black minister in the community, elected chairman. The board appointed Rhody McCoy, a black teacher, as district superintendent. McCoy, in turn, moved to fill administrative vacancies with blacks and members of other racial minority groups, appointing two new African-American principals and one Puerto Rican principal. One of the blacks, Herman Ferguson, assistant principal of a Queens elementary school, was then under indictment for allegedly conspiring to kill a number of moderate black civil rights leaders. He was later convicted.

The majority of the existing principals and teachers in Ocean Hill–Brownsville were Jews. Many felt threatened by the community control experiment and by the local board's efforts to appoint more minority administrators. Some members of the board as well as Superintendent McCoy, in turn, were suspicious of and hostile to the Jewish teachers and administrators and eager to replace them with blacks. Jewish teachers were subject to harassment, particularly in Junior High School 271 where the Afro-American Teacher's Association was well organized. The association's bulletin board at JHS 271 often displayed anti-Semitic literature.

In February 1968, in response to harassment, the school's principal, Jack Bloomfield, and thirty teachers, most of them Jewish, transferred out of the district. After Dr. Martin Luther King's assassination in April, three white teachers were beaten in the hallway of JHS 271 after a school assembly in which Les Campbell, head of the

Afro-American Teacher's Association, spoke. Before Campbell's speech, the school's new black principal advised white teachers to leave the room. Campbell reportedly made a violently antiwhite speech to the students and remaining staff in which he said, "If whitey taps you on the shoulder, send him to the graveyard."[12] After this incident, more than fifty members of the predominantly Jewish white teaching staff stated that they were afraid to return to the school.

In May 1968, McCoy and the community board attempted to fire nineteen Jewish teachers and school administrators. The teachers' union demanded that they be reinstated. After a hearing, an arbitrator ordered that the local board return the teachers to their positions. The local board refused to obey the arbitrator's decision which prompted some 350 white teachers, the bulk of the district's teaching staff, to refuse to return to their classrooms. At the end of May, Albert Shanker, head of the New York teachers union, called a citywide strike of all 57,000 unionized teachers and promised to keep all of New York's schools closed until the Ocean Hill–Brownsville board was compelled to reinstate the teachers who had been dismissed. Within two days, the New York City Board of Education agreed to meet the union's demands.

In September, however, when the dismissed teachers reported for work, Superintendent McCoy met with them and told them that they were not wanted in the district and refused to give them class assignments. During the course of the meeting, in an auditorium packed with local residents, the teachers were subjected to jeering and taunts. As they left the auditorium, they were compelled to pass through a mob of jeering and shoving blacks. To further intimidate the district's Jewish teachers, blacks continued to employ anti-Semitic rhetoric to threaten and frighten them. At McCoy's behest, gangs of young toughs led by Sonny Carson made appearances at schools and meetings. African-American parents picketed the schools carrying signs reading, "Jew Pigs," and referring to Adolph Hitler as the Messiah. Jewish teachers received notes in which they were told, "Watch yourself Jew, crossing streets, drinking tea, etc. You have been marked for elimination." An anonymous handbill placed in the mailboxes of the JHS 271 teachers averred:

"If African American history and culture is to be taught to our black children it must be done by African Americans who identify with and who understand the problem. It is impossible for the Middle East murderers of colored people to possibly bring to this important task the insight, the concern, the exposing of the truth that is a must if the years of brain-washing and self hatred that has been taught to our black children by those bloodsucking exploiters and murderers is to be overcome. The idea behind this program is beautiful, but when the money changers heard about it they took over as is their custom in the black community. If African American history and culture is important to our children to raise their esteem of themselves, the only persons who can do the job are African American brothers and sisters and not the so-called liberal Jewish friend. We know from his tricky, deceitful maneuvers that he is really our enemy and he is responsible for the serious educational retardation of our black children. We call on all concerned black teachers, parents and friends to write to the Board of Education, to the mayor, to the State Commissioner of Education to protest the takeover of this crucial program by people who are unfit by tradition and by inclination to do even an adequate job."[13]

The district's refusal to reinstate the teachers led Shanker and the United Federation of Teachers to call a second citywide strike. During the course of the strike a number of anti-Semitic leaflets were reprinted by the teachers union as it sought to mobilize popular and press support against MCoy and the Ocean Hill–Brownsville board. In November, the citywide Board of Education suspended the Ocean Hill–Brownsville board and reinstated all of the unionized teachers who wanted to return to the district. McCoy resigned several months later. At least in the short term, the union had won.

In the somewhat longer term, however, the tactic of intimidation adopted by the Ocean Hill–Brownsville board and the Afro-American Teacher's Association achieved its desired effect by hastening the departure of Jewish teachers and administrators from the New York City system, thus making room for blacks and Hispanics. Since 1968, the percentage of New York City teaching posts held by Jews has declined from nearly 70% to less than 50%. At the same time, the percentage of New York's teachers who are black or Hispanic has increased substantially. In 1991, under an early retirement plan developed by New York Schools Chancellor, Joseph A. Fernandez, 221 of the city's approximately 1,000 school principals retired from their positions. Three-fourths of the retirees were white, and most of these were Jews. Among their replacements, roughly half were black or Hispanic. This has helped to continue the increase in minority principals, who now constitute 30% of all the city's principals. This increase has come mainly at the expense of Jews.[14]

Obviously, this change to some extent reflects increased levels of education among blacks and Hispanics as well as the expansion of alternative professional opportunities for Jews. That is, more blacks and Hispanics are earning the credentials necessary for teaching and administrative posts in the school system while Jews, especially Jewish women, are abandoning teaching for more remunerative careers in fields such as law, medicine, and business.

Part of the change, however, can also be credited to the use of anti-Semitic appeals to frighten and intimidate Jewish teachers and so to induce them to leave their posts while discouraging other Jews from seeking careers in the New York public school system. A number of Jewish teachers retired rather than return to their inner-city schools after the 1968 strike.

At the same time, the anti-Semitic militancy of blacks functioned to intimidate other political forces and to induce them to endeavor to placate blacks at the expense of the Jews. Thus, Protestants and Catholics, who were not directly affected themselves, have endeavored to placate militant and troublesome blacks by awarding them positions—especially administrative positions—in the New York City school system that were at one time controlled by Jews.

Indeed, the entire Ocean Hill–Brownsville affair arose from an effort by the Lindsay administration to placate blacks by giving them control over a set of administrative functions in the city's educational system that had been controlled by Jews. Some Jews at the time understood this precisely as an effort by elite WASPS—Lindsay, McGeorge Bundy of the Ford Foundation, and the socially prominent Citizens Committee for the Decentralization of the Public Schools— to placate and pacify angry blacks at their expense.[15] The result is that intimidation has been successful, and blacks have been displacing Jews in this municipal service bureaucracy.

Black Anti-Semitism and the University

Black anti-Semitism on the university campus can also be understood in these terms, that is, as an effort by blacks to intimidate Jewish faculty and administrators whose jobs and influence they covet. The Leonard Jeffries affair is a case in point. In recent years, Jeffries, former head of the African American Studies program at the City College of New York (CCNY) who has served as a member of the commission charged with rewriting the New York State public school history curriculum, has achieved a measure of notoriety for his anti-Semitic statements and theories. The best-known incident involved an address by Jeffries to the 1991 Empire State Black Arts and Cultural Festival, sponsored by Governor Cuomo's Black Affairs Committee, the state Martin Luther King, Jr. Commission, and the State University of New York African-American Institute.

In his address, which received a standing ovation, Jeffries delivered a torrent of anti-Semitic comments, claiming that blacks historically had been oppressed by Jews. "Rich Jews," according to Jeffries, "helped finance the slave trade." He claimed to have learned this from the "head Jew at City College." More recently, "There was a conspiracy planned and plotted and programmed out of Hollywood, with people named Greenberg and Weisberg and whatnot . . . Russian Jewry had a particular control over the monies and their financial partners, the Mafia, put together a system for the destruction of the black people." This Jewish conspiracy, according to Jeffries, continues into the present. "There's an orchestrated attack by the Schlesingers, the Shankers, working with white conservatives . . . We're pinpointing their relationships. We're putting it into our African computer. The document is being prepared."[16]

What makes Jeffries even more interesting than his anti-Semitic speeches at conferences are his anti-Semitic attacks on the CCNY campus. Here, Jeffries has used anti-Semitism to intimidate Jewish faculty and the university administration and to attempt to secure additional positions and resources for African Americans at the expense of Jews. In a case that recently came to light, a Jewish academic, Mitchell Seligson, presently director of the University of Pittsburgh's Center for Latin American Studies, interviewed at CCNY in 1984 for the position of director of international studies. Jeffries was part of the group that interviewed the candidate and, according to Seligson, used the opportunity to make anti-Semitic remarks to him both publicly and in private. Seligson reported that several other CCNY professors were present while Jeffries made some of his comments, but not one raised objections.

According to Seligson, Jeffries charged that then City College President Bernard Harleston was a tool of Jewish power brokers and that the entire selection process for the position of director of international studies was illegitimate because it did not produce a black candidate. According to a member of the CCNY faculty, Jeffries also asked Seligson, "Why [would] a Jew-boy like you want to come to a place like this?" After Jeffries's attack, Seligson withdrew his name from consideration at CCNY, citing the "climate of fear on the CCNY campus that I was not prepared to subject myself to." Seligson received a formal apology from the CCNY political science department for Jeffries's comments. No disciplinary action, however, was taken against Jeffries.[17] More than eight years later, in March 1992, the City University Board of Trustees finally removed Jeffries as head of the school's black studies program.[18]

As the Jeffries case suggests, anti-Semitic activity on the part of blacks, sometimes in alliance with members of other racial minority groups, under the rubric, "people of color," has become a persistent factor on some university and college campuses. University campuses, of course, are always on the cutting edge of political dissent, and student organizations speaking for people of color have little patience for yesterday's tired liberal politics of environmental, feminist, consumer, antiwar, or antinuclear protest. These questions are often dismissed, especially on elite campuses, as issues of interest only to bourgeois whites.

The importance of anti-Semitism on university campuses, however, is a function of more than students' continual search for titillating new issues. Since the early 1960s, when barriers to Jewish access were lifted, Jews have achieved positions of influence on university faculties and, to a lesser extent, in university administrations.[19] They have done this primarily by mastering the traditional academic disciplines. On the basis of their research and writing, Jews are among the major figures in most fields of scholarship in the natural sciences, social sciences, and humanities. Jews are prominent among department heads, receive many scholarly grants, and hold distinguished chairs at the nation's most prestigious universities. As a result of their success, Jews have a very substantial stake in the current disciplinary and reward structure of academic life—a reward structure that has given them institutional power, status, and honors.

African Americans, by contrast, have been less well able to break through the barriers to success in traditional American universities. As a result, they have every reason to attack the current disciplinary structure of the university and to demand the creation of new departments, offices, and programs they can control and use as sources of power, status, and honors for themselves.

In recent years, under the rubric of "multiculturalism," African Americans, sometimes in alliance with other "persons of color" (a group whose composition varies from campus to campus), have endeavored to seize control of budgets and to create or capture university programs for the ostensible purpose of promoting teaching and scholarship devoted to the history, politics, literature, and science of non-European peoples. In a similar vein, at many universities, a stratum of black administrators and faculty have organized around affirmative action programs and have endeavored to enlarge their own influence by expanding the size and scope of the programs in their domain. On most campuses, only people of color are deemed qualified to staff Black Studies departments, affirmative action offices, and the like. On some university campuses, however, African-American student and faculty groups are allied with feminists and/or gay-rights activists, resulting in a different set of accommodations.

At a number of colleges and universities, ethnic or multicultural studies are being required of all students. Such a requirement can, presumably, be defended on intellectual grounds and has many sincere proponents. At the same time, however, this requirement also guarantees that a school will be compelled to hire more African-American (and other minority) faculty and administrators to teach and coordinate these programs, perhaps expand its affirmative action efforts to enhance the university's own diversity, and thus to cede control over a larger share of the university's budget to blacks and other people of color. Usually, such a transfer of resources can only come about at the expense of more traditional departments and programs, especially in the social sciences and humanities. Often this is justified by charging that existing programs are "Eurocentric" and badly in need of curricular and administrative overhaul.

This sort of ploy is common in academic politics; it is by no means unique to blacks. Often, members of a field in which there is relatively little student interest will endeavor to develop a course or sequence that can, under some rubric, be required of all students in order to justify the field's faculty positions ("lines," as they are called), administrative support, and share of the university's budget. In many schools, English departments, rather than Ethnic Studies programs, seem to be the most creative and successful practitioners of this stratagem.

The slogans used in academic politics—especially the politics of race—can be quite confusing. Under the rubric of maintaining "diversity," for example, white female faculty members will sometimes demand that faculty positions that might, in fact, have gone to blacks instead be allocated to their white, male spouses.

Similarly, some university administrators who oppose the creation of ethnic studies departments take what seems to be the even more radical position that minority faculty should not be concentrated in one department, creating what they dismiss as an "academic ghetto." Instead, they assert, every department in the university has a moral obligation to recruit black and other minority faculty. Some administrators advocate this position sincerely. For others, however, it is the moral equivalent of Stalin's avowal of "socialism in one country"—a doctrine used to justify breaking the power of the Jews who dominated the Comintern. The doctrine of "minority faculty in *every* department" can be understood as a way of avoiding the necessity of giving minority faculty control of *any* department. In some academic fields, moreover, such as mathematics, physics, and chemistry, virtually no black Ph.D.s are trained and, hence, there is little danger that black faculty can actually be recruited.

At any rate, efforts by African Americans and their allies to gain a larger share of university budgets and faculty positions inevitably create conflicts between blacks and Jews who, despite their historic support for black causes, are now often the most vigorous defenders of the existing disciplinary structure of the university—a structure from which they derive numerous benefits. To some extent, this explains why a number of very prominent liberal and even left-wing Jewish academics moved sharply to the political right beginning in the late 1970s. Some of these neoconservatives, as discussed in Chapter 5, were motivated primarily by support for Israel. Others, however, were less worried about Israel and more concerned with what they deemed to be an effort by blacks and other forces to destroy the university.

Given the prominence of Jews among the defenders of the university's current disciplinary structure, it is not surprising that anti-Semitism has become a weapon often wielded on university campuses by the proponents of multiculturalism and ethnic studies. Indeed, the anti-Semitic weapon permits the opponents of the university's disciplinary structure to claim that the arguments made by that structure's supporters—which are usually couched in terms of "merit" and "excellence"—are nothing more than the special pleading of the Jews.

At the same time, it is worth noting, through anti-Semitic rhetoric and posturing, blacks can intimidate Jewish liberals on campus and compel them to subordinate their own "public interest" agenda to the goals and aspirations of blacks. This is one example of the way in which a politics of anti-Semitism can help African Americans achieve a position of primacy on the political left. We shall return to this topic later in the chapter.

It is worth noting, too, that feminists, who support the creation and expansion of such nontraditional programs as Womens Studies sometimes find themselves allied with blacks against the Jewish (Jewish male, at any rate) defenders of the university's established disciplinary structure. Since many active feminists are Jews, however, organized feminist groups are less well able to make use of anti-Semitic rhetoric against their opponents though, as Letty Cotton Pogrebin has recently pointed out, a measure of anti-Semitism occasionally surfaces in the womens movement.[20]

Usually, of course, the anti-Semitism of African Americans is not constrained by the presence of Jews in their own ranks. Occasionally, however, such a problem does surface, as in the recent case of Julius Lester, a long-time member of the University of Massachusetts African-American Studies department. Professor Lester, a black poet and novelist, discovered that he had some Jewish ancestors, developed an interest in the Jewish religion, and eventually converted to Judaism. This conversion, coupled with Lester's criticism of James Baldwin, whom Lester accused of making anti-Semitic remarks, led to demands by his colleagues—accompanied by what Lester described as anti-Semitic overtures—that he be ousted from the African-American Studies program. Indeed, all fifteen of his colleagues demanded that he be expelled from the department. Lester transferred to the university's Judaic and Near Eastern Studies department. In this way, political order was restored in Amherst.[21]

The relationship between anti-Semitism and multiculturalism was recently symbolized in Atlanta by the prominent display and sale of the ancient anti-Semitic tract *Protocols of the Elders of Zion* at the 1990 Second National Conference on the Infusion of African and African-American Content in the High School Curriculum.[22] An interesting recent case, however, illustrating this linkage between anti-Semitism and ethnic studies, took place not in Atlanta but at the University of Washington in Seattle.[23] In 1990, a faculty-student Task Force on Ethnicity presented a proposal requiring every Washington student to earn at least one-fourth of the humanities and social science credits required for graduation in approved ethnic studies courses. This was deemed necessary in order to combat racism and to sensitize students to the problems of discrimination and oppression.

When Jewish groups asked that the issue of anti-Semitism be included among the topics to be considered under this requirement (i.e., sought a portion of the funds to be spent in this endeavor), minority faculty and student groups, according to University of Washington English Professor Edward Alexander, were vehemently opposed on the grounds that Jews were not "people of color." This meant that they did not share or understand the life experiences of African Americans, Native Americans, or Latinos—the alliance comprising the people of color at that particular university. Presumably, this also meant that Jews should most certainly *not* share in the budgetary outlays and teaching positions to be awarded to officially recognized people of color.

During the subsequent campus debate, one professor of ethnic studies said that he could not accept the inclusion of Jews and anti-

Semitism in the proposed ethnic studies curriculum unless other Semitic peoples, especially Palestinian Arabs, were also included. Another ethnic studies professor helpfully pointed out that Jews could not necessarily even be seen as victims of anti-Semitism because they were not necessarily of Semitic descent. At any rate, she argued, anti-Semitism was historically not as important a problem as white racism.[24]

Several months later, two of the major proponents of the ethnic studies requirement, the Associated Students of the University of Washington (ASUW) and the Black Students Commission, cosponsored a vehemently anti-Semitic speech by one Abdul Alim Musa, who asserted that America was controlled by the Jews who made it their business to keep people of color repressed and powerless. He went on to assert that the "Yahuds are the enemies of humanity" and to predict (and welcome) a second Holocaust in which a popular uprising would lead to the slaughter of America's Jews. Despite some protests, the sponsors of the speech refused to disown Musa's views —except to explain that they should be understood as anti-Zionist rather than anti-Semitic.[25]

In a similar vein, at UCLA, in February 1991, the African-American student newsmagazine, *Nommo*, published an article praising the seemingly ubiquitous *Protocols of the Elders of Zion*. *Nommo* described the *Protocols* in Afrocentric terms, as an account of a conspiracy by "a small group of European people [who] have proclaimed themselves God's 'chosen' by using an indigenous African religion, Judaism, to justify their place in the world." *Nommo* went on to praise hatred for the Jews as "good for Hitler . . . good for Stalin and . . . good for *Nommo*." After a protest by Jewish groups, *Nommo's* editors refused to back down, even to the extent of admitting in print that the *Protocols* were a work of fiction. Instead, the magazine's editors claimed that the Jews were trying to censor them. Their position was supported by the Latino student newsmagazine, *La Gente*.[26] In a subsequent, pregraduation issue of *Nommo*, one of the editors bade farewell to her readers with an attack on "white zionist fucks."[27]

Again, to many of the forces advocating the expansion of ethnic and multicultural studies, Jews are the enemy. Jews have succeeded in, benefit from, and defend the traditional structure of the university—a structure that African Americans, Latinos, and others want to reshape to their own advantage. Anti-Semitism can be a useful way of discrediting and intimidating the defenders of traditional academic values.

Many Jews at major universities have felt the same concern as the Jewish student council member at UCLA who, after a three-hour debate on the *Nommo* article, ending with the council's refusal to criticize it for anti-Semitism, tearfully described how despised she felt on campus—"as if she was wearing a sign that said, 'I'm Jewish, hate me.'" Thus, demands for multiculturalism and anti-Semitism go hand in hand and are likely to continue to do so in the coming years.

Many Jews are too intimidated to object when "people of color" engage in anti-Semitic rhetoric, fearing that they will be branded as racists. Once intimidated, many Jews are afraid to oppose demands for curricular and bureaucratic changes made by the same people of color lest it be said that they are merely defending special Jewish interests against the needs and aspirations of the oppressed. And, this is precisely why anti-Semitism is likely to continue to be such a useful arrow in the quiver of African Americans and other people of color on university campuses.

Of course, both in the university and in the larger society, many Jews feel a moral commitment to black causes that impels them to support the demands and aspirations of African Americans despite the anti-Semitic rhetoric in which these are sometimes couched. As noted previously, moreover, many Jews and Jewish organizations believe that the fundamental interests of Jews are so closely tied, both politically and institutionally, to those of blacks that it is sometimes necessary to support black demands even when, conceived narrowly or in the short term, these seem to be disadvantageous to Jews.

Thus, in the university setting, some Jews can be found supporting black demands for ethinc studies requirements, the appointment of additional African-American faculty and administrators, and so forth. Similarly, in the larger society, Jewish organizations feel compelled, in part by morality and in part by calculation of long-term interest, to support civil rights legislation that promotes racial quotas or their near equivalent in hiring, despite the potential disadvantages to Jews of such policies.

Internal Politics

Anti-Semitism also has come to play an important role in the internal politics of the African-American community. Through the 1960s, black leaders and organizations such as the SCLC, CORE, the NAACP, and the Urban League were closely aligned with Jews and Jewish groups and often heavily dependent upon them for legal advice, organizational leadership, and funding. Jews were critically important to blacks when few other whites would help them. This dependence upon Jews, however, made established black politicians vulnerable to attack by insurgent black political forces who could use anti-Semitic appeals as a way of charging that established blacks had sold out to whites and could not be trusted.

The first major black politicians to successfully use this strategy were Malcolm X in the North, and Stokely Carmichael, head of the Student Nonviolent Coordinating Committee (SNCC), in the South. The Chicago-based Nation of Islam, or Black Muslims as they were often called, led by Elijah Mohammed, began to attract national publicity during the middle and late 1960s. In contrast to the message of established black organizations that emphasized integration and coalition building with whites, Mohammed argued for black separatism and against collaboration with those he dismissed as "white devils."

The Muslim platform of black assertiveness, separatism, and hatred of whites struck a responsive chord with young blacks in Northern urban ghettos. Malcolm X, Elijah Mohammed's chief lieutenant in New York, was the Nation of Islam's most effective preacher and recruiter. Malcolm appealed to young ghetto blacks by preaching self-determination, self-defense, and the use of violence, if necessary, to achieve liberation. Traditional black politicians who were allied with and dependent upon white support were denounced as collaborators who had sold out the black community. Since the most prominent white allies of black causes were typically Jews, Malcolm's rhetoric often contained anti-Semitic or anti-Zionist references. This latter was important because established black leaders had often been compelled to voice their support for Israel as a condition for receiving the support of Jewish organizations for their own objectives.

Indeed, to this day black members of Congress are among the most reliable supporters of aid for Israel and opponents of aid for Israel's enemies on Capitol Hill. For example, in 1981, sixteen of the seventeen black congressmen voted against the Reagan administration's sale of the AWACS airborne control system to Saudi Arabia—a sale bitterly opposed by pro-Israel groups. This black backing is, to a considerable extent, purchased by Jewish campaign contributions and some assistance on issues important to blacks, such as the anti-apartheid campaign. Most black congressmen, however, insist upon keeping a low profile for their help for the Jewish state. Seldom, for example, will a black member of Congress publicly accept an award from an American Jewish organization or allow a Jewish organization to hold the customary testimonial dinner to honor him for his

support for Israel. Most members of the black congressional delegation fear that a Zionist award would be politically damaging.

By attacking Israel, Malcom X was underscoring the difference
between himself and these "kept" black politicians forced to perform
obeisance to a white group in exchange for its support. Thus, in one
speech, Malcolm declared, "The Jews with the help of Christians in
America and Europe, drove our Muslim brothers out of their homeland, where they had been settled for centuries and took over the
land for themselves. This every Muslim resents . . . In America, the
Jews sap the very life-blood of the so-called Negroes to maintain
the state of Israel, its armies, and its continued aggression against
our brothers in the East. This every Black Man resents." In another
speech Malcolm dismissed a question about the Holocaust by criticiz-
ing those who became "wet-eyed over a bunch of Jews who brought
it on themselves."[28]

By attacking Israel and the Jews Malcolm was, in effect, attacking
his more established rivals for power within the black community
who were closely tied to Jewish contributors and who were, as a
result, forced to maintain a supportive posture toward Israel. This
was now excoriated by Malcolm as behavior utterly inappropriate
for a true leader of the African-American people.

This same tactic was used subsequently and for similar reasons by
Malcolm's successor, Louis Farrakhan, who achieved prominence by
referring to Judaism as a "gutter religion."[29] When established black
leaders sought to distance themselves from or to repudiate such comments, or to remind blacks of the support that Jews had given to the
civil rights movement they, in effect, provided ammunition for their
more radical foes—buttressing charges that they had sold out to
whites. For example, when Vernon Jordan, executive director of the
National Urban League, responded to Farrakhan's attacks on Jews
by praising Jews for their past support, he became the target of angry
denunciations and pickets in front of Urban League offices.[30]

In the South, during the same period, anti-Semitic appeals became
an important weapon for Stokely Carmichael, chairman of the Student Non-Violent Coordinating Committee (SNCC). Carmichael was
a New York native and had attended the heavily Jewish, Bronx High
School of Science. Upon graduation, however, he enrolled in a black
college in the South where he became involved in the civil rights
movement. Under its former chairman, John Lewis, SNCC had relied
heavily upon Jewish contributors and field organizers.

However, in the mid-1960s, SNCC, which appealed mainly to
younger, more radical blacks, faced a challenge from more militant
groups like the Muslims and the Black Panthers who accused SNCC

of being insufficiently committed to the revolutionary cause and being too moderate in its tactics. These groups were able to use the
prominence of Jews among SNCC's supporters as evidence of its
insufficient militancy and, so, to undermine its credibility among
young black radicals.

Muslims even went so far as to walk into SNCC field offices in
the South to intimidate the Jewish workers who almost inevitably
formed a significant portion of the staff, and to embarrass their black
coworkers for relying upon the leadership of Jews. In one account
by Dotty Miller, a Jewish graduate of Queens College working for
SNCC in Atlanta, "The Muslim came into SNCC's office and began
denouncing the presence of Jews in the civil rights movement. 'The
only thing wrong with Hitler was that he didn't burn up all the
Jews,' the Muslim said."[31]

In response to this challenge from the left, Stokely Carmichael,
who had replaced Lewis as head of SNCC in 1966, took a much
more black nationalist and antiwhite stance which was continued by
his successor, H. Rap Brown. It was Carmichael who coined the
phrase "black power." Anti-Semitism was part and parcel of SNCC's
turn to the left. After the 1967 Arab-Israeli war, the SNCC Newsletter
presented a series of attacks on Israel as well as a number of anti-
Semitic caricatures and cartoons. A headline in the Newsletter asserted that "Zionists conquered the Arabs' homes and land through
terror, force and massacres." A group of Israeli soldiers was shown
allegedly shooting unarmed Arabs lined up against a wall. One cartoon showed Israeli General Moshe Dayan with dollar signs on his
epaulets. Another cartoon depicted the former heavyweight champion, Mohammed Ali, with a noose around his neck. The hand holding the noose displayed a Star of David and a dollar sign.

In the wake of this newsletter, most of SNCC's Jewish supporters
broke with the organization. However, SNCC's credibility as a militant, black nationalist organization was restored among its radical
young troops. Over the next several years, SNCC, the Black Panthers,
and other organizations seeking to recruit militant young blacks vied
with one another to assert their radical credentials through antiwhite
and, especially, through anti-Semitic appeals. One famous poem,
presented by the Black Panther's magazine stated:

> We're gonna burn their towns and that ain't all
> We're gonna piss upon the Wailing Wall
> And then we'll get Kosygin and DeGaulle
> That will be ecstasy, killing every Jew we see.[32]

The aggressive anti-Semitism of organizations like SNCC, the Nation of Islam, and the Black Panthers represented a serious threat to more mainstream black organizations and politicians. Groups like the SCLC and the NAACP relied very heavily upon Jewish contributors and supporters. This reliance, however, made them vulnerable to charges of insufficient militancy and undue dependence upon whites, especially Jews—charges that have considerable basis in reality. For example, for years the leaders of established black organizations signed Bayard Rustin's annual Black Americans in Support of Israel Committee (BASIC) statement. When Julian Bond sought to succeed Roy Wilkins as head of the NAACP in 1976, he also signed the statement even though he was personally critical of Israel and, as a former leader of SNCC, had formerly been a foe of Israeli policy. Bond believed that signing the BASIC statement was essential if he was to have any chance of winning the NAACP position, given the powerful influence of Jews within the organization.

Jesse Jackson's use of anti-Semitic rhetoric during the 1984 presidential campaign can be understood in very much the same terms. Ostensibly, Jackson was a candidate for the presidency of the United States. Jackson, however, understood that he could not hope to win the presidency. What Jackson actually sought to win was the leadership of the African-American community. Through his presidential campaign, Jackson hoped to make himself the single most powerful black politician in the country and, as a result, a major power broker in the national Democratic party.

In this endeavor, however, Jackson opposed and was, in turn, opposed by the leaders of most major black organizations and the elected black public officials who, taken together, were already the established power brokers and leaders of the black community. Both Mayors Coleman Young of Detroit and Andrew Young of Atlanta, for example, initially opposed Jackson's candidacy, as did Mayor Harold Washington of Chicago and State Representative Julian Bond of Georgia.[33]

Thus, Jackson faced the opposition of the established leaders of the black community—most of whom were committed to supporting Walter Mondale for the Democratic presidential nomination. Jackson's response was to seek to mobilize grass-roots support within the black community by presenting his candidacy as a crusade on behalf of African-American self-respect. Black politicians who refused to support Jackson were castigated as "Uncle Toms" who should be ashamed of themselves.

Jackson's anti-Semitic slurs as well as his refusal to disavow the more vicious anti-Semitism of Black Muslim leader Louis Farrakhan must be understood in this context. Jackson was an insurgent struggling to make himself the dominant force within the black community. Jackson sought to displace black elected officials, organization leaders, and even Coretta Scott King, widow of the martyred Martin Luther King. Anti-Semitic remarks permitted Jackson to distinguish himself from all these individuals who were, indeed, politically linked or financially dependent upon Jews and, thus, vulnerable to the charge of dependence upon whites and insufficient militancy.

Crown Heights

The most recent and most violent manifestation of the role of anti-Semitism in the internal politics of the African-American community is the Crown Heights anti-Semitic riots of August 1991. The riots began with a fatal traffic accident. An auto driven by Yosef Lifsh, a member of an ultraorthodox Jewish sect, the Lubavitcher Hasidim, ran a red light and struck and killed a seven-year-old African-American child, Gavin Cato, and injured his cousin, Angela.

This accident sparked several nights of rioting and looting by local blacks who rampaged through the Crown Heights neighborhood attacking Jews, looting Jewish shops, and shouting "Heil Hitler," "Kill the Jews," and other anti-Semitic epithets. One Orthodox Jew, Yankel Rosenbaum, a twenty-nine-year-old visiting scholar from Australia who had come to New York to study archival material at the Yivo Institute, was dragged from his car and stabbed to death by a gang of young blacks.[34]

What distinguished this series of events from other episodes of violence and rioting that have, unfortunately, come to characterize life in America's urban slums is the role that a small group of African-American politicians played during the rioting and the use they sought to make of the entire affair. These politicians, most notably the Reverend Al Sharpton, Alton Maddox, Vernon Mason, the Reverend Herbert Daughtry, and Sonny Carson, are well-known activists and insurgents in New York black politics. Individually and collectively they have stood ready to use almost any incident that could attract publicity for themselves and demonstrate their own militancy on behalf of black causes and their devotion to the African-American community in contrast to the more moderate—and, thus, politically suspect positions of more established black leaders and officials. As New York's established black politicians sought to restore order in Crown Heights, activists like Sonny Carson urged young black rioters to continue their violent behavior.

Sharpton, Mason, and Maddox, it may be recalled, were the chief defenders of and spokesmen for Tawana Brawley, a black teenager whose tale—ultimately proven to have been entirely fabricated—of kidnapping and torture at the hands of a gang of whites in upstate New York was a media sensation in 1990. Recently, Daughtry played an active role in the effort to convict a white Teaneck, New Jersey, police officer, Gary Spath, of murder for the 1990 shooting death of a black teenager, Philip Pannell. After a trial, Spath was acquitted of all charges in February, 1992.[35]

These insurgent leaders stepped into the Crown Heights affair and, through anti-Semitic appeals, sought to expand their own popular base in New York's African-American community, particularly at the expense of New York's black elected officials, such as Harlem Congressman Charles Rangel and, most notably, Mayor David Dinkins. Daughtry, along with Sharpton and Maddox, had long been leaders of the Brooklyn insurgent opposition to the Harlem "establishment" clique of black politicians with whom Dinkins was associated.

The Booklyn group had felt especially betrayed by Dinkins in 1985 when, in their view, he made a backdoor deal to support former Mayor Edward Koch's reelection in exchange for the latter's support for Dinkins's candidacy for the Manhattan Borough presidency. During Dinkins's successful 1989 mayoral race, Sharpton described him as an "Uncle Tom," while Maddox characterized him as "an Ed Koch in blackface."[36]

From the beginning of Dinkins's administration, the Brooklyn insurgents led by Daughtry, Sharpton, and Maddox had been attacking the mayor for insensitivity to the needs of poor blacks and undue willingness to accept the fiscal constraints imposed upon the city by white bankers and businessmen. For his part, Vernon Mason, who sought a seat on the City Council, attempted to use his well-publicized defense of Professor Leonard Jeffries's anti-Semitic theories as a campaign weapon to boost his appeal among black voters. The true targets of Mason's defense of anti-Semitism can be inferred from the fact that Harlem Congressman Charles Rangel contributed $3000—the maximum permitted by law—to the reelection of Mason's chief foe, incumbent City Councilman Stanley Michels, who is white.[37]

In the typical pattern, Dinkins was closely tied to and dependent upon Jewish contributors and advisors. Jewish financier, Felix Rohatyn, was Dinkins's chief fiscal advisor. During his 1989 campaign for election, and throughout his administration, Dinkins had the strong support of Sandra Feldman, leader of the heavily Jewish, United Federation of Teachers. In addition, Dinkins courted and relied upon the votes of Jews—virtually the only whites in the city willing to cast their votes for a black mayoral candidate. Dinkins took 40% of the Jewish vote in defeating Republican Rudolph Giuliani by a mere 47,000 votes out of some 1.7 million votes cast. As a result, Dinkins frequently attended Jewish ceremonial events and even traveled to Israel during the Persian Gulf War to show his support for the Jewish state.[38]

This close association with and dependence upon Jews made Dinkins vulnerable to charges of "selling out." Dinkins, as was sometimes said in the black community, "wore too many yarmulkes." Thus, from the perspective of Sharpton, Mason, Maddox, and the other insurgents, the Crown Heights affair presented an opportunity to mobilize the support of young blacks by demonstrating their own militancy, while undermining more established black leaders by demonstrating their overreliance on Jews.

Thus, when Mayor Dinkins described the murder of Yankel Rosenbaum as a "lynching" comparable to the shooting of Yusuf Hawkins, a black man killed by whites in Bensonhurst the previous year, Reverend Al Sharpton expressed shock. "It is absurd for the mayor to compare an outright racial fatality/shooting with intent, with the stabbing of Yankel Rosenbaum, who we still don't know was assaulted because of his race or religion," Sharpton declared.[39] Another black activist said, "The mayor does not seem to distinguish premeditated murder from retaliatory murder."[40] For his part, Sonny Carson averred, "This statement does not make any kind of sense. They [the city's Jewish power elite] have a way of convincing the mayor to make statements."[41] Sharpton agreed: "The mayor should quit leaning over to please others."[42] In October 1992, a black man, Lemrick Nelson, charged with Rosenbaum's murder was acquitted by a predominantly black jury even though the individual had been identified by Rosenbaum before he died. Police also had recovered the bloody weapon from the pocket of the accused. Nelson's defense attorney subsequently held a victory party which was attended by several of the jurors. The celebration reinforced doubts about the validity of the verdict.

When Dinkins sought to pay a condolence call on the Cato family he was greeted by rocks and bottles thrown by young blacks. His efforts to address the crowd were drowned out by jeering protestors. During Gavin Cato's funeral, at St. Anthony's Baptist Church in

Bedford-Stuyvesant, radical blacks—including Sharpton, activist lawyer Colin Moore, and the Reverend Herbert Daughtry—attacked Dinkins, who sat quietly in the audience. The mayor left the church by a side door before the services ended.

During Cato's funeral, Al Sharpton, seeking to appeal to militant young blacks, declared that the black community would permit "no compromise, no sellout . . . nothing less than the prosecution of the murderer of this man."[43] Sonny Carson congratulated the youthful rioters and looters saying (to the assembled white media), "You might not like this but I am very proud of them."[44]

New York's established African-American politicians understood the Crown Heights affair as an attack on themselves and sought to respond. For example, establishment blacks organized their own memorial service for Gavin Cato at a church they controlled. Dinkins spoke at this service, held at the First Baptist Church in Crown Heights. The mayor called for understanding and racial harmony and received a warm reception from the congregation.[45] The pastor of the First Baptist Church is the Reverend Clarence Norman, whose son Clarence, Jr., chairman of the regular Brooklyn Democratic party, is a pillar of the New York City black political establishment and one of the mayor's closest political allies.

Jewish organizations, for their part, made constant demands that Dinkins speak out against and repudiate Sharpton, Carson, and Maddox. This Dinkins was unwilling to do because it would only provide additional ammunition for his foes in the black community—confirming that he was merely a stooge for the Jews.[46] The entire Crown Heights affair was a difficult one for Dinkins, who is running for reelection in 1993 and needs Jewish as well as united black support.

A third component of the intrablack politics of the Crown Heights affair involved Caribbean blacks. Immigrants from Haiti and the other islands of the Caribbean have, for the most part, been a conservative force within the black community, more likely to give their support to moderate politicians like Mayor Dinkins than to agitators like Sharpton, Mason, and Maddox. To an increasing extent, however, younger Caribbean blacks have tended to be attracted to the more militant style of African Americans, often to the chagrin of their parents who lament that the children are "becoming American."

Caribbean blacks form a large segment of the black population of Crown Heights, and to insurgent activists like Sharpton, Mason, and Maddox the death of Gavin Cato represented an opportunity to appeal to younger, more militant Caribbean blacks and woo them away from their own, more conservative community leaders. This same calculus had led Carson, Sharpton, and Maddox to organize a well-publicized black boycott of a Korean grocery in 1990 on the ground that the owners had shown disrespect to a Haitian woman.

Anti-Semitism was a useful instrument for this purpose because of some tension between the Caribbean and Hasidic communities over housing and behavior in public spaces. More important, though, Caribbean community leaders in Crown Heights had historically cooperated with Jews in community organizations and even, to some limited extent, in politics. This made them vulnerable to charges of collaborationism and meant that attacks on the Jews could be used to discredit those blacks who cooperated with Jews. Thus, in the Crown Heights affair, radical African-American politicians sought to use anti-Semitism to attack the established leadership of the Caribbean black community.

That this leadership was a target for Carson and the others became clear at Gavin Cato's funeral. At the conclusion of the funeral, Sonny Carson sought to unfurl the Guyanese flag as though he was the true spokesman for Caribbean blacks.[47] Later, when the leaders of the Caribbean community decided to hold their annual Carnival—the West Indian–American Day parade—despite the recent tragedy, Carson sought to appeal to more militant Caribbean blacks and undermine the authority of community elders by denouncing them for planning a celebration so soon after Gavin Cato's death.

Caribbean leaders such as Carlos Lezama responded by denouncing Carson and their other African-American activist challengers for presuming to tell Caribbeans how to conduct their own struggles for justice. Carson's criticism of Carnival, moreover, was condemned as disrespectful to Caribbean people.[48] It is interesting that rather than seek to vie with the anti-Semitic rhetoric of Sharpton, Carson, and Maddox, Caribbean leaders made a point of inviting Hasidic Jews to march in their parade. They were able to deflect the anti-Semitic campaign of the American blacks by appealing to the solidarity of their own ethnic base rather than being forced to veer sharply to the left to protect themselves. For African-American leaders like Mayor Dinkins, however, anti-Semitic attacks from their insurgent foes represent a much more serious challenge that can lead them to diminish their own links to the Jewish community. As noted above, this is what black members of Congress have already done.

Alliance Building

A third role played by black anti-Semitism is in support of efforts by African Americans to forge alliances and coalitions with other groups—some but not all of which may have their own reasons for supporting expressions of antipathy for Jews. When they attack Jews, rather than whites more generally, blacks are, in effect, making themselves available as partners to those whites who are not Jews. Blacks can also serve the useful function of saying what some whites believe but are reluctant to say for fear of being branded anti-Semites.

Anti-Semitism can play a useful role in several types of coalitional efforts on the part of blacks. First, anti-Semitism is useful to the efforts of radical blacks to link themselves to the forces of the Third World on the international scene. During the 1960s, many African Americans came to identify with the aspirations of Third World nations nominally struggling against neocolonialism or American imperialism—evils with which blacks struggling for civil rights in the United States could identify. As Glenn Loury has noted, the various black power movements of that period gave rise to a black nationalist or even Pan-African identity for many blacks, which prompted them to see parallels between their relationship to white Americans and the position of nonwhite Third World people relative to the West.[49] Identification with the Third World allows American blacks to see themselves as part of a worldwide struggle against oppression. Most Third World participants in this struggle, of course, are strongly opposed to Israel, and, hence, anti-Zionism can be an important element of Third World solidarity for African-Americans, as it often is for Western European Socialists.

This pattern became quite evident during the 1991 Persian Gulf War. The Bush administration's decision to send military forces into the Persian Gulf was strongly opposed by virtually all black leaders on the grounds that African Americans would be forced to bear more than their share of the cost of the war both in terms of casualties and in terms of the diversion of badly needed resources from domestic social objectives. Jesse Jackson, for example, told rallies that every American bomb dropped on Baghdad deprived American blacks of roads and schools.

Many prominent African Americans used the war as an occasion to attack Israel and express their solidarity with the Third World. Father Lawrence Lucas, a leftist priest, asserted that the United States had started the war against Iraq primarily to "provide support for

Israel." The Reverend Ben Chavis, executive director of the Commission on Racial Justice of the United Church of Christ, urged blacks to show solidarity with Palestinians. In a similar vein, the Reverend Calvin O. Butts III, pastor of Harlem's Abyssinian Baptist Church, attacked New York Mayor David Dinkins for visiting Israel during the war. Butts accused Dinkins of being more concerned with Jewish voters than with his own community. Congressman Charles Rangel, who accompanied Dinkins to Israel, was forced to end his speech at a Harlem antiwar rally prematurely after he was jeered for defending Israel. Both Dinkins and Rangel, it should be noted, were strong critics of the war.

This sense of identification with the Third World is reinforced by the benefits that blacks can obtain from a Third World alliance. While Third World forces can offer little material help to American blacks, they can offer them a sense of power and association with the world's majority, as well as status and legitimacy on the international scene as representatives of anticolonialist and anti-imperialist groups in the United States. As Jim Sleeper has observed, some blacks are drawn to the international left, "not least for the very non-nationalist reason that here, at last, they find whites who treat them as people of importance."[50]

Delegations of American blacks attend international conferences, visit Third World capitals, and so forth. In these contexts, opposition to Israel and Zionism is universal. Very often African Americans participate in the drafting of resolutions condemning what are presented as the morally equivalent evils of racism, imperialism, Zionism, and apartheid. Generally, Middle-Eastern delegations expect Africans and black Americans to support resolutions in opposition to Zionism in exchange for their support for resolutions opposing apartheid. For example, during the United Nations Womens Conference held in Copenhagen in 1980, "trade-offs" were negotiated in which American black delegates agreed to support Palestinian causes in exchange for Arab support for an antiapartheid resolution.[51]

Of course, opposition to Israel and support for the cause of the Palestinians is not automatically anti-Semitic. However, it is difficult to support the Palestinians and oppose Israel and Zionism without simultaneously opposing Israel's supporters in the United States, most of whom happen to be Jews. It is difficult to be against Zionism without also being against Zionists. It is unusual for blacks who take anti-Zionist positions to not also express anti-Semitism.

At the same time, relationships between American blacks and Israel's enemies inevitably have domestic repercussions leading to conflicts between Jews and blacks in the United States. For example, in 1977, Andrew Young, the U.S. ambassador to the United Nations and, at that time, the highest ranking black official in the Carter administration, held an unauthorized meeting with representatives of the Palestine Liberation Organization (PLO). After vigorous protests by American Jewish organizations, Carter fired Young for violating U.S. policy which forbade such meetings with PLO officials.

In retaliation for the role played by Jews in Young's ouster, a number of black leaders traveled to the Middle east to hold friendly meetings and discussions with Israel's Arab enemies. For example, Joseph Lowery, head of the Southern Christian Leadership Conference, led a delegation consisting of NAACP President Benjamin Hooks and Georgia State Senator Julian Bond. This group presented Libyan dictator, Muammar Qaddafi, an award of appreciation from American blacks called "The Decoration of Martin Luther King."[52]

Closely related to the role that anti-Semitism plays in developing alliances between blacks and Third World forces is the role that it plays in shaping the relationship between blacks and white members of the American Left. Anti-Semitism has helped black radicals achieve a position of primacy on the American Left. Through the 1960s, blacks were a subordinate group on the Left, especially within the Communist party which was dominated by Jewish intellectuals. Harold Cruse, a black Communist, described this situation in his well-known 1967 work, *The Crisis of the Negro Intellectual*. Jewish Communists, said Cruse, felt compelled to ensure their complete political and ideological power over their Negro allies. To this end, according to Cruse, Jewish Communists sought to dominate the field of "Negro studies" and made certain that Jews always held the top Communist party posts in the black community.[53] Through a posture of anti-Semitism, blacks simultaneously link themselves to non-Jewish leftists, many of whom are anti-Zionist if not anti-Semitic, while intimidating Jewish leftists who are, in effect, accused of being insufficiently militant in their support for Third World causes—perhaps even of being closet Zionists. Attempting to disprove this implicit or explicit charge is one reason that some Jewish leftists in recent years have become vehemently and outspokenly anti-Zionist.

Indeed, many American-Jewish leftists are eager to distinguish themselves from "Zionists" and to pretend that anti-Zionism is actually different from anti-Semitism. This fiction can be useful for both black and Jewish radicals. To the extent that blacks attack Zionists rather than Jews, they have an opportunity to build alliances with Jewish leftists which may, under some conditions, be useful. By the same token, to the extent that Zionists rather than Jews are defined as the enemy, Jewish leftists can maintain their own political credentials and sense of solidarity with the oppressed by joining in the denunciation of Israel and its supporters.

The maintenance of these political credentials is so important to some left-wing Jews that they will go to extraordinary lengths to distinguish themselves from the "fiendish" Zionists. Take, as one example among many, the left-wing Jewish journalist, Lenni Brenner. In the chapter devoted to "Blacks and Jews" of his 1986 volume, *Jews in America Today*, Brenner seeks to critically examine the assertion that Jews played an important role in the civil rights movement during the 1960s.[54] Brenner is forced to concede that a large percentage, perhaps more than half of the whites who traveled to the South to participate in demonstrations, sit-ins, and the like, were liberal Jews. However, and this is the important point in Brenner's view, "there did not seem to be any overt Zionist organizational presence" at the demonstrations. In other words, while Jews (like Brenner) may have worked closely with blacks, Zionists most certainly did not. Following this line of thought, the Zionist entity may, even then, have been plotting against the civil rights movement—perhaps its infamous *Protocols* could be consulted on this point.

Finally, black anti-Semitism may occasionally function to create at least de facto alliances between blacks and some non-Jewish white liberals. When blacks denounce Jews, rather than whites more generally, in their efforts to expand their role and influence within universities, municipal service bureaucracies, and other settings, they make it possible for, or even invite, non-Jewish whites to placate them at the expense of the Jews. Indeed, Jews can usually be said to be overrepresented anyway.

As noted above, this type of de facto alliance of blacks and non-Jewish white liberals against the Jews played some role in the Ocean Hill–Brownsville school struggle. Another example is related by Harvard Law School Professor Alan Dershowitz. "Several years ago," Dershowitz asserts, "a coalition of black and third world students [at Harvard University] convened a weekend conference called 'Third World Communities and Human Rights' . . . The sole human rights discussion consisted of a tribunal convened to judge the so-called nation of Israel, for its terrorism and genocide."[55]

The conference's main speaker was an official of the Libyan United Nations mission. Several speakers at the conference made vehement anti-Jewish statements. When the Harvard Jewish Law Students Association protested the conference and the Libyan speaker, members of the association were not only threatened by black students but also were criticized and accused of racial insensitivity by white members of the law faculty and administration who spoke at the conference. Clearly, to some liberal whites, mollifying angry blacks was far more important than the feelings of Jews.

A not dissimilar case involved attorney Jack Greenberg and the Harvard Law School. In 1982, the dean of the Harvard Law School asked a prominent African-American civil rights lawyer, Julius Chambers, to teach an intensive course on race and the law. Chambers indicated that while he could not take enough time off from his practice to teach the entire course, he would be willing to coteach it with his old friend and colleague, Jack Greenberg. Greenberg, of course, was the long-term head of the NAACP Legal Defense Fund and one of the most important civil rights lawyers in America. Chambers had once worked for Greenberg and now was a member of the fund's Board of Directors. Both Greenberg and the Harvard Law School administration agreed to Chambers's proposal and the course was scheduled.

Most members of the faculty and most students welcomed the idea of a course taught by two of the nation's prominent experts in the field. A group of black law students, however, objected to Greenberg's involvement with the course. An ad hoc group, calling itself the Third World Coalition, called for a boycott of the class. In an open letter they asserted, "This course is concerned with the legal system and Third World people in the United States and, therefore, it is extremely important that it be taught by an instructor who can identify and empathize with the social, cultural, economic and political experiences of the Third World community."

The black student leader of the protest, Mohammed Kenyatta, saw the boycott as an opportunity to bring pressure on Harvard to hire more black faculty. The fact that Greenberg was not only white but a Jew as well highlighted the fact that the end of quotas and discrimination at the Harvard Law School had led to the appointment of many Jewish law professors but only two blacks on a faculty of sixty. Significantly, a portion of the white faculty and student body took up the cause of the black students, some stating more or less explicitly that blacks were underrepresented at Harvard and their numbers should be augmented, if necessary, at the expense of those who were overrepresented.[56]

A more recent example of this phenomenon took place at the University of Washington. As mentioned above, during a campus talk sponsored by the Black Students Commission and other student groups, the speaker, Abdul Musa, bitterly attacked Jews as enemies of humanity and called for a second Holocaust. Complaints by Jewish faculty and student groups about the speech could generate no response from a university administration that normally prides itself on its own racial sensitivity and sponsorship of numerous programs to combat racism. From the administration's perspective, however, maintaining good relations with blacks apparently took precedence over the interests of Jews. The university's associate vice-president for student affairs, a non-Jewish white liberal, purportedly dismissed a Jewish faculty member's complaint about the Musa speech by averring that "only a few Jews" were concerned about it.[57]

In this, and the other cases discussed above, non-Jewish white liberals were not necessarily expressing anti-Semitic sentiments of their own. It must be said, however, that at least occasionally some white liberals do welcome anti-Semitic rhetoric on the part of blacks, who are freer to say what others might also think in their heart of hearts. Virtually all Jewish academics, for example, can cite cases in which a small number of their liberal, Gentile colleagues were not displeased to see developments that reduce the influence or numbers of the Jews, who are sometimes viewed as obstreperous and divisive forces in academic departments.

Nevertheless, in the cases discussed above, the motives of the non-Jewish white liberals were undoubtedly pure—they sought to help African Americans and members of other racial minorities overcome the consequences of poverty, deprivation, and discrimination while dealing with the justifiable anger manifested by blacks in response to their history of oppression at the hands of whites. Yet, when blacks express their rage specifically at Jews, rather than whites more generally, whether intentionally or not they make it possible for other whites to conciliate blacks at the Jews' expense.

This has certainly become a very common phenomenon, especially on university campuses. For example, in 1989, the State University of New York at Binghamton appointed Ali Mizrui, a scholar with a long record of anti-Semitic commentary, to a prestigious Schweitzer chair.[58] In 1991, in response to the support of black faculty and despite the concerns expressed by some Jews, Cornell University's administration appointed Mizrui to a visiting chair at that institution. Paradoxically, this same administration had steadfastly refused to bow to demands that the university divest itself of stock in corporations doing business with the racist Union of South Africa. The administration was willing to appease blacks at the expense of

Jewish sensibilities—but certainly not at the expense of investment income.

Blacks and Jews: Shoulder to Shoulder into the Next Century

Blacks are likely to continue to make use of anti-Semitic rhetoric and activities in the years to come. Since affirmative action programs opened the universities—particularly the elite universities—to blacks, a new stratum of black professionals with elite credentials has gradually come of age in the United States. Indeed, one of the most fascinating aspects of the recent televised Senate hearings on Clarence Thomas's nomination to the Supreme Court was the opportunity to see how substantial and influential this new stratum has become. So many African-American witnesses and participants in the Thomas hearings were attorneys, professors, and ranking federal civil servants—many with degrees and honors from the nation's most prestigious universities.

Unfortunately, the interests of this new, postaffirmative action stratum of black professionals are likely to clash with those of Jews. For both groups, the public and quasi-public sectors are now, and will continue to be, the most promising venue within which to acquire position, status, and influence. It would certainly not be surprising if this group used anti-Semitic appeals to endeavor to expand their own influence at the expense of the Jews. Indeed, survey data suggest that levels of anti-Semitic sentiment are already substantially higher within this group than even within any other group of black respondents. Heightened animosity may be the inevitable wave of the future in black-Jewish relations. Jewish support for civil rights will have had the ironic result of helping to create an influential stratum of blacks who will find anti-Semitism to be in their interest.

Of course, just as Jews are constrained from attacking blacks by their dependence upon the Democratic coalition and the domestic state, so blacks are to some extent constrained from attacking Jews by their own dependence upon these same institutions. Blacks may with to end their subservience to Jews within the liberal coalition. Indeed, blacks may endeavor to subordinate Jews within this coalition. Nevertheless, Jews and blacks in America are locked into the need for cooperation as much as they are fated to compete with one another.

Even if this was a possibility, neither group could actually afford to drive the other from the Democratic coalition. The result would be the complete collapse of the Democratic party and a substantial reduction in the influence that both groups presently exercise. This same consideration, by the way, operates as a constraint upon whatever anti-Semitic tendencies exist on the liberal left.

In reality, moreover, neither Jews not blacks can easily break their ties to the liberal Democratic coalition and the domestic state. For Jews, this would mean voluntarily abandoning institutions and positions of power that took the better part of a century to construct—a prospect considerably more daunting than fleeing an inner city neighborhood for the safety of the suburbs.

At the same time, for blacks, the possibility of forming political coalitions outside the present liberal camp seems remote. Of course, in politics no alliance is inherently impossible. By bringing together fundamentalist Protestants with Catholics on the issue of abortion, contemporary Republicans have shown that it *is* possible to unite the previous generation's lynchers and lynchees. Nevertheless, of all the outcomes that could emerge from contemporary political struggles, an alliance between blacks and the groups presently comprising the Republican party seems the most implausible.

Lest blacks and Jews forget that they do have a certain commonality of interests, there are some forces in the United States only too ready to remind the "Zulus" that "Israeli-occupied territory" does, after all, provide them with a measure of security. And, just in case Pat Buchanan is an insufficient warning, it is *very* useful to recall that David Duke and his various friends keep both brown shirts *and* white sheets in their closets.[59]

Anti-Semitic Rhetoric and Political Reality

Because they have generally perceived a long-term commonality of interest—and because they have been satisfied with their own superordinate role in the alliance with blacks—Jews and Jewish organizations have generally been very cautious about publicly expressing whatever private racist sentiments they might harbor.[60] As noted earlier, Jews have felt a stake in making it impossible to question the validity and legitimacy of the demands made by blacks. For reasons discussed above, however, black politicians and leaders have often been far less cautious about publicly airing their own anti-Semitism. This has had a potentially important consequence.

Unfortunately, by making public use of anti-Semitic rhetoric, as a number of observers have noted, blacks have played an important role in also making it possible for others to do the same.[61] Over the past several years, black politicians have made statements that would have led to a frenzy of charges and denunciations if made by a white.

This, first, made it possible for left-liberal whites like Gore Vidal to make use of anti-Semitic rhetoric that, as William Buckley notes, would once have been fatal but is now "no longer professionally suicidal."[62] Eventually, anti-Semitic rhetoric by blacks helped open the way for openly anti-Semitic rhetoric in other political quarters as well.

For reasons discussed above, Jews were reluctant to attack blacks for their use of anti-Semitism. If they could not condemn black anti-Semites as insane extremists, however, then Jews lost the ability to make this charge stick against others. The memory of Auschwitz, as Buckley notes, has become a senior citizen and is fading away. Or, as A. M. Rosenthal has recently observed, blacks helped to make public expressions of anti-Semitism so commonplace that Pat Buchanan's history of anti-Semitic commentary was hardly mentioned by his political rivals in either the Republican or Democratic camps.[63]

Because blacks and Jews are, like it or not, locked into a long-term relationship which neither can easily abandon, black anti-Semitism probably does not represent much of a *direct* threat to American Jews. The same, however, cannot be said for the forces that black anti-Semitism has, indirectly, helped to unleash. We shall examine these in subsequent chapters.

5 The Rise and Fall of the Republican-Jewish Alliance

During the 1970s and 1980s, Republicans launched a major offensive against the Democrats and the domestic state that Jews had played such an important role in building and to which Jews continued to be closely linked. The victories that liberal forces had achieved, especially during the era of the Great Society, had alienated a number of political groups, including business leaders, Southern whites, and large segments of the middle class. This now provided the Republicans with an opportunity to expand and strengthen their own political base while undermining the institutions in which the Democrats had entrenched themselves.[1]

Business attributed many of the problems that it began to encounter during the 1970s to Democratic regulatory programs and to burgeoning social welfare expenditures that increased its labor costs. A number of business leaders started working in the 1970s to politically revitalize the nation's corporate community. This revitalization was expressed through the formation of the Business Roundtable which fought successfully against the efforts of consumer groups to create a consumer protection agency. Business also financed institutions such as the American Enterprise Institute and the Heritage Foundation that propounded the principles of free enterprise. In addition, literally thousands of corporations organized political action committees to attempt to influence national elections.

At the same time, the Democratic party also suffered massive defections because of its identification with racial minorities and various liberal movements. A substantial portion of the Southern white electorate abandoned the Democrats in presidential even if not congressional elections. Many Southerners as well as many Catholics and evangelical Protestants from other regions of the country were offended by the stances of national Democratic politicians on such matters as civil rights, abortion, school prayer, gay rights, and other social issues. Moreover, the 1970s saw the beginning of an erosion of the economic position of large numbers of middle-class voters who had previously been willing to tolerate social welfare spending and high levels of taxation. These now became open to the appeals of politicians advocating tax reduction.

Some of these dissident forces had supported Richard Nixon in 1968 and in 1972 but were demoralized by Nixon's forced resignation in 1974. In 1980, however, Ronald Reagan was able to rebuild and expand the Nixon coalition. Reagan presented a set of proposals designed to link disaffected groups to one another and to the Republican party. Reagan promised middle-class suburbanites that he would trim social programs, cut taxes, and bring inflation under control; he pledged to social and religious conservatives that he would champion the enactment of school prayer and antiabortion legislation; and he promised opponents of the civil rights revolution an end to federal support for affirmative action and minority quotas.

Reagan also promised American business that he would relax the environmental rules and other regulations that Democrats had enacted during the 1970s. Finally, he offered the defense industry greatly increased rates of military spending under the rubric of a need to respond to a growing Soviet threat—a rubric that also pleased large segments of the South and West that benefited from military outlays as well as conservatives who feared the Soviet Union.

During his six years in office, Nixon had worked to take control of the agencies of the domestic state through such devices as reorganization of the executive branch. Once in power, the Reagan administration pursued a somewhat different strategy. After gaining control of the White House in 1981, the Reaganites sought to reward middle- and upper-income voters with favorable economic and fiscal programs that would firmly attach them to the Republican party. In addition, however, rather than attempt to take control over the social service and regulatory agencies in which the Democrats were entrenched, the administration worked to undermine and weaken them.

Central to this endeavor were the tax reductions, domestic spending cuts, and efforts at deregulation promoted by the Reagan and Bush administrations. These Republican policies provided major benefits for upper-income groups while reducing the extractive, distributive, and regulatory capabilities of governmental and quasi-governmental institutions over which the Democrats exercised influence.

In 1981 the Reagan administration sponsored legislation which substantially cut corporate and individual income-tax rates, especially for upper-income taxpayers, and indexed these rates to inflation. Coupled with the administration's military buildup, these tax cuts produced the enormous budget deficits of the 1980s. Five years later, in the 1986 tax reform act, tax rates were further reduced and numerous loopholes—deductions, exemptions, and tax preferences —were eliminated from the federal tax code. By closing the loopholes for influential groups that had made nominally high-income tax rates politically feasible, the 1986 tax reform act has made it difficult for Congress to restore any of the lost revenues.

With the federal government strapped for revenues, the domestic social institutions and programs upon which the Democrats were so dependent came under intense pressure. Funding levels for existing domestic programs were threatened, and it was all but impossible for congressional Democrats to enact new social programs despite demands that more be done to cope with a variety of domestic problems. Thus, Reaganite tax cuts meant a diminution in the flow of resources to institutions, groups, and forces with close ties to the Democrats.

In addition, hoping to simultaneously promote economic expansion and undermine their political foes, the Reaganites undertook to sabotage the regulatory institutions that liberal Democrats had built during the preceding decades. The administration promoted deregulation in the transportation, energy, banking, and financial sectors of the economy, and curtailed enforcement of environmental, health, safety, consumer, and antitrust laws. Consequently, regulatory agencies became less able to intercede against business on behalf of groups disadvantaged by market processes, and the capacity of Democrats to intervene in the domestic economy was reduced.

The Democrats quickly counterattacked, seeking to compel the administration to make additional funds available for domestic social programs either by increasing taxes, reducing military spending, or both. Subsequently, Democrats sought to demonstrate that the Republic program of deregulation had given rise to abusive and dangerous practices in the securities and banking industries. In addition, the Democrats attacked and drove from office a number of prominent Republican politicians through media revelations and congressional investigations. Reagen, himself, was very nearly forced out of office by the 1986 Iran-contra probe, as Nixon had been twelve years earlier by the Watergate investigation.

Democrats, Republicans, and Jews

During the intense struggles of these two decades, many Republicans were aware of the major electoral and institutional role that Jews played in the Democratic party, the liberal media, the domestic state and the public interest groups that supported it. As noted earlier, Jews occupied a prominent place on Richard Nixon's secret "enemies list." On a number of occasions, the president and his close associates seemed convinced that Jews in the national news media and in executive agencies were involved in a conspiracy to undermine the administration. In one notable instance, a White House staffer named Fred Malek was assigned the task of counting the number of Jewish employees in the Bureau of Labor Statistics, an office within the Labor Department, after the agency released economic data that displeased the president.

Despite such private sentiments and despite their awareness of the importance of Jews in the Democratic camp, Republicans made no public use of anti-Semitic rhetoric to mobilize support against their Democratic foes. During the Nixon era, the Republicans thought their interests were best served by refraining from antagonizing Jews. First, the Republicans were already able to make effective use of race baiting as an instrument of rabble-rousing and had no particular reason to indulge in anti-Semitism as well. Opposition to the civil rights movement and the Democratic party's civil rights programs had intensified white antipathy toward blacks throughout the nation and in the South, in particular. This made racist appeals, once the staple of Southern politics, a useful tactic in other parts of the nation. Moreover, appeals to white racism could play an important role in the Republican electoral college strategy (the so-called Southern strategy) designed to create an impregnable electoral base in the South.

Blacks were quite vulnerable to this tactic. African Americans controlled few institutions through which to defend themselves and were mainly dependent upon the private and public institutions and media controlled by their white liberal allies, including Jews. Thus, coded appeals to white racism—from Nixon and Reagan's allusions to "welfare queens" to George Bush's "Willie Horton" commercial—became staples of Republican campaigns during the 1970s and 1980s.

At the same time, Jews were very heavily defended by the media and other institutions over which they exercised influence. Indeed, the Jews had only recently demonstrated their capacity to protect themselves and to discredit their opponents. During the late 1950s and early 1960s, anti-Semitism had been successfully defined by the Jews as a form of extremism in which only politicians on the lunatic fringe engaged. As a result, any effort to make political use of anti-Semitism seemed fraught with risk.

In the late 1970s, some Republicans calculated that the liberal camp could more easily be undermined by inducing the Jews to defect than by assailing them. After all, a number of wealthy Jews had been long-standing Republican contributors. Moreover, some Jews were antagonistic toward affirmative action programs, were nervous about the implications for Israel's security of the Democrats' turn toward pacifism, and were offended by black anti-Semitism. In the 1970s, Republicans were encouraged to seek the support of Jews by a number of prominent Jewish intellectuals who moved to the Republican side, used their journals and writings to endeavor to convince other Jews to do the same, and assured Republicans that they *could* successfully woo Jewish support. As a result, Jews were invited to join the Republican party rather than being subjected to attack during the Republican offensive of the 1970s and 1980s.

Unfortunately, from both the Republican and Jewish conservative perspectives, few Jewish voters, organizations, or political activists ever deserted the Democrats or joined forces with the Republicans. Indeed, Jewish conservatives were quite embarrassed in 1984 after they incorrectly predicted that Ronald Reagan would win a substantial share of the Jewish vote. Jews never became a significant part of the Republican electoral coalition.

However, political struggle involves more than votes and elections. In fact, in recent years, the role of electoral politics in the American political process has, in some respects, been reduced. Though Jews did not become important in Republican electoral politics, two small but extremely significant groups of Jews became major factors in the regime, or system of governance, that the Republicans created in the 1980s. As shown below, during the era of the "Reagan revolution," despite their reluctance to vote for Republican candidates, Jews played important roles in implementing the administration's economic and foreign policy objectives. The association of Jews with Reaganism, especially in the realm of foreign policy, helped to heighten the anti-Semitism of forces on the political left but produced a measure of philo-Semitism on the right, most notably among Protestant fundamentalists.

In the mid and late 1980s, the financial activities of the Jews came under attack from a coalition of liberals and conservatives, and their power was broken. Subsequently, in the wake of the Soviet Union's collapse, the value of Jews to Republican foreign policy efforts also declined sharply. This opened the way for Republicans to become less concerned about Jewish sensibilities. Moreover, against the backdrop of the new acceptability of anti-Semitic rhetoric in the late 1980s and 1990s, some Republican conservatives seized the opportunity to publicly raise questions about the activities of the Jews that they had been more reluctant to voice twenty years earlier.

Jews and Republican Economic Policy

The first area in which Jews became important in the Republican regime of the 1980s was economic policy. Although Jews play a major role in the liberal political camp, during the 1980s a small group of Jewish bankers and financiers became important allies of the Reagan administration and key agents in its economic and fiscal programs. Jews presided over the great expansion of liquidity—money and credit—that fueled the economic boom and expansion of equity values of the Reagan era. The Reagan administration had come into office praising the virtues of free market competition and unfettered capitalism and promising to restore national prosperity by lowering taxes, reducing government interference in the economy, and curbing burdensome regulation of business. Jewish financiers played a critical role in helping the administration to fulfill its pledges. In turn, the administration, for a time, protected these financiers from attack by their corporate and political foes.

Soon after the 1980 election, the Reagan administration moved to bring about free financial markets by appointing John Shad as head of the Securities and Exchange Commission. Shad, former vice-chairman of E. F. Hutton & Co., was known for his free market views and suspicion of the government's efforts to regulate the securities industry. Shad brought to the SEC such free marketeers as Charles Cox and Gregg Jarrell, economists trained at the University of Chicago. These economists fully accepted the views of the "Chicago School" of economics, and believed that unfettered competition provided for the most efficient allocation of capital and, ultimately, best served the public interest.[2]

Under the leadership of Shad and his cohorts, the SEC moved to deregulate the securities industry. Deregulation had several components. First, a number of longstanding SEC investigations, such as a two-year-long probe of allegations that Citicorp, one of the nation's largest banking corporations, had used complex foreign currency transactions to avoid taxes, were brought to a close. This, of course, signaled to Wall Street that a more permissive climate had developed at the SEC.

Subsequently, in October 1982, at Shad's urging, the Reagan administration secured the enactment of legislation that opened the way for trading in stock futures, a commodity invented by Chicago commodities trader, Leo Melamed, who, in turn, had been inspired by the theories of Nobel Prize–winning economist, Milton Friedman of the University of Chicago. The most popular futures, S&P 500 index futures, allowed investors to make highly leveraged bets on the future level of the Standard and Poor's index of 500 stocks. Using index futures, an investor was only required to put up 10%–15% in cash as opposed to the 50% down payment required of individual stock purchasers.

This new instrument was seen by the Reagan administration and by SEC Chairman Shad as an excellent means of promoting liquidity in equities markets, and as a way of making it easier for companies to acquire the capital they needed to finance the acquisition of new plants and equipment. For similar reasons, the SEC supported the rise of computerized "program" trading. Despite complaints about rapid market price fluctuations caused by computerized trading and many calls for regulation, Chairman Shad and his advisors felt that computerized trading promoted liquidity by permitting major institutional investors to buy and sell enormous blocks of stock in a short period of time.

In addition to promoting trading in equities and liquidity in the marketplace, the SEC also stepped back its day-to-day supervision of the stock market. Under Chairman Shad, the SEC reined in the division of market regulation which was directly responsible for such supervision, refused to follow a recommendation by its own staff attorneys that it investigate and crack down on abuses such as bogus trading designed simply to produce tax losses, and ended a program to construct a computer surveillance system that would have permitted the SEC to follow the names of all buyers and sellers involved in trades on the floor of the New York Stock Exchange.

Moreover, the Reagan administration and SEC looked favorably upon the great wave of corporate takeovers and mergers—many hostile—that was taking place in the 1980s. In 1984, Treasury Secretary Donald Regan stated the administration's position in a letter to Congressman John Dingell. Dingell was chairman of the House Energy and Commerce Committee and chief congressional overseer of the SEC and, by extension, of Wall Street. Dingell's committee was then considering antitakeover legislation. Regan asserted that corporate mergers and takeovers worked to the overall advantage of the economy and the American public. Takeovers, according to Regan, provided a way of disciplining corporate management and holding it accountable for its actions. Takeovers promoted economic efficiency by reorganizing assets and management resources. Finally, takeovers helped to identify undervalued assets and allowed shareholders to realize the real value of their investments. In other words, they greatly enhanced the value of equities.[3] Regan's statement was quite consistent with the viewpoint of the "Chicago School." Corporate mergers and takeovers promoted economic efficiency and, moreover, contributed to the stock market boom that was delighting hundreds of thousands, perhaps millions, of the administration's middle- and upper-middle-class constituents.

Consistent with the administration's positive view of mergers and acquisitions, the SEC ended its long-standing policy of requiring that the public disclosures required to be filed by individuals seeking to gain control of a firm show precisely how the financing of the takeover was to be accomplished. Under the Shad regime, financing arrangements could be left vague. In a number of cases, a letter from a major investment bank, such as Drexel Burnham, indicating that it was planning somehow to arrange the financing was sufficient. For example, in January 1986, when financier Carl Icahn announced that he was launching an $8 billion hostile takeover bid for Phillips Petroleum, he had very little money. Instead, he paid Michael Milken of Drexel Burnham the sum of $1 million for a letter indicating that Drexel was "highly confident" that it could raise the money for the takeover through junk bond sales if necessary. This "confidence" was adequate for the SEC.

Finally, during the first six years of the Reagan era, the SEC also looked with favor on the explosion of low-grade, high yield corporate bonds that came to be popularly known as "junk bonds." Under Chairman Shad and his free marketeer cohorts, the SEC viewed junk bonds as major additional sources of market liquidity. Moreover, as junk bonds came increasingly to fuel corporate takeovers which drove up stock prices, the Reagan administration and free marketeers within the SEC saw them as the driving force behind the process that was creating one of the greatest bull markets in American history, again to the delight of the upper-middle-class electorate whose support the president courted.

Thus, deregulation of the securities industry opened the way for the use of new financial techniques and instruments that the administration hoped would enhance the supply of credit and availability of funds needed to finance economic expansion, especially at a time when the administration's own program of massive deficit spending was reducing the availability of money to private borrowers.

The administration also hoped that deregulation would promote the reorganization of the economy along more rational and efficient lines, and contribute to a boom in equity values. In these ways, financial deregulation was seen as making a major contribution to restoring the international competitiveness of American business and to the general prosperity of the nation, or at least that segment of the nation fortunate enough to own equities or to be able to take advantage of the new financial opportunities being made available.

In implementing its policies, the administration found itself in a de facto alliance with a small, but powerful, group of Jewish bankers and financiers. This group of individuals created or perfected the new financial instruments that, taken together, served the administration's interests by expanding the supply of credit during the 1980s that, in turn, fueled the great bull market of that era. For example, Jewish financiers and traders perfected the stock index futures that greatly increased liquidity in the financial system by allowing for highly leveraged securities transactions.

Similarly, Michael Milken of Drexel Burnham Lambert created the market in high yield, low-grade securities and pioneered the use of these so-called junk bonds to raise the billions of dollars in capital needed for corporate mergers and acquisitions, especially for hostile takeover bids and leveraged buy-outs. James Schneider and Paul Levy of Drexel Burnham perfected the unregistered exchange offer which allowed financially troubled companies to rapidly raise billions of dollars in new capital by substituting new, nominally less valuable securities—usually junk bonds—for old ones without being subject to the lengthy process of SEC registration.

Such Jewish financiers as Saul Steinberg, Victor Posner, Carl Icahn, Nelson Pelz, the Belzberg family, Sir James Goldsmith, and others were among the leaders in hostile takeover efforts. Of the major actors in the area of corporate takeovers, only two—T. Boone Pickens and Cincinnati-based Carl Lindner—were not Jews. Jewish arbitrageurs—Ivan Boesky came to be the most famous—became major factors in the acquisition of huge blocks of stock, easing the way for takeover attempts. Jews pioneered program trading that, among other things, permitted corporations to generate excess revenues in their pension funds that could then be employed for other corporate purposes.

During the 1980s, the Reagan administration and the Jewish financiers enjoyed a perfect marriage of convenience. The administration was concerned with promoting economic growth and enhancing prosperity among its upscale constituents, even if this came at the expense of blue-collar workers and corporate managers whose firms were absorbed or simply put out of business. For their part, the Jewish financiers saw an unprecedented opportunity to acquire wealth and power with the blessing and protection of the federal government.

Ironically, given the charges of "insider trading" that eventually sent several to prison, most of the major Jewish bankers and financiers of the 1980s had been outsiders on Wall Street. They had been kept at the margins of the banking and securities industries by the informal arrangements and accommodations that perpetuated WASP control. With some obvious exceptions, through the 1970s Jews and Jewish firms in the securities industry occupied niches that were deemed somewhat unsavory—and were less profitable—than those filled by their WASP colleagues.

For example, trading in low-grade bonds was traditionally disdained by major investment houses and left to Jewish firms. When Michael Milken joined what was then called Drexel Firestone and sought to develop a market in low-grade bonds, his colleagues in the bond department objected vigorously on the grounds that it was unseemly for the firm to be involved with such securities. Some of Milken's colleagues apparently also objected to working with a Jew and demanded that his office be moved to another floor.

As outsiders, on the margins of the banking and securities industries, Jews were better able to see and make use of the new opportunities made available by the financial deregulation and permissive climate of the Reagan era. Whereas traditional investment bankers would offer advice and financial assistance to clients involved in mergers and acquisitions, the Jewish upstarts were willing to participate in such acquisitions themselves. The parvenu Jews saw the incredible possibilities inherent in the junk bonds that established firms disdained. The Jews honed the art of risk arbitrage, another field snubbed by WASP Wall Street. Jewish newcomers and a few of their non-Jewish allies saw the possibility of using junk bonds to finance hostile takeover attempts.

In their endeavors, the Jewish financiers enjoyed the blessing and protection of the Reagan administration. The administration courted the financiers and protected them from a hostile Congress. Indeed, the Jewish financiers were treated by the administration and the SEC as valuable advisors and political allies. For example, both Ivan Boesky and Michael Milken were frequently invited to participate in SEC-sponsored conferences and advisory panels to discuss the securities industry and to offer their ideas regarding the economy and the state of corporate and public finance. Michael Milken continued to be featured on SEC panels even after he became the target of a major SEC insider trader investigation.

Several of the Jewish financiers and their business cohorts became active in Republican party affairs, particularly, of course, as contributors and fund-raisers. For example, George Roberts and Henry Kravis, partners in the leveraged buy-out firm of Kohlberg, Kravis, Roberts & Co., one of Michael Milken's most important clients, were major Republican contributors. Each donated many thousands of dollars to Republican campaigns in the 1980s, and $100,000 to the 1988 Republican presidential campaign.[4]

The activities of the Jewish financiers, of course, particularly their involvement in the wave of corporate takeovers that took place between 1985 and 1986 when nearly one-fourth of the corporations that had been listed in the Fortune 500 disappeared, provoked intense criticism from a number of quarters. Long-established investment banks resented the growing wealth and financial power of the newcomers. The largest and most powerful corporations in America found themselves vulnerable to hostile takover bids which, even when unsuccessful, could cost hundreds of millions of dollars to defeat. Firms targeted or threatened by corporate raiders sought protection through legislation that would make hostile mergers and acquisitions more difficult as well as laws that would hinder the plant closings often associated with corporate takeovers.

Often, such firms were able to mobilize the support of their workers and unions who feared job losses as well as that of the communities in which their plants were located. These communities, of course, feared plant closings and the erosion of their tax bases. Thus, for example, when T. Boone Pickens, with the financial backing of Michael Milken, sought to acquire Phillips Petroleum, local politicians organized prayer vigils and groups of demonstrators wearing "Boone Buster" T-shirts to greet Pickens when he arrived for a shareholders meeting at Phillips' headquarters in Bartlesville, Oklahoma.[5]

With the backing of this unusual coalition of established bankers, corporate managers, union leaders, and local government officials, congressional Democrats were only too happy to attack the activities of the corporate raiders and their financial backers who were now seen as politically vulnerable props of Reagan's fiscal program. Many of Reagan's opponents in the Democratic party and the liberal media understood that it was the de facto alliance between the administration and the Jewish financiers that made sufficient money and credit available to fuel economic expansion despite the huge budget deficits that would otherwise have diminished the availability of capital to private concerns.

The administration's opponents understood also that the activities of the Jewish financiers were at least partially responsible for the great boom in stock prices that contributed so significantly to the prosperity and sense of financial well-being (a false sense in the official Democratic view) felt by the millions of relatively affluent Americans who were the core of the president's political constituency. By attacking the activities of the Jewish financiers, Democrats hoped to disrupt Reagan's economic policies, which were damaging to their own constituents, while also undermining the president's electoral standing by demonstrating to his upper-middle-class supporters that the White House was presiding over what critics called a "swiss-cheese economy" that was bound to collapse.

Thus, Democrats and the national media pointed to hostile acquisitions as a prime example of the Reagan administration's subservience to wealthy and greedy financial speculators and indifference to the adverse impact of its economic programs on ordinary citizens. Congressional Democrats not only gave their support to antimerger and plant closing legislation but also launched investigations designed to show that, under the Shad regime, the SEC had consistently ignored its responsibility to oversee securities markets. Democrats charged that the SEC had failed to act in the face of what Representative John Dingell characterized as the "biggest series of stock market abuses since the 1929 crash."[6]

For its part, the Reagan administration was anxious to block congressional efforts to restrain the operations of the Jewish financiers. In a sense, the relationship between the White House and the Jewish financiers was similar to the contemporaneous relationship between the administration and the Japanese. Japanese bankers were purchasing a substantial percentage of the U.S. government securities that funded the administration's huge budget deficits. Realizing the White House's dependence upon the Japanese, the administration's foes fanned anti-Japanese sentiment and called for the enactment of protectionist legislation. Reagan's opponents calculated that disrupting the administration's alliance with Japan would make it impossible for the president to continue the program of deficit spending financed by Japanese securities purchases upon which the government was so heavily dependent. In turn, because it *was* dependent upon Japanese securities purchases, the White House sought to protect Japanese corporations from the protectionist sallies launched by congressional Democrats.

In a similar vein, from the administration's perspective, "merger mania," junk bonds, trading in stock index futures, and the like were essential ingredients of the economic growth and prosperity that the Reaganites wanted to foster. Hence, the administration worked to protect the financiers by preventing the enactment of antimerger and plant closing legislation as well as other congressional bills aimed at curbing their activities.

Ultimately, the White House could not protect the Jewish financiers from a series of criminal investigations of allegations that a number of them had engaged in illicit insider trading. The investigations began in 1985 as a result of an anonymous letter to Merrill Lynch and Co. accusing two of its brokers of trading on inside information. Merrill, Lynch conducted an internal investigation that revealed that the brokers in question were copying enormous trades in takeover stocks by a bank in the Bahamas and turned the information over to the SEC.

Democratic politicians were not the instigators of the anonymous tip that began the insider trading probe that ultimately destroyed Drexel Burnham and the financiers. Nevertheless, the Reagan administration's political foes seized the opportunity to point to the scandal as conclusive evidence of the avarice and predatory practices condoned by the White House. The Reaganites, it was said, had presided over "a decade of greed." The insider trading scandals became an issue in the 1988 elections, though they obviously did not prevent a Republican victory.

Fearing an explosion in Congress and the news media, the SEC was forced to act and eventually traced the trades to Dennis Levine, a managing director at Drexel Burnham Lambert and a close associate of many of the major Jewish financiers. Under pressure, Levine agreed to cooperate with federal authorities and led investigators to Ivan Boesky. Boesky, in turn, led prosecutors to a number of others, including, most important, Michael Milken. A number of securities traders and financiers, including Boesky and Milken, eventually received heavy fines and lengthy prison terms for illegally trading in securities on the basis of inside information of pending mergers and takeover attempts. Appeals from these verdicts continue to this day. Drexel Burnham Lambert was destroyed and forced into bankruptcy.

There can be little doubt that Boesky, Milken, and the others traded on the basis of inside information, sometimes exchanged with one another and sometimes acquired via outright bribery. At the same time, however, it is difficult to resist observing that much of the securities industry depends upon the acquisition of information that others do not have. Just as relatively few wealthy individuals ever emerge completely unscathed from a full-scale Internal Revenue Service audit of their tax filings, few major investment bankers and financiers could truly claim *never* to have traded on the basis of inside information. Insider trading is an activity in which certain classes of individuals are more likely than not to engage by the nature of their business, an enterprise in which success depends upon having access to information that is not universally available.[7]

Thus, when against a backdrop of anonymous tips, congressional pressure, and complaints by corporate managers, union leaders, and local politicians, the SEC and federal investigators led by Rudolph Giuliani, a politically ambitious federal prosecutor, launched probes of insider trading, there was little doubt that the practice existed. The main issue was obtaining evidence, and this was accomplished by allocating enormous investigative and prosecutorial resources to the problem, making unprecedented use of the RICO statute that had been designed for use against the Mafia, and granting immunity or plea bargaining with some individuals in exchange for their cooperation in netting others.

While innocence and guilt are legal questions, the decision to investigate and prosecute—especially to invest substantial investigative and prosecutorial resources—is always a political question. Why investigate these individuals and this activity rather than all the other possible areas of criminal conduct? Why devote substantial resources to one set of investigations rather than another?

In the United States, as elsewhere, criminal investigations often serve as weapons in partisan warfare. Indeed, the use of the courts and prosecutors as political instruments dates back to the Alien and Sedition Acts in the early days of the Republic. During the 1980s and 1990s, Democrats and Republicans often used "ethics probes," sometimes resulting in criminal indictments, in their partisan warfare. It is difficult to resist the suspicion that through insider trading probes the Reagan administration's political opponents had found an effective means of attacking and destroying the financial agents upon whom it relied.

Some of the financiers believed that they had come under attack because they were Jews. Paul Levy, formerly a specialist in unregistered exchanges at Drexel, has been quoted as observing, "There is a lot of anti-Semitism at work. People [on Wall Street] see Drexel as a bunch of Jewish guys who have been making too much money."[8] Others pointed to palpable anti-Semitic sentiment among the executives of the corporations that were actual or potential takeover targets. It apparently did not go unnoticed in executive suites across the country that virtually all the takeover specialists and their financial backers were Jews.

At least one popular novel of the 1980s was predicated upon an upsurge of anti-Semitism sparked by financial scandals. More interesting, though, is that many of the nonfiction works written about the financial practices of the early Reagan era focus much more heavily upon the *practitioners* than the *practices* themselves. Every book, of course, mentions the ethnic background of the financial villains of the 1980s, but some go beyond this to describe the people or events that seem to the author to epitomize the spirit of the times. Intentionally or not, these descriptions are usually laced with anti-Semitic stereotypes. The financiers emerge as the sorts of typical Jewish parvenus who often served as the villains of the nineteenth-century novels discussed in Chapter 3.

In one popular and well-written account of the period, the behavior of the financiers at a social affair is described in great detail—presumably to help the reader better understand their financial machinations. Apparently, a large number of attractive young women were invited to this event. The author quotes an attendee who points out that these were the sorts of beautiful women that the financiers must have dreamed about in high school but were unable to attract.[9] No explanation is given for this youthful failure, but the reader can easily surmise that the Jewish financiers could only attract the blond Gentile women of their dreams when their bank accounts had grown large enough to overcome their more undesirable Jewish characteristics. Students of popular culture might also note that the behavior and instincts attributed to these blond Gentile women have changed markedly over the past century. Whereas in nineteenth-century works describing Jewish avarice the blond heroine was usually repulsed by her Jewish suitor despite his wealth—remember the lovely Estelle Washington—her late twentieth-century sister seems to be more readily available.

The administration's Democratic opponents were too closely linked to Jews themselves to be able to make overt use of anti-Semitic rhetoric against the Republicans. Nevertheless, some of the terms that were employed to characterize the activities of the Jewish financiers, such as "decade of greed" or "predatory business practices," were undoubtedly intended by some of their users to serve as euphemisms for "sharp Jews." In the not-so-secret code of American ethnic politics, "greedy" or "predatory" businessman is just as certainly a synonym for Jew as "welfare queen" is for black.

Nevertheless, even though a measure of anti-Semitic rhetoric was used in the campaign against them, the Jewish financiers were not attacked primarily because they were Jews. Rather, the fact that a group of "greedy" and "predatory" Jews played an important role in its implementation simply made it easier for the foes of Reaganomics to bring it under attack.

The destruction of Drexel Burnham and the Jewish financiers not only helped to undermine Reaganite economic policy but also severed one of the major ties linking Jews and the Republicans. After the demise of Michael Milken and the others, Jews were no longer useful economic allies for the Reagan administration. Moreover, the destruction of the Jewish financiers diminished the importance of Jewish financial support for Republican politicians—an important reason for Republicans to take Jewish sensibilities seriously during the Reagan years. These factors by themselves, perhaps, might not have had a decisive impact upon the relationship between Jews and the Republicans. As shown below, however, a second and far more important connection that developed between Jews and the Republicans in the 1980s—this in the area of foreign policy—had a parallel history.

Jews and Republican Foreign Policy

During the early 1980s, their support for Israel led an important group of Jews to become major factors in the national security regime created by the Republicans. Just as they had sought to use economic and fiscal policy against the Democrats, during the 1980s, the Republicans attempted to use the military and national security apparatus as a political weapon. And, just as Jewish financiers helped implement Republican economic policy, so a group of Jewish "hawks" came to play an important role in the enactment and implementation of Republican foreign policy.

In the years after World War II, there had been a bipartisan consensus in the United States on questions of foreign and military policy. Democrats and Republicans agreed on the need to maintain powerful military forces and a capacity for covert intelligence operations. The leaders of both parties were prepared to deploy these forces to contain the Soviet Union and its allies and to fight left-wing insurgent movements. The Vietnam War destroyed this consensus. Antiwar forces gained influence within the Democratic party and were able to impose limits on both military expenditures and American intervention in Third World conflicts. Reagan Republicans regarded Democratic "neo-isolationism" as posing dangers to the nation as well as opportunities for their party.

The Reagan defense buildup of the 1980s was an effort to attach social forces with a stake in defense programs to the GOP, while creating a governing apparatus that could supplant institutions of the domestic state linked to the Democrats. Thus, the Reagan administration adopted policies of military Keynesianism to stimulate the economy, used military procurement as a form of industrial policy, and maintained funding for social programs administered by the Veterans Administration while seeking to slash drastically spending on welfare programs administered by domestic agencies.

Republican presidents Reagan and Bush also sought to reassert their prerogative to deploy American military force abroad, to conduct covert intelligence operations, and to support guerrilla movements fighting Soviet-backed regimes. Thus, without seeking the prior approval of Congress, the Reagan administration sent troops to invade Grenada and aircraft to bomb Libya. Also, American ground troops were sent to intervene in Lebanon in 1982, and American naval forces were sent into action in the Persian Gulf in 1988. Most significantly, despite the bitter opposition of the congressional Democratic leadership, the Bush administration launched a massive air and ground assault that destroyed the armed forces of Iraq in 1991.

In addition, large quantities of American arms were supplied to pro-Western forces in Angola and Afghanistan. Moreover, the Reagan and Bush administrations rebuilt the CIA's capacity to engage in covert operations by greatly expanding its budget and personnel, and by attempting to circumvent congressional scrutiny of intelligence operations, particularly in Central America where the White House worked to undermine the Sandanista regime in Nicaragua.

Besides strengthening military and intelligence agencies, Republican presidents also made efforts to develop alliances with foreign governments that could help them to achieve political goals they were unable to realize through America's own governmental institutions. The most important of these was a tacit alliance with the government of Japan. The Reagan and Bush administrations kept America's borders open to a flood of Japanese goods. In turn, the Japanese government helped fund the American budget deficit by purchasing U.S. Treasury securities through its central bank and by encouraging private Japanese financial institutions to do the same. It was this alliance with Japan that permitted both the Reagan and Bush administrations to maintain high levels of military spending without raising taxes.

The White House also entered into joint ventures with the leaders of Israel and Saudi Arabia. In the first case, the Reagan administration and the Israelis cooperated in channeling arms to Iran. In the later case, the administration sold advanced weapons to Saudi Arabia while the Saudi royal family helped to finance the Nicaraguan contra forces. Later, the Saudi regime played a critical role in America's successful war against Iraq. In both instances, arrangements with a foreign government were used by the White House to circumvent the opposition of its foes in Congress.

A number of these Republican ventures enjoyed considerable success. President Reagan oversaw the largest peacetime military buildup in the nation's history. Military spending provided major segments of industry and regions of the country with a continuing stake in the success of the Republicans and helped fuel the longest period of economic expansion in the postwar period. In addition, Ronald Reagan and George Bush, whose standing in the polls reached an unprecedented 90% approval rating after the Persian Gulf War, demonstrated that it was possible, despite the trauma of Vietnam, for a politician to increase his popularity at home by using American forces abroad.

Congressional Democrats, of course, sought to block Republican efforts to use the national security apparatus as a political weapon. Liberal Democrats resisted the Reaganite military buildup, arguing that Reaganite military policies, especially the Strategic Defense Initiative, would provoke an arms race with the Soviets and served to diminish more than to enhance American security. Democrats asserted that the nation's security would be better served by arms control agreements, and they demanded that the administration pursue serious negotiations with the Soviet Union to achieve reductions in both nuclear and conventional forces. To this end, they gave their support to what became the largest peace movement since the end of the Vietnam War and to its key proposal—the nuclear freeze.

Though the freeze proposal ultimately failed, throughout the course of the Reagan and Bush administrations, until Bush preempted the issue with his own 1991 proposals for massive arms cuts in the wake of the political, economic, and military collapse of the Soviet Union, arms control continued to be a central issue for the Democrats. In addition to its implications for foreign policy, arms control promised to reduce the Republicans' ability to derive political benefits from military spending while making more money available for domestic programs.

Not long after the defeat of the nuclear freeze proposal, the administration's opponents in Congress found a new way to attack the Reagan military buildup. Congressional Democrats charged that waste and fraud were rampant in the military procurement process, suggesting that much of the money being appropriated for defense was actually going to line the pockets of unscrupulous defense contractors. In televised testimony, witnesses displayed toilet seats, coffee pots, and hammers for which defense contractors billed the American taxpayer hundreds or even thousands of dollars. This attack was equivalent to conservative crusades against welfare fraud—an effort to discredit a major spending program by focusing upon the abuses that inevitably accompany it. The Democratic campaign against waste and fraud in military procurement helped undermine support for the Reagan buildup and, coupled with the pressure of the growing federal budget deficit, permitted Congress to hold increases in defense spending to the rate of inflation after Reagan's first term.

Congressional Democrats also worked to block efforts by the president to deploy military forces abroad and to use alliances with foreign governments to further his policy goals. Thus, opponents of the Reagan administration sought to compel the president to end U.S. military involvement in Lebanon and criticized him for failing to use the procedures outlined in the War Powers Act to secure congressional approval for the deployment of American forces in the Persian Gulf. Moreover, congressional Democrats attacked the administration's alliances with foreign dictators. For example, Congress played a key role in the sequence of events that led to the ouster of the Philippine dictator, Ferdinand Marcos, an ally of successive American administrations. In addition, as noted previously, the administration's opponents used protectionism to attack the alliance with Japan upon which the Republican fiscal regime depends.

Finally, congressional Democrats attacked the administration's Nicaragua policy by compelling the CIA to stop mining harbors, insisting that the agency withdraw a training manual that advocated the assassination of Sandinista cadres, and publicizing charges that the contras were engaged in drug smuggling and routinely violated human rights. They ultimately were able to restrict President Reagan's efforts to aid the contras by enacting a series of amendments—the Boland amendments—to foreign military assistance bills.

This is why conservative forces within the Reagan administration undertook to build an alternative intelligence apparatus attached to the National Security Council. This apparatus enabled them to conduct covert operations such as aid to the contras that the Congress had refused to approve, as well as activities such as the sale of weapons to Iran that Congress would certainly not countenance.

Critics in Congress called the network put together by CIA Director William Casey, Marine Colonel Oliver North, and retired Air Force General Richard Secord a "state within the state." This characterization is not inappropriate because that apparatus had some of the administrative, extractive, and coercive capacities of a governmental intelligence agency. The network was able to conduct covert operations because it was staffed by retired military officers and CIA operatives, and it had ties to foreign intelligence officials and arms merchants. Lacking access to tax revenues, it was financed by gifts from foreign governments, contributions from wealthy American conservatives, and the profits from weapons sales to Iran.

Jews and the National Security Regime

It was in the context of this bitter struggle between Republican administrations and Democratic Congresses over military and defense policy that Jews—both American Jews and Israel itself—came to be important to the Republicans. Since the creation of the state of Israel, Jewish groups have lobbied on behalf of American economic aid and military support for the Jewish state. During the 1960s, the pro-Israel lobby became a major factor on the Washington scene, achieving substantial influence in Congress and in the White House.

During the 1970s, American Jews faced a difficult choice. As liberal Democrats, Jews strongly supported expansion of the domestic welfare state. Until the Vietnam War, liberal Democrats saw no inconsistency between a liberal stand on domestic issues and a staunch anticommunism and support for high levels of defense spending. This was the guns *and* butter Democratic liberalism of such politicians as "Scoop" Jackson, Hubert Humphrey, and Lyndon Johnson. During the Vietnam War, however, Democratic liberals moved to a posture of antimilitarism, while Republicans began to take sole possession of the principle of a strong national defense and rigid anticommunism.

This created a dilemma for American Jews. Israel was heavily dependent upon American military assistance. Many liberal Democrats, though, espoused cutbacks in the development and procurement of weapons systems, a curtailment of American military capabilities and commitments, and what amounted to a semireturn to isolationism. These policies all appeared to represent a mortal threat to Israel and, hence, were opposed by many Jews who supported Israel.

Beginning in the 1970s, Republican politicians made overtures to such Jews, seeking to woo them away from the Democrats. During the 1972 presidential campaign, Republican appeals to Jewish groups emphasized the threat that would be posed to Israel if McGovern won and instituted massive cuts in American military spending. White House speech writer Pat Buchanan, who was many years later during the Persian Gulf War to write a famous attack on the pro-Israel lobby, wrote a memo suggesting that Defense Secretary Melvin

Laird point out to Jewish groups that cuts in American defense spending would mean that weapons systems vital to Israel's security such as the F-14 and F-15 would not be built. Most Jews supported McGovern in the 1972 presidential election. However, he was rejected by many of the major contributors upon whom Democrats rely in American politics. Though these individuals applauded many of McGovern's views in the arena of domestic politics, they saw him as insufficiently supportive of Israel and as favoring foreign and military policies that would undermine Israel's security.[10]

During the next several years, Republicans told Jewish groups that every dollar spent on American defense represented twenty-five cents spent on Israel's defense. Republicans did not have to invent this point. A number of Jews ascertained for themselves that Israeli security required a strong American commitment to internationalism and defense. Among the most prominent Jewish spokesmen for this position was Norman Podhoretz, editor of *Commentary* magazine. Podhoretz had been a liberal and a strong opponent of the Vietnam War. But by the early 1970s he came to realize that "continued American support for Israel depended upon continued American involvement in international affairs—from which it followed that an American withdrawal into [isolationism] represented a direct threat to the security of Israel." This was one major reason that Podhoretz broke with liberals who "were loud in calling for a continued American commitment to the security of Israel, but simultaneously favored cuts in the defense budget which, if implemented, would make such a commitment impossible to carry out."

In 1976, Podhoretz gave his strong support to Pat Moynihan's Senate campaign in the New York Democratic primary against liberals Bella Abzug and Ramsey Clark. This campaign gave Podhoretz an opportunity to promote the notion of "an inextricable connection between the survival of Israel and American military strength." Abzug and Clark were castigated for professing to support Israel while opposing "the defense appropriations out of which aid to Israel had to come."[11]

Podhoretz and other neoconservative Jewish intellectuals were instrumental during the 1970s and 1980s in developing justifications for increased defense spending, as well as linking American military aid to Israel to the more general American effort to contain the Soviet Union. Israel was portrayed as an American "strategic asset" that could play an important role in containing Soviet expansion into the Middle East.

A number of Jewish neoconservatives became active in the Committee on the Present Danger, a group formed to lobby for increased levels of defense spending and the strengthening of America's defense capabilities against what they asserted was a heightened threat of Soviet expansionism. The founders of this committee were the veteran diplomat Paul Nitze, former Under Secretary of State Eugene Rostow, and former Treasury Secretary Charles Walker who had become a prominent corporate lobbyist serving a number of major defense contractors who, in turn, provided the financing for the committee.

The Committee on the Present Danger, in effect, was an alliance between cold warriors like Nitze who believed in the need to contain the Soviet Union and was concerned that the Carter administration was permitting American defenses to weaken, the defense industry represented by Walker, which had an obvious pecuniary interest in heightened levels of defense spending, and pro-Israel forces who had come to see high levels of defense spending and an interventionist U.S. foreign policy as essential to Israel's survival and who hoped to make support for Israel an element of America's effort to contain the Soviet Union. Each of these allies had a stake in asserting that Soviet expansion represented a "clear and present danger" to the United States. For cold warriors, this was political gospel as well as a route through which they hoped to return to power in the bureaucracy. For the defense industry, this was the key to high profits. For the Israel lobby, opposition to the USSR was a rubric through which to justify the expansion of American military and economic assistance to Israel.

During the period preceding the 1980 election, the committee became a major actor in the Reaganite camp. The Reaganites, as we have seen, had their own reasons for advocating the expansion of defense spending. Ronald Reagan became a member of the committee as did a number of key associates. After Reagan's 1980 electoral victory, several key Reagan appointees in the national security area were drawn from the committee's membership. These included Richard Allen, Reagan's first national security adviser, CIA Director William Casey, and Deputy Secretary of Defense Richard Perle. Thus, the Committee on the Present Danger became the vehicle through which the alliance of cold warriors, defense contractors, and pro-Israel groups became part of the Reagan coalition and gained access to the government.

During the Reagan years, American and Israeli Jews played an important role in support of the administration's foreign and defense policies. The pro-Israel lobby became an important part of the political constituency that supported the administration's massive defense buildup and hard-line opposition to the Soviet Union. Pro-Israel forces helped to garner both congressional and popular support for the administration's policies. At the same time, Israel itself became an arm of American foreign policy—acting on behalf of the administration in areas where congressional Democrats had blocked action in which the administration wished to engage. Though the Reagan administration occasionally clashed with pro-Israel Jews and with Israel, for the most part Jews' involvement with the Republican national security regime was rewarded with favorable treatment.

It is interesting but perhaps not surprising given the foregoing, that during this period pro-Israel forces found themselves in alliance with traditionally anti-Semitic but fervently anti-Communist Christian fundamentalists. On the other hand, the enemies of the Reagan regime on the political left made increasing use of anti-Semitic rhetoric during this same period.[12]

The Israel Lobby and the Republican National Security Regime

It is conventional to regard the Israel lobby as a major force in the formulation of American foreign policy where the direct interests of Israel are concerned. The Israel lobby is widely credited with securing billions of dollars in American military and economic assistance for Israel. During the 1980s, however, the role of the Israel lobby was much broader. This lobby served as a major component of the anti-Communist coalition supporting the Reaganite arms buildup and policy of vigorous anticommunism. The Israel lobby, along with several important strongly pro-Israel liberal Democrats, such as former Representative Stephen Solarz of New York, helped Reagan to bring about the largest peacetime arms buildup in American history despite the fact that Congress was controlled by Democrats who were nominally opposed to the president's plans.[13]

In Congress, the Israel lobby worked to secure support for Reaganite programs from Democratic senators and representatives who would have been expected to oppose them. For example, the foreign aid bill passed by Congress in 1984 contained provisions for aid to El Salvador that were opposed by the congressional Democratic leadership. Democratic leaders were then pressing the administration to drop its support for the Salvadorean government. Since the foreign aid bill, however, also contained provisions for some $2.5 billion in aid to Israel, pro-Israel lobbyists pressed vigorously for its passage.

This linkage of aid to Israel with other foreign aid sought by the administration was not accidental. Since Israel is the major recipient of American foreign aid, national administrators expect the Israel lobby to help secure the passage of every foreign aid bill, and they normally receive it. The Israel lobby has, for years, served as the U.S. foreign aid program's major domestic constituency. Indeed, in a briefing to a world hunger board at the State Department in 1984, John K. Wilhelm, a career official of the Agency for International Development, was quoted as saying that the active support of the pro-Israel lobby was "vital" to securing congressional support of the entire American foreign aid program.[14]

Another key instance in which the Reagan administration sought and received the assistance of the Israel lobby involved the 1983 introduction of American forces into Lebanon. After Reagan sent marines into Beirut in the wake of Israel's invasion of Lebanon, congressional Democrats began to demand an immediate American withdrawal. Reagan did not wish to bow to congressional pressure to withdraw the troops but, at the same time, did not want simply to ignore Congress. Instead, he sought congressional authorization to keep the marines in Lebanon for another eighteen months. Uncertain of winning Senate passage of this bill, Reagan called upon AIPAC for support.

AIPAC lobbied a number of senators whose positions were uncertain and was widely credited for playing an instrumental role in the passage of the bill. After the vote, Reagan called Tom Dine, the head of AIPAC, to thank him. According to the *Jerusalem Post*, Reagan said, "I just wanted to thank you and all your staff for the great assistance you gave us on the War Powers Act Resolution . . . I know how you mobilized the grassroots organizations to generate support." Dine replied by promising to continue to work with the administration in the future.[15] During the Reagan era, the pro-Israel lobby also worked vigorously on behalf of congressional support for the administration's arms buildup, especially the Strategic Defense Initiative (SDI) program in which Israel had a strategic as well as a financial interest.

As we shall see, the relationship between Jews and the Republican administration soured during the Bush presidency. On one critical occasion, however, pro-Israel forced played an important role in securing congressional support for the administration's goals in the area of foreign and military policy. This was, of course, the January 1991 congressional vote on the use-of-force resolution authorizing President Bush to undertake offensive military action against Iraq after its invasion of Kuwait.

In December, the White House worked with a number of Republican and Democratic supporters of Israel to establish the Committee for Peace and Security in the Gulf. This organization was led by Richard Perle, a staunch supporter of Israel and a former deputy secretary of defense in the Reagan administration. Also prominent in the committee's leadership were Ann Lewis, a liberal Democratic activist (and sister of Massachusetts Congressman Barney Frank), and former Representative Stephen Solarz of New York, a senior Democratic member of the House Foreign Affairs Committee. Solarz later served as a cosponsor of the use-of-force resolution. In 1992, as a result of redistricting Solarz lost the Democratic congressional primary in what was now a predominantly Hispanic district.

In the days prior to the vote, the White House worked closely with AIPAC to lobby congressional Democrats. AIPAC mobilized its national network of campaign contributors, political activists, and important constituents to bring pressure on wavering Democrats. In the end, ten Senate Democrats and eighty-six House Democrats supported the president. AIPAC was widely credited with having played a key role in bringing about this result. AIPAC, which is usually eager to claim credit for a successful outcome in order to maintain its reputation as Washington's most powerful lobby, publicly denied this, pointing out that Jewish members of Congress were evenly divided in the final vote. However, some administration sources indicated that because of the extreme sensitivity of the issue, AIPAC was anxious to camouflage its role to avoid providing evidence for the accusation, made by some politicians on both the left and right, that the Persian Gulf War was fought at the behest of the Jews to protect Israel.[16]

In addition to supporting the Reagan administration's defense policies in Congress, pro-Israel forces promoted and publicized the importance of strengthening America's defenses and vigorously opposing the expansion of Soviet power. In this endeavor, a particularly important role was played by "neoconservative" Jewish intellectuals who used their access to the print and broadcast media to promote national defense. Of course, the importance of defense became a major theme of Norman Podhoretz's *Commentary* magazine. But in addition, such magazines as the *New Republic* and the op-ed pages of the *New York Times* and *Washington Post*, to say nothing of the various syndicated television panel discussion programs, began to focus on the Soviet threat and the importance of bolstering America's defenses.

Pro-Israel forces and their intellectual allies who sought to link Israel directly to the global struggle against communism by characterizing Israel as a "strategic asset" to the United States in a critical and volatile part of the world. American support for and alignment with Israel was portrayed as a way of combating Soviet influence in the Middle East. This position was also promoted by a number of Jewish officials in the Reagan administration. Three of these officials— Richard Perle, Stephen Bryan, and Michael Ledeen—continue today to be active in the Jewish Institute for National Security Affairs (JINSA). Throughout the Reagan years, JINSA worked through high-ranking Jewish officials to promote a strong relationship between Israel and the U.S. Defense Department.[17]

Israel, for its part, was willing to serve as a strategic American asset in exchange for American economic and military support. Just as pro-Israel forces in the United States aligned themselves with the Reagan administration, so did Israel's own government endeavor to become part of the Reagan administration's supporting cast. The Israeli government worked with the administration to carry out military and intelligence tasks that the administration could not undertake on its own, not only in the Middle East but in Central America, Africa, and other parts of the world.

For example, with the blessing of the Reagan administration, the Israeli government was actively involved in supplying arms to Iran during the Iran-Iraq war and later in the arms sales that were at the heart of the Iran-contra affair that came close to toppling the Reagan administration. Israel was also involved in supplying arms and training to UNITA forces in Angola and supplying arms and military advice to a number of U.S.-supported Latin American regimes and movements during the 1980s. At the same time, pro-Israel forces in the United States worked to justify Israeli activities and Reagan administration policies. For instance, with at least the tacit approval of the Reagan administration, Israel sold a substantial quantity of military equipment to the right-wing Guatemalan government. When the media and liberal members of Congress raised questions about this relationship, the Israeli role was defended by pro-Israel groups in the United States who asserted that tales of human rights abuses by Guatemalan government forces were exaggerated.[18]

In a similar vein, Israel played an important role in supplying arms to Nicaraguan contra forces after the Reagan White House was compelled to halt its overt aid to these forces. Israel had played a role in American efforts to help the contras since the first days of the Reagan administration. For example, during the early 1980s, the Israeli government had provided the United States with large quantities of Soviet bloc arms captured during the invasion of Lebanon. These arms were then turned over to the contras. After Congress enacted the Boland amendment in 1984 prohibiting American aid to the contras, Israel continued, with clandestine American financing, to provide large quantities of arms and training in their use to contra forces.[19]

At the same time that the Israeli government worked with the White House to provide arms for the contras, pro-Israel groups in the United States cooperated closely with the administration's effort to undermine support for the Sandanista regime and bolster public support for its anti-Communist policies in Latin America. The Reagan administration sought the help of pro-Israel forces in publicly promoting its Latin American policies and securing congressional support for them. Pro-Israel forces were asked to portray these policies as part and parcel of the same struggle against communism as Israel's fight against the P.L.O.

Jewish groups, including the Anti-Defamation League, obliged. They worked with the White House Office of Public Liaison to publicize charges that the Sandanista government was anti-Semitic. In particular, the Sandanistas were accused of setting fire to a synagogue in Managua, lending support to and accepting assistance from the P.L.O., and expropriating the property of Nicaraguan Jews. These charges were echoed by Israeli conservatives eager to justify their involvement in Central America. In May 1984, Michael Kleiner, a Knesset member of the right-wing Herut Party of the Likud bloc, was brought to the United States by the conservative U.S.A. Foundation to address a conference on the persecution of Jews in Nicaragua. Kleiner announced that the conservative movements in the United States and Israel had joined to bring freedom to Central America and charged that the P.L.O. had trained the Sandanistas. Kleiner's remarks were entered into the *Congressional Record* by Senator Jesse Helms.[20]

The use of foreign governments to effect American foreign and military policies became a standard pattern during the Reagan years. Because the U.S. government was bitterly divided, with Democrats controlling Congress, and administration was not free to conduct American foreign, military, and intelligence policy as it wished with the agencies nominally established for those purposes. Instead, the administration turned to private contractors, foreign governments, and the like. Israel became a major proxy in the American global struggle against the Soviet Union and cooperated closely with American military and intelligence services. The relationship became strong and institutionalized, especially in the intelligence area. The pro-Israel lobby, of course, used Israel's role as a strategic asset to justify demands for additional American support for Israel.

The place of pro-Israel forces and Israel in the Reaganite coalition and their support for anticommunism and militarism brought them into an improbable alliance with other hard line anti-Communist forces, notably the Christian fundamentalists, who previously had been viewed by Jews as anti-Semites. Though fundamentalists, by definition, read the Bible literally, as we observed earlier, the Bible takes a number of different positions on similar topics and presents many different emphases. Because of their own fierce opposition to communism and implacable hatred of the Soviet Union, Christian fundamentalists were happy to support Israeli anticommunism and militarism and, as a result, to emphasize those portions of their liturgy that seemed to support rather than attack the Jews. In particular, fundamentalist Christians asserted that the return of the Jewish people to the State of Israel was a precondition for the second coming of Christ.

Of course, this would result in the conversion of Jews to Christianity and their disappearance as a separate and distinct group. The second coming and conversion of the Jews, however, seemed far enough in the future that Israelis and pro-Israel Jews in the United States saw no difficulty in working with conservative Christians to pursue a policy of vigorous American opposition to the Soviet Union, military expansionism, and support for Israel.

Close relations between Israel and Christian fundamentalists began to develop after the conservative Likud bloc came to power in Israel in 1977, and strengthened after Reagan's presidential victory in the United States in 1980. After Reagan took office he received a telegram signed by Reverend Jerry Falwell and other prominent Christian fundamentalist leaders urging him to give his full support to Israel which, they said, "from a religious, moral and strategic perspective," represented "our hopes for security and peace in the Middle East."

The Begin government awarded Falwell the Zabotinsky Award for service to Israel and brought him and other leaders of the Christian right to Israel frequently as honored guests. Falwell strongly supported Israeli annexation of the occupied territories and moving the Israeli capital to Jerusalem. "There is no question that Judea and Samaria should be part of Israel," Falwell declared. Moreover, "I believe that the Golan Heights should be annexed as an integral part of the state of Israel," he said.[21]

Obviously, not all Jews were comfortable with their new allies. Many Jews viewed Christian fundamentalists as anti-Semites whose ultimate aim was to make America a Christian country and to convert the Jews to Christianity. Jewish fears were heightened by the occasional anti-Semitic lapses of evangelical leaders. Jerry Falwell, for example, publicly observed, "A Jew can make more money accidentally than you can make on purpose." Similarly, the Reverend Bailey Smith, president of the Southern Baptist Covnention, was widely quoted as asserting that God does not hear the prayers of Jews. Even though Smith apologized for his remarks and embarked on a trip to Israel to make amends, to some American Jews Smith's comments simply revealed what religious fundamentalists really thought.

Nevertheless, to Israel and pro-Israel forces in the United States, the fundamentalists were useful allies. Their fierce anticommunism made them natural supporters of the pro-Israel lobby's efforts to promote American military preparedness, and made them natural allies of Israel's conservative government and demonstrated willingness to fight the Soviet Union's clients in the Arab world. Fundamentalist leaders on tours of Israel were often greeted by Israeli "hawks" like General Ariel Sharon, shown captured Soviet weapons, and taken on tours of battlefields where Israeli forces were said to have vanquished the Communists. To both sides, politics was far more important than theology.

On the other hand, the role of Jews and Israel in the Reaganite coalition enhanced the anti-Zionism of the left. Just as forces of the right had traditionally used anti-Semitic appeals to attack liberal regimes linked to Jews, now liberal forces used anti-Zionism to attack Jews and Israel for their support for a right-wing regime. This had begun during the Nixon era, when not only left-wing radicals attacked Israel but opposition to Israel and support for the Arabs in general and the P.L.O. in particular became a staple among non-Jewish American liberals—liberal church groups in particular. For example, in 1973, the liberal National Council of Churches opposed the shipment of arms or military supplies to Israel during the Yom Kippur War. One member of the National Council's governing board expressed the view that "Israel might have to die in the cause of peace."[22]

Similarly, in 1975, when the United Nations issued its resolution equating Zionism with racism, the National Council expressed its own support for the United Nations. In 1978, after Israel retaliated for a P.L.O. terrorist attack that killed thirty-seven civilians with air strikes against Arab refugee camps, the National Council condemned the Israeli action and called on the United States to stop supplying Israel with military equipment. A resolution to deplore the deaths of the Israelis killed in the initial attack was considered and rejected. In 1980, the 250-man board of the National Council split almost evenly on the question of whether Israel should continue to exist. And, of course, in 1981, the National Council strongly condemned Israel's bombing raid against Iraq's nuclear reactor.

In 1986, writing in *The Nation*, Gore Vidal aimed a bitter attack precisely at the linkage between pro-Israel forces, the Reagan administration, and conservative forces in the United States. "Let me spell it all out," said Vidal. "In order to get military and economic support for Israel, a small number of American Jews . . . have made common cause with every sort of reactionary and anti-Semitic group in the United States, from the corridors of the Pentagon to the TV studios of the evangelical Jesus-Christers . . . There is real madness here; mischief too."[23]

The relationship between Israel and its supporters and conservative political forces in the United States also helps to explain why segments of the American liberal media adopted on anti-Israel posture during the 1980s. Though it maintains an official posture of neutrality and objectivity, the elite American media has tended since the Vietnam War to oppose incumbent administrations, especially those with a conservative orientation. Prior to the Vietnam War, the national news media had maintained a close relationship with national politicians. Indeed, since the time of Franklin Roosevelt, presidents had used the national media to enhance their own power.

During the early stages of the Vietnam War, the media generally gave the war positive coverage, presenting the official government account as fact. Soon, however, American officials in Vietnam who disapproved of the way the war was being conducted leaked information critical of administration policy to reporters. Publication of this material infuriated Presidents Kennedy and Johnson. On the one occasion, President Kennedy went so far as to demand that the *New York Times* reassign its Saigon correspondent. The national print and broadcast media—the network news divisions, the national news weeklies, the *Washington Post* and *New York Times*—discovered, however, that there was an audience for critical coverage among segments of the public skeptical of administration policy.

At the same time, growing opposition to the war among liberals led members of Congress to break with President Johnson. These shifts in popular and congressional sentiment encouraged journalists and publishers to continue to present critical news reports. Through this process, journalists developed a commitment to "investigative reporting," while a constituency emerged that would rally to the defense of the media when they came under White House attack. The media discovered that in alliance with liberal political forces who would rally to their defense when they came under attack, they could enhance their power and autonomy in American government and politics by aggressively investigating, publicizing, and exposing instances of official misconduct.

Conservative forces responded to media criticism by denouncing the press as biased and seeking to curb it or, as in the case of Bush administration policy during the Persian Gulf War, to prevent it from operating. Liberal forces, however, have welcomed media investigations and critical news accounts and have stood ready to come to the media's defense. Over the years, as a result, there developed an alliance between the national media and liberal forces in national politics. This, rather than some inherent liberal bias, explains why the media seem so often to be aligned with liberal forces against the White House.

Thus, when Israel was ruled by Labor party governments and had good relations with liberal Democrats in the United States, it generally received positive coverage from the American media. However, after the conservative Likud government came to power in Israel in the late 1970s, and as Israel came increasingly to be identified with the Reagan administration's foreign policies in the 1980s, it came under increasing media attack. Indeed, some of the same journalists, including many Jews like Mike Wallace of "60 Minutes," who had strongly supported Labor's Israel, became very critical of Likud's Israel.[24]

In recent years, for example, the Palestinian uprising against occupying Israeli forces on the West Bank and in the Gaza Strip generally has been portrayed by the elite national media as a case of "freedom fighters" opposing brutal Israeli oppressors.[25] In the days leading up to the Persian Gulf War, the American media gave much attention to the Palestinian cause, often giving credence to the rather contorted Palestinian line linking Iraq's invasion of Kuwait with the Israeli occupation of the West Bank. This was especially marked on ABC-TV where Ted Koppel's "Nightline" program provided a great deal of positive exposure for Palestinian views, as though the Palestinian issue actually had some relationship to the Gulf crisis.

By the beginning of 1992, however, when it had become abundantly clear that Israel was no longer allied with the Republican White House, and especially after Labor returned to power in the early summer, a number of liberal columnists and commentators who had previously been severe critics of Israel began to change their tone. For example, compare New York Times columnist Anthony Lewis's euphoric column endorsing the views of the new Rabin government with his harsh denunciations of Israel and its leadership during much of the preceding decade.[26] Perhaps, now that Israel's

Labor party has returned to power and Israel has begun to resume its historic relationship with the Democrats, America's liberal media will eventually decide that the Palestinians are terrorists rather than freedom fighters after all. Liberal pundits, to be sure, were sharply critical of the Rabin government's decision in January 1993 to deport four hundred Palestinians it accused of having ties to Hamas, an Islamic fundamentalist group involved in terrorist activities.

The Collapse of the Jewish-Republican Alliance

After 1985, and even more so after 1988, the arms buildup lost its place as a centerpiece of the Republican agenda. Republican presidents instead turned to arms control negotiations as a way of avoiding further increases in military spending. This, coupled with the collapse of the Soviet Union in 1990–1991, reduced the importance to the Republicans of both the pro-Israel lobby in domestic affairs and of the State of Israel as an instrument of American foreign policy.[27] This latter point became abundantly clear during the Persian Gulf War when the United States compelled Israel to refrain from participating. Ironically, just as the success of the black-Jewish alliance in the civil rights movement had made black anti-Semitism possible, so the success of the Jewish-Republican alliance in the Cold War now helped to diminish the Republicans' dependence upon the Jews. In effect, the Jews had become expendable.

The earliest manifestation of the diminished importance of the Jews in the Republican camp was the Pollard case. Jonathan Pollard was a Jewish defense analyst employed by the U.S. navy, who was caught passing secret American intelligence data to the Israelis. Included in the information provided to Israel by Pollard was data on U.S. code-breaking techniques, satellite data that enabled Israel to stage its 1985 bombing raid against P.L.O. headquarters in Tunis, and information on U.S. agents operating in Israel.

Pollard's activities were completely illegal but not unusual. During the period of close cooperation between America and Israel, Israeli espionage activities were, for the most part, ignored by the United States.[28] For their part, Israeli authorities ignored the activities of American spies in Israel. In the Hobbesian world of sovereign nations, it is an accepted fact of life that friendly powers will spy upon one another. Generally, a quiet protest is the most severe penalty imposed when one ally becomes too aggressive in its inquiries into the affairs of another. Pollard's activities were an only slightly more egregious version of what had become commonplace during the era of close cooperation between America and Israel. That period was now over, however, and the U.S. government treated Pollard with unprecedented severity, presumably as an example and a warning to Israel and its Jewish supporters in America.[29]

Pollard had agreed to a plea bargain arrangement in which he would plead guilty, fully cooperate with federal authorities in assessing the damage to U.S. interests resulting from his espionage activities, help in identifying other spies, and refrain from disclosing other classified information. In exchange, the government agreed to tell the judge that the information provided by Pollard was of considerable value in assessing the damage caused by his espionage activities and the enforcement of the espionage laws and to recommend a reduced sentence—most likely a suspended sentence—for Pollard's wife and what was termed a "substantial period of incarceration" for Pollard. The phrase "substantial period" was understood to mean that Pollard would receive less than the life sentence that could theoretically result from an espionage conviction.

Though after the plea bargain Pollard cooperated fully with federal authorities, the government effectively reneged on its agreement. Prosecutors asserted that Pollard had shown no remorse for his crime and argued that he should receive an especially harsh sentence because he had spied for Israel. They told the presiding judge Aubrey Robinson that "because the foreign nation involved is a U.S. ally," a lenient sentence would represent "a potentially damaging signal to individuals . . . contemplating espionage activities in the United States."[30] In other words, because there were potentially many American Jews who might consider spying for Israel, Pollard must receive an especially harsh sentence.

On the day of Pollard's sentencing, Defense Secretary Caspar Weinberger wrote to the judge, "It is difficult for me . . . to conceive a greater harm to national security than that caused by Pollard." Weinberger called for a harsh sentence to provide "a measure of protection against further damage to the national security."[31] Pollard was sentenced to life imprisonment—a term exceeding any ever meted out to an individual convicted of spying for an American ally and greater than most prison terms given Soviet spies. Pollard's wife was sentenced to two concurrent five-year terms.

The initial reaction of American Jewish organizations was to distance themselves from Pollard as they had from the Rosenbergs during the 1950s. American Jews were concerned that the Pollard case would be used by anti-Semites as evidence that Jews put their loyalty to Israel ahead of their loyalty to the United States. To show that this was not true, American Jewish organizations quickly condemned Pollard's actions and supported the government's prosecution of the case.

However, after Pollard had served several years of his life sentence in federal prison, Jewish organizations were emboldened to raise questions about the unusually harsh treatment he had received. In 1991, Pollard's family organized an appeal of his conviction. Arguing before a federal appeals court, Pollard's attorney, former Assistant U.S. Attorney General Theodore Olson, asserted that the U.S. government had breached its plea bargain agreement with Pollard by first agreeing not to request a life sentence in exchange for Pollard's guilty plea and then "doing everything it could to secure a life sentence." Olson pointed particularly to the letter from then Defense Secretary Caspar Weinberger to the presiding judge in Pollard's original trial, Aubrey Robinson, accusing Pollard of treason, a crime which is punishable by life imprisonment or even death under federal law. This despite the fact that Pollard had never been formally charged with treason.

A large number of American Jewish leaders signed a friend of the court brief submitted by Pollard's attorneys. These included Elie Weisel, Arthur Hertzberg, and former World Jewish Congress President Philip Klutznik as well as the heads of the three major rabbinical seminaries in America. American Jews had initially feared an anti-Semitic backlash from the Pollard case. By 1991, however, some had come to see the Pollard case itself as a direct attack upon the American Jewish community. In April 1992, a three-judge federal appellate panel rejected, by a 2–1 vote, Pollard's appeal of his life sentence. Ironically, the two judges on the panel who voted against Pollard—Laurence Silberman and Ruth Ginsburg—are both Jewish. A non-Jewish judge, Stephen Williams, dissented, asserting that Pollard's sentence represented "a fundamental miscarriage of justice."[32] In September 1992, the Washington Board of Rabbis called upon the president to commute Pollard's sentence. The board attacked "the justice of [Pollard's] punishment and the circumstances which resulted in his unreasonable sentence."[33] Pollard's attorneys also appealed his sentence to the U.S. Supreme Court, charging that the government had breached its plea bargain agreement with Pollard.

Through its harsh treatment of Pollard, the administration had, in effect, sent a signal to Jews that their importance to and power in the government was now diminished. Indeed, the most immediate impact of the Pollard case was felt by American Jews working in defense and diplomatic agencies. Edward Luttwak, an American Jewish defense analyst, has been quoted as saying that the Pollard case has had "a disastrous effect" on American Jews working in the defense establishment.[34]

As they once investigated individuals having ties with Communist and other hostile governments, U.S. security officers now probe deeply into the backgrounds and activities of individuals with ties to Israel. Since most American Jews have ties to Israel—they have visited Israel, have relatives in Israel, or at the very least have made contributions to organizations that have links to Israel—the potential result is to undermine the position of Jews in American government and policy-making capacities—long a major source of Jewish influence in the United States. According to some reports, a number of Jewish Defense Department employees lost their security clearances in the wake of the Pollard affair.

American Jewish organizations began slowly to rally to Pollard's defense because they began to fear that, through its actions during and especially after the Pollard case, the government was calling the legitimacy of all Jewish support for Israel into question. For many years it was possible to be simultaneously 100% American and 100% pro-Israel. The administration seemed, now, to be asserting that any Jew who vehemently supported Israel was a potential Pollard—someone whose loyalty to the United States was questionable. Also affected by the Pollard affair were Soviet Jewish emigré scientists and engineers who found it difficult to obtain security clearances and, hence, to find work. The tightening of security clearance procedures undertaken in the wake of the Pollard case virtually precluded American citizens born in "hostile" countries from obtaining the high levels of clearance needed to work as physicists or engineers on defense contracts or for firms holding defense contracts. In effect, this was a ban on Russian Jews—the only emigre group boasting large numbers of engineers and physicists born in a hostile country.[35]

The second manifestation of the Republican regime's new attitude toward its erstwhile Jewish allies was President George Bush's attack on the pro-Israel lobby. In the summer of 1991, Israel sought some $10 billion in loan guarantees from the United States to facilitate the construction of housing for Russian Jewish emigrants flooding into Israel. In August, the Bush administration decided to postpone the Israeli request for a four-month period in order to force the Israelis to stop building new settlements in occupied Arab territories and to ensure the Shamir government's cooperation with American efforts to arrange a Middle East peace conference in October. Though American Jews were divided on Shamir's settlements policies, pro-Israel forces in the United States moved to bring pressure on Congress to provide immediate loan guarantees for Israel despite President Bush's opposition.

A major lobbying effort by AIPAC, the Conference of Presidents of Major American Jewish Organizations, the National Jewish Community Relations Advisory Council (NJCRAC), and other groups brought hundreds of pro-Israel activists to Washington in August and early September and seemed to result in expressions of support for immediate provision of the loan guarantees by enough senators and representatives to ensure passage and, if necessary, to override a presidential veto.

On Steptember 12, however, President Bush held a nationally televised press conference in which he vigorously defended his decision to defer the Israeli request and bitterly attacked the pro-Israel lobbyists who were seeking congressional support to countermand Bush's decision. During the press conference, the usually affable Bush pounded his fist on the lectern and demanded that Congress defer to him on this sensitive foreign policy question.

Bush depicted the Israeli leadership as greedy and ungrateful. During the Persian Gulf War, according to Bush, American soldiers had "risked their lives to defend Israelis in the face of Iraqi Scud missiles." Moreover, said Bush, "during the current fiscal year alone, and despite our own economic problems, the United States provided Israel with more than $4 billion in economic and military aid—nearly $1,000 for every Israeli man, woman and child." Later, Bush failed to correct a reporter who implied that the loan guarantees to Israel involved a direct transfer of funds from the U.S. Treasury that could be better spent on urgent domestic needs. Bush also suggested that previous American aid given to Israel had been used improperly to build Jewish settlements in the occupied territories of the West Bank. "It is our goal to support the welfare of the new [Russian Jewish] immigrants and to have peace, not to choose one humanitarian goal at the expense of the other," the president said.

As to the pro-Israel lobby in the United States: "I'm up against some powerful political forces," the president declared, "but I owe it to the American people to tell them how strongly I feel about deferral." Later in the press conference Bush said, "We're up against very strong and effective . . . groups that go up to the Hill. I heard today there were something like a thousand lobbyists working the other side of the question. We've got one lonely little guy down here doing it."[36]

In the wake of the Bush press conference, congressional sponsors of the loan guarantee package agreed to the president's demands. Republicans quickly moved to follow the president's leadership. As for the Democrats, even Israel's strongest backers feared that if they pushed for immediate passage of the loan guarantee package, Democrats would be vulnerable to the election-year charge of seeking to spend American dollars abroad when they were needed at home. Indeed, nationally syndicated columnists Rowland Evans and Robert Novak urged Republicans to make use of the president's strong stand against aid to Israel to counter the Democratic charge that Bush was more interested in foreign affairs than domestic problems. Here was an issue where the Democrats rather than the Republicans seemed to be focused on needs halfway around the world rather than more pressing needs at home. The chance of using the Israel loan guarantee issue to undermine the Democrats' "Come home, America" campaign that prompted Republicans to quickly line up behind the president, and their fear that this would happen, led Democrats to cave in quickly.

Pro-Israel groups were angered by the president's attack but felt that they could not oppose him. Public opinion polls indicated that Americans supported the president's position by a 3–1 margin and, indeed, that nearly half of all Americans surveyed opposed providing *any* economic aid for Israel. Opposition to such aid was quite striking. According to the September 26, 1991, NBC News/*Wall Street Journal* Poll, while voters by 58%–32% favored economic aid to the Soviet Union, and by a margin of 55%–29% supported economic aid to Poland, voters *opposed* economic support for Israel by a 46%–44% margin. The same poll indicated a general weakening of public support for Israel. Among those surveyed, 34% saw Israel as the greatest impediment to a Mideast peace settlement, while 33% thought that the Arab nations were the chief stumbling block. In addition, by a margin of 49%–31%, voters believed that Israel should give up occupied Arab territories in the West Bank, Gaza Strip, and Golan Heights in return for a peace treaty.[37] Subsequent polls indicated a steady erosion of public support for assistance to Israel.[38]

While previous presidents, including Reagan, had conflicts with Israel and American Jewish groups, the Bush speech marked the first time in nearly forty years that an American president had questioned the legitimacy of pro-Israel lobbying efforts by American Jews. This switch was especially notable given the Republicans' ten years of close relationship to the pro-Israel lobby, including their reliance upon that lobby only the summer before to obtain a favorable vote on military intervention in the Persian Gulf.

American Jews, even those who themselves opposed the Shamir government's settlements policy, were angered by Bush's remarks and feared that the president's comments would fuel not only anti-Israel but also anti-Semitic sentiment in the United States. Anti-

Semitic columnists like Patrick Buchanan—who later became a candidate for the Republican presidential nomination—applauded the president's stand and took the opportunity to lash out at Israel and its friends in America. "In going pubic," wrote Buchanan, "rather than engaging the Israeli lobby on its preferred turf, the back rooms and corridors of Congress, President Bush did the right thing." Even if Bush fails to stop the loan guarantees, Buchanan continued, Bush will have "exposed Congress for what it has become, a Parliament of Whores, incapable of standing up for U.S. national interests, if AIPAC is on the other end of the line."[39]

The White House contributed to the growing apprehension felt by American Jews by expressing concern over the large number of anti-Semitic telephone calls and letters generated by the president's comments. Of course, by expressing this concern, the White House, in effect, warned American Jews that they would be taking a real risk if they continued to oppose the president on the loan guarantee issue.[40]

After Bush succeeded in forcing the congressional sponsors of the loan guarantee package to agree to a four-month delay, the president moved to calm the fears of American Jews. In a September 17, 1991, letter to Shoshana Cardin, chairwoman of the Conference of Presidents of Major Jewish Organizations, Bush expressed dismay that some of his remarks during the previous week's press conference had "caused apprehension within the Jewish community." Bush went on to say, "My references to lobbyists and powerful political forces were never meant to be pejorative in any sense."[41]

Though most American Jewish leaders publicly professed to be satisfied with Bush's letter, there was a general feeling among American Jews that the president was being a bit disingenuous. Some Jews noted that even after the September 17 letter, White House officials continued to hint that, if necessary, Bush would appeal to the American public for support against the pro-Israel lobby again. Alfred Moses, President of the American Jewish Committee, called the president's "continuing threat to go to the American public" on this issue an "ominous sign."[42] For the first time in a half-century, a major public official had used the threat of popular anti-Semitism against American Jews. The Israeli government continued to press for loan guarantees, but American Jews feared that they would lose an all-out fight on the issue.[43]

For its part, the Bush administration continued to attack the Israeli government and paint it as an unworthy and unreliable ally. In April 1992, the United States charged that Israel had illegally sold American Patriot missile technology to China and other nations.[44] This made it even more difficult for American Jews to seek additional assistance for Israel. By March 1992, Israel's American supporters had given up the struggle and the loan guarantee request was dead.[45] Not surprisingly, the administration then discovered that the Israelis had not sold Patriot technology to China after all.[46]

As noted earlier, after Israel's Labor party, led by Yitzhak Rabin, returned to power during the summer of 1992, the Bush administration agreed to provide the loan guarantee package in exchange for Israel's commitment to support American policy goals in the Middle East. In particular, the Israelis were expected to cooperate with the American-sponsored Middle East peace conference.[47] In its dealings with the Rabin government, the actions of the White House were governed primarily by its conceptions of American foreign policy interests, especially the administration's desire to expand American influence in the Arab world. The views and sensibilities of American Jews were weighed far less heavily. Noting that the political influence of American Jews had waned dramatically, the Rabin government took the unprecedented step of actually asking Israel's Jewish supporters in the United States to *reduce* their efforts to sway United States policy. Rabin feared that the activities of American Jews on Israel's behalf were coming to be counterproductive.[48]

A third manifestation of the Republicans' new indifference to Jews was the American-sponsored Middle East peace conference that began in November 1991. The United States forced Israel to participate in the conference though the Israeli government felt that it had little or nothing to gain and stood only to lose territory. As the conference began, the U.S. maintained an "even-handed" posture that could only hurt the Israelis who rely upon American support. Indeed, the Bush administration's anti-Israel posture became so pronounced that the *Wall Street Journal* in March 1992 observed that the White House had obviously adopted what it termed a pro-Arab policy. "The White House seems to be veering to the view that in the post–Cold War world Israel has diminished strategic importance, and the Arab regimes have increased importance."[49]

Throughout the year, the administration barely bothered to conceal its hope that the hard-line Shamir government would be defeated in the 1992 Israel elections and replaced by a presumably more compliant Labor government . Yitzhak Rabin's electoral victory in 1992 was welcomed by the Bush White House which moved quickly—using the carrot of loan guarantees and the stick of threatened new arms sales to the Arabs—to encourage Rabin to make territorial concessions to Israel's neighbors that had been rejected by Shamir. Consistent with White House hopes, Rabin proved far more willing than his predecessor to make concessions to the Arabs to avoid antagonizing the Americans.

At the time of this writing, it remains to be seen what will develop from the peace conference. As the November 1992 elections approached, some Republican members of Congress urged the president not to antagonize Jewish voters in an election year.[50] Major Jewish Republican contributors also voiced complaints.[51] The White House, however, understood the ethnic arithmetic of American politics. As former Secretary of State James Baker expressed it in his eloquent response to American Jews who criticized his anti-Israel posture, "Fuck them [the Jews]. They didn't vote for us."[52]

During the months preceding the November 1992 election, the Bush administration was forced to deemphasize its foreign policy commitments because of charges initiated by Pat Buchanan and echoed by the Democrats that America's domestic needs were being neglected while the president focused on foreign issues. As a result, the Middle East peace conference was left to flounder in a sea of empty rhetoric as the clock ran out on the Bush administration.[53] Ironically, Pat Buchanan had, at least temporarily, helped the Jews. What Middle East policy will be pursued by the new Clinton administration remains to be seen. Pro-Israel groups, though, point to the prominence of Jews and such staunch friends of Israel as Samuel Berger and former State Department official Richard Schifter on Clinton's campaign staff and among his key foreign policy advisors as indicating the likelihood that Democratic policy will be favorable to Israel.[54] Some of Israel's supporters, on the other hand, were concerned when Clinton named Warren Christopher to serve as secretary of state. Christopher was seen by pro-Israel groups as insufficiently sensitive to Israel's interests.[55]

Thus, a marriage born of convenience between Republicans and some Jews came to an end. Many Jewish Republicans, including some prominent neoconservatives, shifted their support to Clinton and the Democrats in 1992, refusing to back Bush.[56] Others remained in the Republican camp but without much enthusiasm.[57] What is the long-term significance of these events? Twenty years ago, when Republicans began to court Jewish support, there appeared to be a number of good reasons to woo the Jews—and some very strong reasons to avoid attacking them. Today, there may be less reason for the first and, perhaps, fewer barriers to the second.

6   Another Fatal Embrace?

B etween the 1930s and the 1980s, Jews became extremely influential in American politics while anti-Semitism was relegated to
the margins of American political life. In the contemporary United
States, however, anti-Semitism has begun to reemerge as a prominent political force, and in all likelihood will grow in importance in
the coming years. This is so for three reasons. The first is the end of
the hegemony and internal unity of the liberal coalition that had all
but outlawed anti-Semitic expression. The second is a reduction in
the constraints on conservative anti-Semitism and its increasing role
as a weapon in struggles within the conservative coalition. The third
is the linkage between racism and anti-Semitism in radical populist
ideology coupled with the increased permeability of the political process to the forces of the radical right.

Disarray in the Liberal Coalition

Between the 1930s and the 1960s, the United States was ruled by a
liberal Democratic regime, initially constructed by Franklin D. Roosevelt, in which Jews played prominent roles in the government and
as activists and financial contributors in partisan politics. Their importance to—and high visibility in—the Democratic coalition often
made Jews the targets of attacks by the Roosevelt administration's
opponents. However, the Democratic New Deal regime was able to
protect Jews from their various foes while providing them with a
number of significant economic and political opportunities.

Thus, during the 1930s, FDR found Jews to be useful allies and
gave them access to positions of great power in his administration
and political apparatus. Jews became important officials and advisors
in the executive branch as well as important figures in the Democratic party. Roosevelt also ruthlessly suppressed neo-Nazi forces in
the United States and, perhaps even more important, built a powerful
military machine that helped to destroy Nazi Germany.

During the 1940s and 1950s, Jews and their political allies again
withstood the assault of right-wing forces that sought to link Jews
with international communism. Through this linkage, forces on the

political right hoped to undermine the Democratic postwar regime with which Jews were closely associated. During the course of the ensuing struggle, Jews and their allies were extremely successful. It was during this period that Jews succeeded in having anti-Semitic rhetoric declared to be completely out of bounds in American political debate. At the same time, Jews used their influence in the Democratic postwar regime to secure American support for the construction of the State of Israel. Subsequently, once again at the behest of American Jews, the United States committed itself to the economic support and military defense of the Jewish state.

During the 1960s, Jews joined with other liberal Democrats and with blacks in the civil rights and anti–Vietnam War movements. Through this alliance, Jews were able to weaken their conservative Southern adversaries as well as their Northern white working-class rivals within the Democratic party, and to virtually destroy the traditional party machines upon which these forces depended for their power. In addition, the programs of Lyndon Johnson's Great Society enlarged the welfare state and expanded the influence of Jewish professionals and academics in policy-making and administrative processes at the national, state, and local levels. Through their participation in the civil rights movement, moreover, Jews overcame many of the institutional barriers that had blocked their way in the United States since the end of the nineteenth century. For example, in the 1960s, the doors of the elite universities were opened to Jewish faculty and students, and most other forms of discrimination were outlawed.

Within the Democratic party, the influence of Jews increased substantially during the 1960s and 1970s. As liberal forces undermined the traditional party machines around which the Democrats had been organized, their place was taken by a congeries of liberal political groups and movements, growing out of the peace movement and the civil rights movement. These groups had charged that traditional Democratic machines were unresponsive to public—as opposed to selfish private—interests, and were insensitive to the needs of new constituencies such as women, minorities, and young people. Liberal public interest groups were organized to promote such causes.

Very often, affluent, well-educated, young Jewish professionals who, as college students, had gained their political experience in the antiwar and civil rights movements, played leadership roles in these groups. The rise of public interest groups coupled with the political reforms of the 1960s and 1970s gave Jews a more powerful role in the Democratic party than they ever previously possessed.

In addition, the important changes in regulatory policy and governmental and bureaucratic organization that liberal Democrats were able to bring about during the 1960s and 1970s gave these organizations enormous power in the national government and the entire domestic economy. Jews became important actors in the permanent government consisting of federal domestic agencies, consulting firms, public interest groups, and quasi-public institutions such as "think tanks," universities, charitable foundations, and the elite media.

As we saw earlier, however, the successes that Jews and their allies were able to achieve during the 1960s and 1970s undermined the stability of the Democratic coalition in national politics. Jews had allied themselves with blacks, at least in part, to eliminate discrimination against themselves. However, Democratic civil rights policies led to the defection of millions of white voters from the Democratic party. And, ironically, as we have seen, the increased prominence of African Americans in the Democratic coalition led to an upsurge of black anti-Semitism.

At the same time, liberal Democratic regulatory programs, especially in such areas as consumer protection, occupational safety, and environmental protection led large segments of business to mobilize against the Democrats. This they did by organizing literally thousands of political action committees and taking a vigorous part in political campaigns at every level.

As the Democratic coalition frayed during the 1970s and 1980s, the Republicans launched a full-scale attack against it. Though the Republicans ultimately were not able to take control of Congress, they did succeed in seizing control of the White House for a long period of time. In 1992, it required the one-two punch of a severe and sustained economic recession and an extraordinarily inept Republican incumbent to hand the Democrats control of the White House. Even so, Clinton won a scant 43% of the popular vote. At the very least, the coalition through which Jews rose to power in the United States has been shaken. It has lost its ability to reliably control the White House, for many years its political command center. Moreover, a major division has developed within it between blacks and Jews.

At this time, there is no way to foretell what success President Clinton and his allies will have in restoring the vitality of the liberal coalition. Much, of course, will depend upon the behavior of the economy. If the Clinton administration, through prudent economic programs and luck, is able to restore domestic prosperity, then Americans' support for liberalism and the Democrats also will be restored. If, on the other hand, the problems of the American economy prove to be structural and long term—and there is, of course, every reason to fear that this is so—then liberal Democracy's 1992 victory will be short-lived. Indeed, the Democrats will then be blamed for the problems they did not solve. Under such circumstances, both the capacity of the Democratic coalition to defend Jews from attack and the capacity of the Jews to rely upon the Democratic coalition for this purpose would be greatly diminished.

Conservative Anti-Semitism

Since the days of Richard Nixon and Spiro Agnew, conservative politicians have understood full well that Jews were among the leaders of the enemy camp. However, they have been constrained from making anything of this. Nixon remained silent despite his personal feelings about Jews because the liberal coalition had the capacity to declare anti-Semitic commentary to be "extremist" and to use this charge to destroy politicians found guilty of engaging in anti-Semitic activities.

Subsequently, during the Reagan era, conservatives hoped to win Jewish electoral support and, more important, courted and won the support of Jewish financiers and pro-Israel forces for the administration's fiscal, defense, and foreign policy agendas. As we have seen, Jewish financiers played an important role in Reaganite fiscal policy, helping to fund the nation's huge budget deficits and to restructure the nation's economy. At the same time, pro-Israel forces provided crucial support for the administration's military buildup while Israel served as an important adjunct to American foreign policy.

This, in turn, stimulated anti-Semitism (expressed as anti-Zionism) on the liberal left, further weakening the liberal coalition. Even today, left-liberal church groups continue to attack Israel. For example, in January 1992 the leaders of fifteen liberal church groups urged President Bush to deny Israel's request for loan guarantees for the construction of housing for Russian immigrants until it stopped building settlements in the occupied territories. The church leaders asserted in their statement that "the continuation of settlements [by Israel] poses an enormous obstacle to the fragile peace process." The signers of the statement included leaders of the American Baptist Church, American Friends Service Committee, Episcopal Church, Evangelical Lutheran Church, Maryknoll Fathers and Brothers, National Council of Churches, Presbyterian Church, Roman Catholic Conference of Major Superiors of Men, Unitarian Universalist Association, and the United Church of Christ.

By the 1990s, the factors that served as constraints upon the capacity of conservatives to attack Jews had eased, if not disappeared altogether. This is what permitted President George Bush to appeal to the American people to stand with him against the machinations of the Israel lobby while he shifted American foreign policy away from its long-standing posture of support for Israel toward the acceptance of a Palestinian state and the demand for Israeli return of occupied Arab territories.

To make matters worse, the easing of constraints on conservative anti-Semitism is taking place at precisely the same time that conflict within the defeated Republican party is generating anti-Semitic impulses. Anti-Semitism emerged in Democratic factional politics in the wake of the success of the liberal Democratic coalition. Anti-Semitism is emerging as a weapon in factional struggle with the Republican party as the constituent parts of the former Reaganite coalition struggle for supremacy.

Created during the late 1970s, the Reaganite coalition brought together a variety of different types of conservatives, including pragmatic businessmen seeking to reduce regulatory costs and undermine the power of organized labor, middle-class suburbanites seeking tax relief, social conservatives advocating an agenda of school prayer and an end to abortion, predominantly Jewish neoconservatives whose major concerns were support for Israel and opposition to affirmative action, and old-line "paleoconservatives" whose ideology rested on fear of communism and opposition to big government and who, in some cases, had never reconciled themselves to Roosevelt's New Deal, much less Johnson's Great Society.

During the Reagan era, these forces coexisted. By the time of the Bush Administration, however, serious strains had begun to develop in the conservative alliance.[1] In particular, under the banner of "America First," paleoconservatives led by Patrick Buchanan have sought to subordinate their factional rivals and to win a dominant role in the Republican party. Buchanan and the paleoconservatives are the intellectual, and sometimes the sociological, heirs to what once was the Taft wing of the Republican party. They are fiercely nationalistic. Most want to see the size and role of government in American society drastically reduced. They advocate economic protectionism—indeed, some virtually preach autarky—and warn of a coming trade war with Europe and Japan. They are socially conservative—some, like Buchanan, are conservative Catholics who reject the reforms mandated by liberal popes and the Vatican II conference. Though they were rabidly anti-Communist, paleoconservatives opposed an activist, interventionist foreign policy and were suspicious of the national security state erected after World War II.[2]

Robert Taft and his followers had hoped that the end of World War II would allow the dismantling of Roosevelt's domestic welfare state. Instead, they saw Northeastern Republicans cooperate with Democrats in the construction of an enormous national security state that, if anything, made government an even more pervasive force in American society than had the New Deal. Though most became reconciled to the national security state as necessary to the world-wide struggle against communism, with the demise of the Soviet Union paleoconservatives see an opportunity for American global retrenchment and, thus, for a reduction in the size, capacity, and pervasiveness of the American national state.

Like Taft, the paleoconservatives draw much of their support from small town and rural Protestants and some urban Catholics who are disturbed by the social changes that have taken place and continue to take place in the United States, undermining religious values, the moral order, and long-established social hierarchies. Though Reagan and Bush payed lip service to the concerns of these groups by praising the right-to-life movement and other moral goals, both lacked a genuine commitment to social issues that eventually became apparent and led to a sense of betrayal among social conservatives.

Paleoconservatives also draw support from conservative Southerners because of their opposition to further federal intervention to secure preferential treatment for racial minorities. Campaigning in the South in 1992, Buchanan played on the anger of lower-middle-class whites against the elites—Republican as well as Democratic—who allegedly supported civil rights programs at the expense of ordinary white voters. In Louisiana, Buchanan said, "Mr Bush promised he would veto a quota bill, and then . . . he caved in . . . Now if you belong to the Exeter-Yale-GOP club, that is not going to bother you greatly because, as we know, it is not their children who get bused out of South Boston into Roxbury. It is not their brothers who lose contracts because of minority set-asides. It is not the scions of Yale and Harvard who apply to become FBI agents and construction workers and civil servants and cops who bear the onus of this reverse discrimination." Even Louisiana State Republican officials who supported Bush were filled with admiration for Buchanan.[3]

In some respects like Taft, paleoconservatives also draw upon the support of national, as opposed to international capital, that is, firms and enterprises that produce mainly for the U.S. domestic market rather than for export, or that have been defeated or face defeat by foreign competitors on the world market and view a protected national market as their best hope for survival.

Reaganomics, as practiced by the Reagan and Bush administrations, was an economic policy heavily linked to and dependent upon free trade. The Reagan and Bush administrations ran enormous budget deficits financed through heavy borrowing in credit markets. Among the major purchasers of the U.S. government securities that have financed the huge American deficits was the Japanese central bank. These debt purchases, in turn, were the price the Japanese government has been required to pay for open admission to the U.S. market for Japanese products—a quid pro quo formalized in the 1985 U.S.–Japan Dollar Yen Accord. Of course, in addition to their dependence upon free trade as a mechanism through which to finance their budget deficits, Reaganites also saw free trade as a route to industrial restructuring in the United States.

Their advocacy of free trade earned the Reaganites the support of those sectors of American business, most notably finance, aerospace, and the multinationals that benefit from open borders and the absence of protectionism. At the same time, other industries, including autos, steel, consumer electronics, and other industries that could not compete successfully with foreign imports began to look favorably at the idea of protectionism. These industries, or their surviving remnants, provide a base of support for paleoconservatives as national capital once did for Taft Republicanism.

Finally, blue-collar workers, if not their union leadership, are a base of support for paleoconservatives that was not readily available to Taft in the 1940s and 1950s. Blue-collar unionized workers were among the major victims of Reaganomics. Policies of free trade damaged or even destroyed the very industries that had employed millions of unionized workers. In effect, American workers were left to compete freely on the world market with European and Asian workers. The result was inevitable—a loss of jobs and real income. Though they are advocates of protectionism, labor union leaders are too heavily committed to the Democrats to support a Pat Buchanan. Workers, however, have no reluctance to give their enthusiastic support to a political force that advocates protectionism and "America First," especially if that force is also committed to patriotism and social conservatism.[4]

Anti-Semitism has begun and will continue to play a role in this developing struggle for control of the Republican party, especially in the wake of Bush's defeat in 1992. Moreover, should the paleoconservatives succeed in seizing control of the Republican party, anti-Semitism will almost certainly be an arrow in their quiver against the Democrats.

In Republican factional struggle, anti-Semitism is a weapon that the paleoconservatives can exploit against the neoconservatives as well as other forces that are linked to the neoconservatives. The predominantly Jewish neocons are the chief intellectual spokesmen for all the aspects of Reaganite Republicanism that the paleoconservatives find objectionable.

First, the neocons are soft on social issues. Few neoconservatives attach much moral significance to the issues of abortion or school prayer and pragmatically advocate doing little to concretely advance these causes in order to avoid alienating middle-class suburban voters. Indeed, many neocons are fond of saying privately that social issues are merely useful bait with which to attract the votes of the riff-raff. By helpfully reminding conservative Protestants and Catholics of the true character and aims of the Jews (as revealed by the portions of their liturgy they have chosen to overlook in recent years), paleoconservatives can disrupt the improbable alliance between conservative Christians and Jews and bring the former over to their own camp. Paleoconservatives are already making very substantial headway on the religious right. The Reverend Jerry Falwell, for example, has indicated that though he backed Bush in 1992, he is "front-row center for Buchanan in 1996."[5] Since backing Buchanan and continuing to support Israel are probably incompatible, we shall see where Falwell will assign his priorities.

Second, the neocons are internationalists. Many neocons were at one time liberal Democrats or, in some cases, even Socialists or Marxists. One major factor that drew them inexorably to the right was their attachment to Israel and their growing frustration during the 1960s with a Democratic party that was becoming increasingly opposed to American military preparedness and increasingly enamored of Third World causes. In the Reaganite right's hard-line anticommunism, commitment to American military strength, and willingness to intervene politically and militarily in the affairs of other nations to promote democratic values (and American interests), neocons found a political movement that would guarantee Israel's security. Neocons continue to be important among internationalist forces, arguing that American leadership and willingness to use military power is necessary to prevent chaos and to protect democracy and human rights in the post–Cold War world. This is, of course, precisely what the paleoconservatives want to end. They want to limit America's foreign commitments as the first step toward dismantling the national security state.

Finally, the neocons are free traders and are often the intellectual spokesmen for forces advocating policies of free trade and economic internationalism. Paleoconservatives are protectionists and receive the support of protectionist forces in the economy such as portions of the textile industry, the steel industry, and the congeries of small- and medium-size firms represented by the Business and Industrial Council.[6] Neocons advocate programs and policies that will promote economic stability by linking the interests of the United States, Japan, and Europe. Here, they speak the language of international economic cooperation also favored by the American financial community as well as by free trade interests among America's multinationals and aerospace industries.

The neocons were alienated by the Bush administration. Most, however, have remained in the Republican camp, and many have close ties to such leaders of the Republican center as former Vice-President Dan Quayle, former Education Secretary William Bennett, former Housing Secretary Jack Kemp. Their continuing identification with Republican centrists like Quayle, Bennett, and Kemp and their policies makes the Jewish neocons extremely useful targets for the paleoconservatives.

By attacking the Jews, paleoconservatives can simultaneously attack virtually every form of heresy that, from their point of view, has contaminated Republican politics during the Reagan and Bush years as well as the Jewish and non-Jewish heretics that have been the dominant forces in the party. Obviously, labeling internationalism, free trade, and pragmatism on social issues as "Jewish" positions is calculated to undermine and silence support for them. Moreover, just as blacks can use anti-Semitism to brand as "Jewish interests," views that have been presented in universalistic terms, so can paleoconservatives use anti-Semitism to expose the internationalist and other views of their opponents as special Jewish interests rather than larger public goals. Indeed, paleoconservatives like Joseph Sobran are fond of asserting that, in one way or another, the positions taken by the neoconservatives are simply ideological covers for their support for Israel.[7]

This is why, after a long hiatus, anti-Semitism has once again become a significant phenomenon on the political right. The most noteworthy expression was, of course, Pat Buchanan's charge that the Persian Gulf War was promoted by the Israeli Defense Ministry and its "amen corner" in the United States, and his subsequent description of Congress as "Israeli-occupied" territory. Later, ignoring the many non-Jewish conservatives who advocated American military intervention in the Persian Gulf, Buchanan identified four influential individuals who played key roles in bringing about the American attack on Iraq. These were A. M. Rosenthal, former executive editor of the *New York Times;* Richard Perle, former assistant secretary of defense and a leading Reagan-era hawk; columnist Charles Krauthammer; and former Secretary of State Henry Kissinger.[8] All are Jews and one, Perle, a leading neoconservative defense strategist. With these assertions, Buchanan is linking internationalism and, by extension, the maintenance of the national security state, to the machinations of the Jews.

Buchanan, however, is simply the most visible tip of the iceberg. For example, in a 1986 article in the *New Republic,* John Judis reports a speech delivered at the 1986 meeting of the Philadelphia Society, an old-line conservative forum, by the paleoconservative Stephen Tonsor, attacking the neocons as interlopers who had only recently been left-wingers. Tonsor said, "It is splendid when the town whore gets religion and joins the church. Now and then she makes a good choir director, but when she begins to tell the minister what he ought to say in his Sunday sermons, matters have been carried too far."[9] In the same article, Judis quotes a number of conservatives, including syndicated columnist Russell Kirk, as asserting that neoconservatives, as distinguished from true conservatives, were mainly interested in the defense of Israel. "That lies in back of everything," said Kirk. Similarly, the *National Review*'s recent issue on anti-Semitism provides a number of examples of efforts by Buchanan and other paleoconservatives, such as former *National Review* editor Joseph Sobran, to use anti-Semitic rhetoric to attack their idelogical and factional rivals in the Republican camp.

To paleoconservatives, the disruption of the established Republican coalition and its replacement with one that they lead is a necessary first step to the defeat of the Democrats and the reversal of six decades of errors. Thus, Bush's defeat is an opportunity rather than a calamity. According to Sidney Blumenthal, the magazine *Chronicles,* which has emerged as the leading journal of the Buchananite right, editorialized even before the election, "We have to shoot the elephant in such a way that he falls on the donkey and crushes it. It might take a generation just to haul away the rotting carcass, but we would be able, for the first time since 1932, to breath clean air."[10] And part of this process of shooting the elephant is to accuse it of having a Jewish problem.

Obviously, Buchanan and his followers did not expect to win the Republican presidential nomination in 1992. Their interest was 1996 and beyond. Bush's defeat in the 1992 presidential election has weakened the centrists and given forces on the Republican right the opportunity to argue that the party needs to nominate a "real" conservative in 1996. Religious fundamentalists led by Pat Robertson's Christian Coalition have already taken control of Republican state party organizations in Iowa, Georgia, and Minnesota. It should be noted that although Robertson seeks to portray himself as a mainstream conservative, his 1981 treatise, *The New World Order*, presents a picture of communism and capitalism as parts of a single conspiracy organized originally by rich Jews including the Rothschilds, Paul Warburg, and Jacob Schiff.[11] Paleoconservatives are seeking control of the Republican National Committee (RNC) and see an opportunity to drive out the centrist "holdovers from the days of Jake Javits and Nelson Rockefeller."[12] The January 1993 victory of Haley Barbour, a centrist, in the struggle over the RNC chairmanship, is one hopeful sign that the forces of the Republican Far Right may still be defeated.

Even before the 1992 election, members of the conservative camp lost no opportunity to point out that Bush's then heir-apparent, Vice-President Dan Quayle, was heavily dependent upon his chief of staff, neoconservative William Kristol, the son of the leading neoconservative Irving Kristol. Similarly, Buchanan lost no opportunity to attack the predominantly Jewish neocons. In one of his nationally syndicated columns, Buchanan said of the neocons, "Like the fleas who conclude they are steering the dog, their relationship to the [conservative] movement has always been parasitical." *Wall Street Journal* editorial page editor Robert Bartley is reported to have commented that in his 1992 primary campaign Buchanan seemed to be running against Irving Kristol rather than George Bush.[13]

To his credit, former Vice-President Quayle refused to abandon his support of Israel. In a speech commemorating the Holocaust, Quayle said, "America has more than interests where Israel is concerned. We have shared values, cherished traditions, a true friendship."[14] Similarly, in a speech to an AIPAC conference, Quayle addressed the audience as "fellow Zionists."[15] Members of the Christian right have been less hesitant to distance themselves from the Jews. For example, at a November 1992 meeting of Republican governors, Mississippi Governor Kirk Fordice declared that the United States was a "Christian nation." South Carolina Governor Carroll Campbell corrected Fordice by describing American values as Judeo-Christian. "I just wanted to add the Judeo part," said Campbell. Fordice appeared to glare at Campbell and replied, "If I want to do that, I would have done it." Pat Buchanan's sister and campaign manager, Angela "Bay" Buchanan, subsequently told interviewers on "Face the Nation" that Fordice was correct and had "no need to apologize."[16]

Should the Buchananite wing succeed in its efforts to seize control of the Republican party—and Buchanan's strong showing in the 1992 Republican primaries and the prominent place given to him at the 1992 Republican convention suggest that it might—anti-Semitism would certainly become a weapon in its attack on the Democrats. Paleoconservatives are fully aware of the prominence of Jews in the liberal Democratic camp. It has certainly never escaped the notice of paleoconservatives that Jews are among the most important leaders of the liberal Democratic opposition. The Clinton administration, like others before it that have sought "change," has drawn heavily upon the talents of Jews. Rubin, Reich, Kantor, Rivlin, Kunin—the list goes on and on. This extraordinary importance of Jews, first in the Clinton campaign and now in the Clinton administration potentially makes anti-Semitism all the more attractive as a weapon in the paleoconservative arsenal.

As has so often been the case, the more prominent the relationship between Jews and the political regime, the better the opportunity for the government's opponents to attack it by attacking the Jews. If Clinton's programs prove unpopular and his efforts to revive the domestic economy falter, there is not much doubt that some of the Democratic coalition's opponents will point out the administration's (and the nation's) Jewish problem. Richard Nixon kept his enumeration of the Jews quiet and off the record. Can anyone doubt, however, that if the time seems propitious, Pat Buchanan will be more than happy to count the Jews publicly and *very* loudly?

If any reminder is needed, Buchanan's strong showing in the primaries demonstrates once again that a record of anti-Semitism is no disqualification to political office in the United States today. As in the case of Louisianians voting for David Duke, the voters of New Hampshire and the other primary states did not give their votes to Buchanan *because* he was an anti-Semite. On the other hand, the fact of his anti-Semitism *did not prevent* 37% of the New Hampshire Republican electorate or roughly 30% of the Republican electorate in a number of other states from supporting Buchanan. It is also worth noting that while President Bush and his supporters attacked Buchanan for many of the positions he has taken in recent years, they were silent on the issue of anti-Semitism. They understood full well that this was no disqualification.

Radical Populism and Anti-Semitism

Finally, neo-Nazi groups, that had been relegated to the lunatic fringe of American politics, returned to prominence with the candidacy of David Duke in the Louisiana gubernatorial election. Of course, Duke insisted that his neo-Nazi and Ku Klux Klan activities were simply youthful indiscretions. However, he made no great effort to purge himself of past sins or to deny the validity of the positions he took in the past.[17]

Duke's disavowals were not taken too seriously by the candidate or his core followers in the white working class.[18] He simply hung his brown shirt and his hooded robe in the closet for the duration of the campaign so as not to seem too strident for the more delicate sensibilities of lower-middle- and middle-class voters as he sought to move his appeal up the class structure. When pressed about his views on Jews, Duke took the Buchananite road of pointing to the power and influence of the Israel lobby and pro-Zionist forces in the United States as the problems with which he was concerned, not Jews per se.

Anti-Duke forces among liberals, Jews, and blacks have pointed with pride to the fact that he lost the Louisiana gubernatorial race by a wide margin, receiving only slightly more than 40% of the vote against his opponent's approximately 60%. This is said to represent a repudiation of Duke and his views. However, this ignores the fact that Duke won 55% of the white vote. This is what is significant about the Duke candidacy—not that he lost—but that a neo-Nazi and Klansman could win 55% of the white vote in a statewide election. This means that more than 700,000 Louisianians, primarily drawn from the working and lower-middle classes, were prepared to give their votes to Duke despite (and in some cases because of) the fact that he could reasonably be suspected at least of, shall we say, cordially disliking Jews and blacks.

At the very least, the Duke vote suggests that there is a what might be called permissive climate for anti-Semitism in the United States. Large numbers of working-class and lower-middle-class voters seem to be willing to support an anti-Semitic candidate so long as he maintains a respectable appearance. A permissive climate is all that is needed. In the 1920s and 1930s, most Germans who voted for Hitler did not do so *because* of his anti-Semitism. Rather, his anti-Semitism—which was an attraction to some—simply was no disqualification to millions of others.[19]

No better indication of the Jews own awareness of the potential for electoral anti-Semitism—poll data to the contrary notwithstanding—is the way in which Jewish organizations approached the Louisiana gubernatorial election. Though individual Jewish political activists and major Jewish organizations were heavily involved in the effort to defeat Duke, particularly by mobilizing as many black voters as possible, most kept a low public profile "for fear of inadvertently helping the Duke candidacy," according to the *Jewish Observer*. The *Observer* goes on to note: "Instead of intervening directly in Louisiana politics, Jewish activists individually furtively funneled tens of thousands of dollars to [Duke's opponent, former Louisiana Governor Edwin] Edwards or to various Democratic party groups which contributed to the successful defeat of Duke."[20]

While it is not known precisely how much money Jews contributed to the anti-Duke effort, a number of Jewish donors are known to have given $5000 each to groups opposing Duke. At one fundraiser attended by Jewish leaders, Duke's opponent, Edwards, raised about $36,000, according to Jews active in the anti-Duke endeavor. Much of this effort was kept behind the scenes for fear of creating an anti-Semitic backlash. According to Rabbi Edward Cohn, head of the New Orleans Rabbinical Council, Jews were "the backbone of fund raising efforts [for Edwards]." However, said Rabbi Cohn, "We tried to be as invisible as possible."[21]

Duke, of course, was defeated, but none too overwhelmingly. His defeat was a result of two factors. First, one-fourth of Louisiana's electorate is black. This means, of course, that a racist candidate faces the daunting task of capturing almost 70% of the white vote (assuming equivalent turnout levels among blacks and whites) to actually win a statewide contest. This is one of the reasons why Jewish organizations, along with other white liberal groups during the 1960s, were such vigorous supporters of the civil rights movement. The enfranchisement of millions of Southern blacks was seen as a bulwark against the sort of right-wing politicians that the South often produced and as a way of undermining the power of the conservative coalition in Congress. This latter goal was also achieved. Southern Democrats are now obliged to take liberal positions on domestic issues in order to maintain the support of their black constituents. This is one reason that the Congress is now a liberal bastion in American politics.[22]

The second reason for Duke's defeat is that he was opposed by most middle- and upper-middle-class voters as well as the Louisiana business community. Most polls showed Duke support waning as respondents moved further up the class structure. Radical populists often make use of anti-Semitic appeals precisely because anti-Semitism, unlike communism or other appeals to the underclasses, can serve as a way of mobilizing the hoi polloi that does not directly threaten the status and property of the well-to-do. Populist anti-Semites attack a segment of the privileged class and exploit popular hatred of that class and the political regime, while hoping to avoid the furious opposition of the privileged stratum as-a-whole. Perhaps some members of the bourgeoisie can even be enlisted in the radical populist cause while others are kept on the sidelines out of apathy or fear of coming under attack themselves as associates or confederates or relatives of the Jews.

Nevertheless, the well-to-do are inherently distrustful of rabble-rousers or any issues and forces that threaten to swell or arouse popular participation in politics. Especially in the United States, the, better classes have usually worked to depress popular participation and keep it within safe channels. The upper classes are only willing to tolerate rabble-rousers in very hard times when they feel their backs to the wall. Otherwise, even if they have no love for Jews, and even if they will not associate with them socially, respectable conservatives will work against anti-Semitic rabble-rousers because potentially such politicians threaten their own political power.

This is precisely what happened in Louisiana. The non-Jewish business community opposed Duke fearing that the populist forces he led posed a threat to their own political, economic, and institutional power. Every major economic and political interest in the state banded together behind the candidacy of Edwin Edwards, making available to him millions of dollars, the support of all the major newspapers, television and radio stations, and all of Louisiana's established political, religious, and social leaders. This total alliance of the haves—not his anti-Semitism—was able to defeat Duke, though, again, none too overwhelmingly.[23] Had any significant segments of Louisiana's political, economic, or social elite deserted to Duke's side, an American state might now have a Nazi governor.

Rather than serve as a defeat, the Duke campaign will undoubtedly be a spur both to Duke and to other radical populists. Duke has now set the precedent and shown the way. Racism and anti-Semitism are not automatically politically fatal. So long as a radical populist is not too strident to offend their sense of order and what is respectable, working- and lower-middle-class voters will not shrink from supporting him. Duke entered a number of 1992 Republican presidential primaries but was, of course, overshadowed by Buchanan, who took most of Duke's issues and voters.[24]

Nevertheless, this is not the end of the line for Duke or radical populism. One Duke clone, Shawn Slater, is already active in Colorado. Slater, the Colorado leader of the Knights of the Ku Klux Klan, already has a high level of name recognition throughout the state and hopes to run for statewide office in the near future. Slater is well-spoken and clean-cut in the Duke mold, and in order to appeal to lower-middle- and, perhaps, even middle-class voters does not make use of racial slurs in his speeches. He endeavors to present a positive image, asserting that he is for Christian whites rather than against Jews and blacks. Thomas Robb, the national leader of the Knights, whose headquarters is in Arkansas, describes Slater as "just the kind of bright, stable young man we think can articulate our viewpoint and reach a mass of people."[25]

The conditions for Duke and other radical populist anti-Semites are now and will continue to be ripe in the United States for the forseeable future. This is because of three factors: economics, political sociology, and political structure.

First, throughout the world, radical populists usually become prominent during economic hard times. When large numbers of blue-collar workers cannot adequately clothe their families and white-collar workers cannot find jobs commensurate with their level of training and ambition, they are happy to listen to radical solutions to their problems. Economic dislocation is already providing the impetus for attacks on foreigners, including Jews, in Western Europe.

Can anyone doubt that America is in for a long period of hard times? Whatever Clinton does, the world has entered a period of political and economic transformation which, among other things, includes an erosion of the economic power and prosperity of the United States. America's competitive composition has already declined and continues to deteriorate. Among the major losers have been blue-collar workers and less skilled white-collar employees. As America's wealth declines, the opportunities for political entrepreneurs of all sorts will increase, and there is no doubt that radical Populists will be among them.

Second, the political sociology of American politics has changed.

At one time, the forces of radical populism had three major targets—Catholics, blacks, and Jews. In the nineteenth and early twentieth centuries, radical Populist forces were sometimes more concerned with anti-Catholicism—or opposition to "Papists" as they called it—than anti-Semitism. And, of course, hatred of blacks overshadowed everything else.

Today, despite the arrival of new immigrants from Asia and Latin America, Jews are much more exposed. Anti-Catholicism has disappeared from the ideology of right-wing populism, which now emphasizes the superiority of white Christians as a group, precisely in order not to lose the support of Catholics. Radical Populists draw support from among Catholics (Catholics are now actively recruited for membership in the Klan), and, indeed, working-class Catholics gave their votes to David Duke in large numbers. Moreover, though racism is still the lead card in the radical Populist deck, in the ideology of contemporary radical populism, presumably as a product of their alliance in the civil rights movement, Jews and blacks are now inseparably linked rather than discrete objects of hatred.

For example, organizations such as the Ku Klux Klan, David Duke's National Association for the Advancement of White People (NAAWP), and the Christian Identity movement, a congeries of sometimes-violent radical populist groups organized around a set of quasi-religious doctrines, agree that Jews are the motive power or evil force behind blacks. According to the Anti-Defamation League, a typical recruit to one of these groups is usually drawn by hatred of blacks. He or she soon learns, however, that "behind the blacks lurk the Jews," who are actually "the more dangerous enemy." The following is an excerpt from a recorded telephone message by the Invisible Empire, one of the major Klan groups, in Pensacola, Florida, reported by the ADL, which illustrates the point.

Listen Whitey, the Jews have taken over America and you are too damn ignorant to see it. They are pouring out your tax money to the niggers and you are too damn brainwashed to know it. The Jews are pouring out pro-nigger, pro-Jew poison over the Jew-owned TV and you are so damn stupid that you swallow it. The Christ-killing Jew has seized the reins of government and passed laws to imprison you if you raise your hand against the nigger, and you don't have the brains to do a damn thing about it . . . He has filled your schools with stinkin niggers and you have taken it lying down. You are now reaping your reward . . . you no longer have what it takes to hunt down the white-hating instigators who are destroying you.[26]

These groups and their ideologies were only recently assumed to be curiosities on the lunatic fringe of American politics. Yet, it is hard to completely dismiss them when one of their number has shown how easy it is, during a period of even comparatively mild economic recession, to move from the lunatic fringe to the mainstream of American electoral politics.

The ease with which this transition was accomplished points to a third reason why conditions in America are favorable to radical populism. This is the set of changes that has taken place in recent years in America's political structure to make the electoral process more open and permeable, especially to forces that can muster reasonably large numbers of enthusiastic supporters. These changes include the virtually complete demise of partisan loyalty and the established party organizations that once served as political gatekeepers in the United States as well as the permeability of party nominating processes. This makes it possible for well-organized outsiders to pose electoral challenges to established forces in both primary and general elections. The only barrier to entering American electoral politics today is money. In the absence of established party organizations, any group that can raise enough money can participate in the electoral process. And, in recent years, of course, the perfection of direct mail fund-raising methods have allowed groups on the Populist right such as Duke's NAAWP to accumulate large amounts of money from small contributions.[27]

Moreover, the rules governing public funding of presidential campaigns are made to order for small, well-organized groups of fanatics who can invest enormous time in fund-raising. During the 1980s, Lyndon LaRouche's campaigns became eligible to receive nearly $1 million in federal matching funds. By December 1991, the New Alliance Party, a small group of fanatics founded and led by the reclusive left-wing anti-Semite, Fred Newman, was already eligible for more than $600,000 in federal matching funds. Most of the money raised by New Alliance fund-raisers was obtained in tiny donations on street corners and shopping mall tables, or through the party's numerous small enterprises, from "contributors" who had little or no idea to what they were contributing.[28] For the past half-century, liberal reformers have worked to create a more open political process that would allow full play for the activities of liberal social protest groups without the interference of party "bosses" or restrictive electoral laws. They have succeeded. But this same openness also permits full play for the activities of social protest groups on the political right.

And then, of course, there is the mass media. The media like to present themselves as the new political gatekeepers, having displaced party organizations in that capacity. The official media position is that the public is best served when the views of all groups and individuals are fully aired. Presumably, then, in the ensuing competition among various ideas and positions, poor ideas will be exposed and will wither while good ideas will flourish. Perhaps over the long term this is true. In the short run, however, the media usually succumb to what might be called the "National Enquirer effect." They are inexorably drawn to politicians and groups who present outlandish, radical, and unusual ideas because these are thought to attract viewer interest and higher ratings.

The media are drawn to the radical populists because they are titillating. They say things that should not be said. There is a hint of danger, of suppressed violence, of menace that the media find irresistible. An articulate, well-groomed radical populist is a media dream come true—the forbidden fruit in an attractive package. This is why David Duke, for most of his life a loser and lunatic—LSU's campus Nazi—could, after transforming his image to meet media requirements, find himself in front of a national television audience on "Meet the Press," "Nightline," and the other interview programs. And were the ideas presented by Ted Koppel and his distinguished brethren able to slay Duke's in the competition of the free marketplace where the best ideas win? Of course not. How pale and dull Koppel's liberal clichés sounded in the face of Duke's self-assured presentation of his oh-so-interesting new ideas.

Given the absence of other barriers to entry in American electoral politics, and given the media's fascination with them, the radical populists will be sure to have at least a public relations field day in the years to come. Of course, Duke and the other radical populists represent a real political threat only if times are very hard. Only then will the upper-middle classes and the business community overcome their distaste for rabble-rousers.

If Clinton and the Democrats are able to deal forcefully and effectively with America's long-term economic problems, the threat from the far—and near—right will certainly recede as it did during the late 1930s. If, however, times are hard—as they may well be for America in the coming decades—it is not much of a leap to imagine that some respectable conservative groups would be willing, as they were during the early 1930s, to swallow their distaste and support forces that propose a "real" alternative to the contemporary liberal regime. As Buchanan has ably demonstrated, one wing of the Republican party is already quite comfortable with Duke's ideas, if not with Duke.

If this happened, the unthinkable would quickly become thinkable. An alliance of radical populists and respectable conservatives would almost inevitably make vigorous use of anti-Semitic themes to attack the liberal Democratic regime, and the Jews would find themselves locked in the fatal embrace of yet another state.

Some believe that the defeat of Duke in 1991 coupled with Buchanan's defeat in the Republican primaries and the Democrats' return to power in 1992 indicates that the crisis has passed and that anti-Semitism will again wane. As one Jewish political activist put it after the 1992 election, "This is very different from how we started two years ago with David Duke, Patrick Buchanan and talk of 'America First.' We're ending with a very comfortable feeling . . . "[29]

What is notable, however, about Buchanan, Duke, and America First is not that they were defeated but that they became so prominent in the first place. Observing the resolution of the Missouri crisis in 1820, Thomas Jefferson noted that the Missouri Compromise was significant not because it was achieved but, rather, because it *had* to be achieved. Though the surface tranquility of American politics may be restored, we should know, as Jefferson knew in 1820, that we have heard a fire bell in the night.

Prior to the 1991 Louisiana gubernatorial election, New Orleans Rabbi Edward Cohn scheduled a postelection assembly for the students of his religious school. Cohn feared that he might have to explain to his young students what a Duke victory would mean for them.[30] Fortunately, even though a substantial majority of the white electorate supported Duke, the explanation was not needed. Perhaps next time.

Notes

Chapter One

1. Seymour Martin Lipset, "A Unique People in an Exceptional Country," in S. M. Lipset, ed., *American Pluralism and the Jewish Community* (New Brunswick, N.J.: Transaction Publishers, 1990), 3–30.

2. Ze'ev Chafets, *Members of the Tribe* (New York: Bantam, 1988), chap. 2. In the 1992 national elections, thirty-three Jews, including twenty-eight Democrats and five Republicans, were elected to the House of Representatives. One, Willis Gradison (R.-Ohio), subsequently resigned to take a job in private industry. Significantly, too, four of the seven subcommittee chairmen of the House Foreign Affairs Committee, which deals with foreign aid legislation, are Jews.

3. See Samuel Walker, *In Defense of American Interests: A History of the ACLU* (New York: Oxford, 1990), 219–226.

4. For a discussion of what American Jews might have done, see Rafael Medoff, *The Deafening Silence* (New York: Shapolsky, 1987), Chaps. 8–10. See also Yehuda Bauer, *American Jewry and the Holocaust* (Detroit: Wayne State University Press, 1981); and David Wyman, *The Abandonment of the Jews* (New York: Pantheon, 1984). The British case, which was comparable in a number of respects, is discussed in Bernard Wasserstein, *Britain and the Jews of Europe* (Oxford: Oxford University Press, 1988).

5. Arthur Hertzberg, *The Jews in America* (New York: Simon and Schuster, 1989), 345–346.

6. See Marcia Graham Synott, *The Half-Opened Door: Discrimination and Admissions at Harvard, Yale and Princeton, 1900–1970* (Westport, Conn.: Greenwood Press, 1979). Also Dan Orren, *Joining the Club: A History of Jews and Yale* (New Haven: Yale University Press, 1985). Data on the rise and fall of Jewish quotas are presented in Marcia Graham Synott, "Anti-Semitism and American Universities: Did Quotas Follow the Jews?" in David Gerber, ed., *Anti-Semitism in American History* (Urbana: University of Illinois Press, 1986), 233–274.

7. See Larry Cohler, "Bush Bids for Jewish Votes," *Washington Jewish Week*, August 13, 1992, 5.

8. The National Council of Churches of Christ, messages of September 14 and November 14–15, 1990. The latter is excerpted in Micah L. Sifry and Christopher Cerf, *The Gulf War Reader* (New York: Random House, 1991).

9. National Council of Churches of Christ, message of December 30, 1991.

10. For a useful summary of Buchanan's columns and televised comments, see James M. Perry, "Buchanan, Fighting Bush, Is Himself Attacked for His Views about Jews, Israel and the Nazis," *Wall Street Journal*, February 13, 1992, A20. Buchanan's views are discussed at some length in William Buckley, Jr., "In Search of Anti-Semitism," *National Review* 42, no. 24, December 30, 1991, 31–40. Buckley's article and responses to it are also published in William F Buckley, *In Search of Anti-Semitism* (New York: Continuum, 1992).

11. Perry, "Buchanan, Fighting Bush." Buchanan's remarks in Georgia are reported in R. W. Apple, Jr., "Tsongas Appears to Gain in States with Voting Today," *New York Times*, March 3, 1992, A18.

12. Larry Yudelson, "Pat Buchanan, Out of the Closet?" *Washington Jewish Week*, March 12, 1992, 8.

13. Earl Raab, "What Do We Really Know about Anti-Semitism and What Do We Want to Know" (New York: American Jewish Committee, 1989). Also Jerome A. Chanes, "Is Anti-Semitism in America on the Rise or on the Decline?" *Jewish Post and Opinion*, February 14, 1990. The most recent survey data, reported by the Anti-Defamation League in November, 1992, appear to show a slight increase in the percentage of respondents who feel that Jews have too much power in the United States (31% agree with this proposition). However, there seems to have been some decline over the past several years in the percentage of respondents who feel that Jews run the media or are irritating and too clannish. Blacks continue to be much more likely than whites to manifest anti-Semitic attitudes. The data are reviewed in Debra Nussbaum Cohen, "ADL Surveys Views of Jews," *Washington Jewish Week*, November 19, 1992, 3.

14. Joseph A. Schumpeter, *Capitalism, Socialism and Democracy* (New York: Harper & Row, 1975), 263.

15. The classic argument for American exceptionalism is Louis Hartz, *The Liberal Tradition in America* (New York: Harcourt, Brace, 1955). The claim that American exceptionalism has virtually excluded anti-Semitism is made frequently. See e.g., Lipset, "A Unique People." The most optimistic statement of this view is given by Charles E. Silberman, *A Certain People* (New York: Summit Books, 1985).

16. Some argue that contemporary liberals have also "betrayed" the Jews. See Ruth Wisse, "The Unchosen," *New Republic*, June 15, 1992, 15–19.

17. For a recent overview of theories seeking to explain the origins of anti-Jewish sentiment, see Herbert Hirsch and Jack Spiro, eds., *Persistent Prejudice: Perspectives on Anti-Semitism* (Fairfax, Va.: George Mason University Press, 1988). An older but still valuable treatment is Isacque Graeber and Steuart Britt eds., *Jews in a Gentile World: The Problem of Anti-Semitism* (New York: Macmillan, 1942). See also Gavin I. Langmuir, *Toward a Definition of Anti-Semitism* (Berkeley: University of California Press, 1990); Dennis Prager and Joseph Telushkin, *Why the Jews?* (New York: Simon and Schuster, 1983); Shmuel Almog, ed., *Anti-Semitism through the Ages* (Oxford: Pergamon

Press, 1988); and Robert Wistrich, *Between Redemption and Perdition* (London: Routledge, 1990).

18. For a review of recent poll findings, see Tamar Lewin, "Study Points to Increase in Tolerance of Ethnicity," *New York Times*, January 8, 1992, A12.

19. Ibid.

20. The columnist, of course, is Joseph Sobran. See Buckley, "In Search," 29.

21. Hannah Arendt, *The Origins of Totalitarianism*, rev. ed. (New York: Harcourt, 1967).

22. Paul Johnson, *A History of the Jews* (New York: Harper, 1987), 207–208. Also Selma Stern, *The Court Jew* (New Brunswick, N.J.: Transaction Press, 1985), 208–209.

23. David Biale, *Power and Powerlessness in Jewish History* (New York: Schocken, 1987), 65.

24. Ibid., 67.

25. Ibid., 79.

26. Ibid.

27. Johnson, *A History*, 170.

28. Biale, *Power*, 70–71.

29. Discussed in ibid., 105.

30. Arendt, *Totalitarianism*, 24–25.

31. Biale, *Power*, 103–104.

32. John A. Crow, *Spain: The Root and the Flower*, 3d rev. ed. (Berkeley: University of California Press, 1985), 110.

33. Ibid., chap. 4.

34. Ibid., 112.

35. Edward Peters, *Inquisition* (Berkeley: University of California Press, 1989), chap. 3.

36. Cecil Roth, *The Spanish Inquisition* (New York: Norton, 1964), chap. 1.

37. On Halevi, see Henry Kammen, *Inquisition and Society in Spain in the Sixteenth and Seventeenth Centuries* (Bloomington: Indiana University Press, 1985). Also Roth, *The Spanish Inquisition*, 26.

38. Norman Stillman, *The Jews of Arab Lands* (Philadelphia: Jewish Publication Society, 1979), 55.

39. Ibid., 57–58.

40. Ibid., 51.

41. Ibid., 43.

42. Bernard Lewis, *The Jews of Islam* (Princeton: Princeton University Press, 1984), 134.

43. Biale, *Power*, 70.

44. Lewis, *Jews*, 22–23.

45. Johnson, *A History*, 281–282.

46. See Stern, *The Court Jew*.

47. Johnson, *A History*, 254.

48. Ibid.

49. Ibid., 255–257. Also Stern, *The Court Jew*, chaps. 1–3.

50. See Richard Davis, *The English Rothschilds* (Chapel Hill: University of North Carolina Press, 1983). Also S. D. Chapman, *The Foundation of the English Rothschilds* (London: Macmillan, 1977).

51. Fritz Stern, *Gold and Iron: Bismarck, Bleichroeder and the Building of the German Empire* (New York: Knopf, 1977).

52. See Howard M. Sachar, *The Course of Modern Jewish History*, rev. ed. (New York: Vintage, 1990), chap. 5.

53. Cecil Roth, *The History of the Jews of Italy* (Philadelphia: Jewish Publication Society, 1946), chaps. 9 and 10.

54. Sachar, *The Course*, 115–116.

55. Michael Marrus, *The Politics of Assimilation: A Study of the French Jewish Community at the Time of the Dreyfuss Affair* (Oxford: Clarendon Press, 1971), esp. chaps. 3 and 6.

56. See Robert F. Byrnes, *Anti-Semitism in Modern France, Volume I* (New Brunswick, N.J.: Rutgers University Press, 1950), chaps. 1 and 2. Also Zeev. Sternhell, "Roots of Popular Anti-Semitism in the Third Republic," in Frances Malino and Bernard Wasserstein, eds., *The Jews in Modern France* (Hanover, N.H.: University Press of New England, 1985), 103–134.

57. See Harold Pollins, *Economic History of the Jews in England* (Rutherford, N.J.: Fairleigh-Dickinson University Press, 1982), esp. chap. 6. Also Geoffrey Alderman, *The Jewish Community in British Politics* (Oxford; Clarendon Press, 1983).

58. Colin Holmes, *Anti-Semitism in British Society 1876–1939* (New York: Holmes and Meier, 1979), chap. 5.

59. On Disraeli's role in British politics, see R. J. White, *The Conservative Tradition* (London: Black, 1950). Also E. Feuchtwanger, *Disraeli, Democracy and the Tory Party: Conservative Leadership after the Second Reform Bill* (Oxford: Clarendon Press, 1968); M. Pinto-Duschinsky, *The Political Thought of Lord Salisbury* (London: Constable, 1967): and R. T. MacKenzie, *British Political Parties*, 2d ed. (New York, St. Martins Press, 1963).

60. J. A. Hobson, *Imperialism: A Study*, 3d ed. (London: Allen and Unwin, 1938), 56–57.

61. Holmes, *Anti-Semitism in British Society*, 11–12.

62. Quoted in James Curran and Jean Seaton, *Power without Responsibility: The Press and Broadcasting in Britain*, 3d ed. (London: Routledge, 1988), 44.

63. Graham Storey, *Reuters' Century* (London: Max Parrish, 1951), chaps. 9 and 10.

64. Peter Pulzer, *The Rise of Political Anti-Semitism in Germany and Austria*, rev. ed. (Cambridge, Mass.: Harvard University Press, 1988), 13.

65. See W. E. Mosse, *Jews in the German Economy* (Oxford: Clarendon Press, 1987), chap. 8. Also Donald Niewyk, *The Jews in Weimar Germany* (Baton Rouge: Louisiana State University Press, 1980), chap. 2.

66. Niewyk, *The Jews*, chap. 2.

67. Ibid., chap. 4.

68. Fritz K. Ringer, *The Decline of the German Mandarins: The German Academic Community, 1890–1933* (Cambridge, Mass.: Harvard University Press, 1969), esp. chaps. 3 and 4.

69. Niewyk, *The Jews,* chap. 2.

70. Ibid.

71. Ezra Mendelsohn, *The Jews of East Central Europe between the World Wars* (Bloomington: Indiana University Press, 1983), 85–102.

72. Benjamin Pinkus, *The Jews of the Soviet Union* (Cambridge: Cambridge University Press, 1988), chap. 1. Also Sachar, *The Course,* 332–358.

73. Louis Rapoport, *Stalin's War against the Jews* (New York: Free Press, 1990), chaps. 3 and 4.

74. Ibid., 61–97.

75. On Smolar, see Peter Meyer et al., *The Jews in the Soviet Satellites* (Syracuse: Syracuse University Press, 1953), chap. 11.

76. Ibid.

77. For an excellent discussion of the Hungarian case, see Peter Vardy, "The Unfinished Past—Jewish Realities in Postwar Hungary," in Randolph Braham, ed., *The Tragedy of Hungarian Jewry* (New York: Columbia University Press, 1986), 133–190.

78. Cecil Roth, *A History of the Jews in England* (Oxford: Clarendon Press, 1941), chaps. 3 and 4.

79. Mendelsohn, *The Jews of East Central Europe,* chap. 2. Also, Lucy S. Dawidowicz, *The War against the Jews* (New York: Holt, 1975), 379–382.

80. Johnson, *A History,* 259. Also Hillel Levine, *Economic Origins of Anti-Semitism: Poland and Its Jews in the Early Modern Period* (New Haven: Yale University Press, 1991).

81. Meir Michaelis, *Mussolini and the Jews* (Oxford: Clarendon Press, 1978), chap. 2.

82. For an example, see Alexander Stille, *Benevolence and Betrayal* (New York: Summit, 1991), chap. 1.

83. Ibid., 24.

84. See Adrian Lyttelton, *The Seizure of Power: Fascism in Italy 1919–1929,* 2d ed. (Princeton: Princeton University Press, 1987), 50.

85. See Michaelis, *Mussolini,* chaps. 9–11. Also Liliana Picciotto, "The Jews during the German Occupation and the Italian Social Republic," in Ivo Herzer, ed., *The Italian Refuge* (Washington, D.C.: Catholic University Press, 1989), 109–140. Also Paul Bookfinder, "Italy in the Overall Context of the Holocaust," in Herzer, ed., *The Italian Refuge,* 95–108; Dawidowicz, *The War,* 368–371; and Jonathan Steinberg, *All or Nothing: The Axis and the Holocaust 1941–43* (London: Routledge, 1990).

86. Byrnes, *Anti-Semitism,* chap. 7.

87. Sternhell, "Roots," 111.

88. Ibid., 108.

89. Byrnes, *Anti-Semitism,* 298–304.

90. Sternhell, "Roots," 115–117.

91. On the Dreyfus case, see Arendt, *Origins*, chap. 4. Also Albert Lindeman, *The Jew Accused* (Cambridge: Cambridge University Press, 1991); and Jean-Denis Bredin, *The Affair: The Case of Alfred Dreyfus* (New York: Braziller, 1986).

92. See Paula Hyman, *From Dreyfuss to Vichy* (New York: Columbia University Press, 1979), 16–17. Also William Cohen and Irwin Wall, "French Communism and the Jews," in Malino and Wasserstein, eds., *The Jews,* 81–102.

93. See Michael Marrus and Robert Paxton, *Vichy France and the Jews* (New York: Basic Books, 1981).

94. Pulzer, *The Rise,* 316–317.

95. Ibid., 315–316.

96. Ibid., 317–318.

97. Daniel Lerner et al., "The Nazi Elite," in Harold Lasswell and Daniel Lerner, eds., *World Revolutionary Elites* (Cambridge, Mass.: MIT Press, 1966), chap. 5.

98. See Kammen, *Inquisition and Society.* Also Roth, *The Spanish Inquisition;* and Peters, *Inquisition,* chap. 3.

99. Roth, *The Spanish Inquisition,* chap. 2.

100. Peters, *Inquisition,* 84.

101. Crow, *Spain,* 150–151.

102. Roth, *The Spanish Inquisition,* chap. 3.

103. Karl A. Schleunes, "Retracing the Twisted Road: Nazi Policies toward German Jews," in Francois Furet, ed., *Nazi Germany and the Genocide of the Jews* (New York: Schocken, 1989), 54–70. The best statement of the "intentionalist" view is Dawidowicz, *The War.* Also see the discussion in Michael Marris, *The Holocaust in History* (New York: Meridian, 1987), chap. 3.

104. Karl Schleunes, *The Twisted Road to Auschwitz 1933–39* (Urbana: University of Illinois Press, 1970), chap. 7.

105. Raul Hilberg, *The Destruction of the European Jews* (New York: Holmes and Meier), chap. 2. Also Martin Gilbert, *The Holocaust* (New York: Henry Holt, 1985), chaps. 3–5.

106. Johnson, *A History,* 484–489. Also Hilberg, *The Destruction,* chap. 2.

107. Richard Breitman, *The Architect of Genocide: Himmler and the Final Solution* (New York: Knopf, 1991).

108. Hannah Arendt, *Eichmann in Jerusalem* (New York: Viking, 1963).

109. Raul Hilberg, "The Bureaucracy of Annihilation," in Furet, ed., *Nazi Germany,* 119–133.

110. Hilberg, *Destruction,* 30–36.

111. Hilberg, "Bureaucracy," 120–130.

112. Detlev J. K. Paukert, *Inside Nazi Germany, Conformity, Opposition and Racism in Everyday Life* (New Haven: Yale University Press, 1987), 220–221. Also Michael Geyer, "The Nazi State reconsidered," in Richard Bessel, ed., *Life in the Third Reich* (New York: Oxford, 1987), 57–68: and Robert Gal-

lately, *The Gestapo and German Society: Enforcing Racial Policy* (Oxford: Clarendon Press, 1990).

113. Johnson, *A History*, 487.

114. Hilberg, "Bureaucracy," 127–129.

115. Rapoport, *Stalin's War against the Jews*, 54. See also Yakov Rapoport, *The Doctor's Plot of 1953* (Cambridge, Mass.: Harvard University Press, 1991); and Benjamin Pinkus, *The Soviet Government and the Jews 1948–67* (Cambridge: Cambridge University Press, 1984).

116. Pinkus, *Jews*, 145–209.

117. Ibid., 140–142.

118. Meyer, *Jews*, 250.

119. Ibid., chaps. 11 and 12.

120. Ibid., 483–485.

121. Pulzer, *Rise*, chaps. 10 and 18–20.

122. See Pinkus, *Jews*, chap. 1; and Sachar, *The Course*, chaps. 12–14.

123. Government-sponsored pogroms in Russia are discussed in John D. Klier and Shlomo Lambroza, eds., *Pogroms: Anti-Jewish Violence in Modern Russian History* (Cambridge: Cambridge University Press, 1992).

Chapter Two

1. Discussed in Stephen Birmingham, *Our Crowd: The Great Jewish Families of New York* (New York: Harper, 1967).

2. Richard Franklin Bensel, *Yankee Leviathan: The Origins of Central State Authority in America 1859–1877* (New York: Cambridge University Press, 1990), 248–249.

3. Bensel, *Yankee Leviathan*, 252–253. Also Ellis Paxson Oberholtzer, *Jay Cooke: Financier of the Civil War* (Philadelphia: Jacobs, 1907).

4. For an excellent discussion, see Barry E. Supple, "A Business Elite: German-Jewish Financiers in Nineteenth-Century New York," *Business History Review* 31, no. 2 (Summer 1957): 143–178.

5. Bensel, *Yankee Leviathan*, chap. 5. Also, Irwin Unger, *The Greenback ERA: A Social and Political History of American Finance 1865–1879* (Princeton: Princeton University Press, 1964); and Robert Sharkey, *Money, Class and Party: An Economic History of Civil War and Reconstruction* (Baltimore: Johns Hopkins University Press, 1959).

6. Margaret G. Myers, *The New York Money Market: Volume I, Origins and Development* (New York: Columbia University Press, 1931), 353–355.

7. Supple, "Business Elite," 155.

8. Oberholtzer, *Jay Cooke*, vol. 2, chap. 16.

9. Birmingham, *Our Crowd*, 117–119.

10. Supple, "Business Elite," 156; Birmingham, *Our Crowd*, 159–160.

11. Eric Foner, *Reconstruction: America's Unfinished Revolution 1863–1877* (New York: Harper, 1988), chaps. 6–9.

12. Bensel, *Yankee Leviathan*, 395.

13. See Foner, *Reconstruction*, chap. 8.

14. B. U. Ratchford, *American State Debts* (Durham, N.C.: Duke University Press, 1941), chaps. 7 and 8. Also Michael Perman, *The Road to Redemption: Southern Politics, 1869–1879* (Chapel Hill: University of North Carolina Press, 1984).

15. Reginald McGrane, *Foreign Bondholders and American State Debts* (New York: Macmillan, 1935).

16. See Dolores Greenberg, *Financiers and Railroads* (Newark, N.J.: University of Delaware Press, 1980), 131. Also McGrane, *Foreign Bondholders,* 287–289.

17. William Scott, *The Repudiation of State Debts* (New York: Crowell, 1893). Also Henry Clews, *Twenty-Eight Years in Wall Street* (New York: Irving, 1888.

18. See Richard Nelson Current, *Those Terrible Carpetbaggers: A Reinterpretation* (New York: Oxford, 1988), 145.

19. The Moses family was quite prominent in South Carolina. Several of its members had distinguished themselves during the revolutionary war. See Barrett A. Elzas, *The Jews of South Carolina* (Philadelphia: Lippincott, 1905).

20. See Francis B. Simkins and Robert H. Woody, *South Carolina during Reconstruction* (Chapel Hill: University of North Carolina Press, 1932).

21. Current, *Carpetbaggers,* 224.

22. John S. Reynolds, *Reconstruction in South Carolina* (Columbia, S.C.: State Co., 1905), chap. 6. Also Walter Allen, *Governor Chamberlain's Administration in South Carolina* (New York: Putnam's, 1888), chap. 12.

23. Current, *Carpetbaggers,* 329.

24. Ibid., 222–223. After 1876 and the termination of Radical Reconstruction in South Carolina, a number of the most prominent black politicians were jailed or exiled from the state. See Reynolds, *Reconstruction in South Carolina,* chap. 11.

25. Greenberg, *Financiers and Railroads,* chap. 2.

26. Supple, "Business Elite," 171.

27. Birmingham, *Our Crowd,* 189–191.

28. Ibid., chap. 14.

29. See Ron Chernow, *The House of Morgan: An American Banking Dynasty and the Rise of Modern Finance* (New York: Atlantic Monthly Press, 1990), chap. 5. See also Supple, "Business Elite," 170–171.

30. Birmingham, *Our Crowd,* 257–258.

31. Ibid., chap. 30.

32. Ibid., 123.

33. McGrane, *Foreign Bondholders,* 310–311. Also Clews, *Twenty-Eight Years,* 274–279; and Scott, *Repudiation,* 102–107.

34. Current, *Carpetbaggers,* 363–364.

35. Ibid., 366.

36. Richard Hofstadter, *The Age of Reform* (New York: Knopf, 1955), 70–82.

37. See, e.g., Frederick Cople Jaher, *Doubters and Dissenters* (New York:

Free Press, 1964), 130–140. Also Walter Nugent, *The Tolerant Populists* (Chicago: University of Chicago Press, 1963).

38. William H. Harvey, *Coin's Financial School* (Chicago: Coin Publishing Co., 1894).

39. William H. Harvey, *A Tale of Two Nations* (Chicago: Coin Publishing Co., 1894).

40. Ignatius Donnelly, *Caesar's Column* (Cambridge, Mass.: Harvard University Press, 1960 [1889]).

41. See Michael N. Dobkowski, *The Tarnished Dream: The Basis of American Anti-Semitism* (Westport, Conn.: Greenwood, 1979), 181–182.

42. Ibid., 177.

43. Quoted in ibid.

44. Hofstadter, *Age of Reform*, 80.

45. Barbara Solomon, *Ancestors and Immigrants: A Changing New England Tradition*, rev. ed. (Boston: Northeastern University Press, 1989), 39.

46. Ernest Samuels, ed., *The Education of Henry Adams* (Boston: Houghton Mifflin, 1973), 238.

47. Quoted in Louise Mayo, *The Ambivalent Image: Nineteenth Century America's Perception of the Jew* (Rutherford, N.J.: Farleigh-Dickinson University Press, 1988), 58.

48. Dobkowski, *Tarnished Dream*, 86.

49. Brooks Adams, *The Law of Civilization and Decay* (New York: Macmillan, 1896).

50. Solomon, *Ancestors and Immigrants*, chaps. 6 and 7. Also John Higham, *Strangers in the Land: Patterns of American Nativism 1860–1925*, 2nd ed. (New Brunswick, N.J.: Rutgers University Press, 1988), 102–105.

51. Quoted in Solomon, *Ancestors and Immigrants*, 111.

52. Discussed in E. Digby Baltzell, *The Protestant Establishment: Aristocracy and Caste in America* (New Haven: Yale University Press, 1987), 106.

53. Ibid., 107.

54. See Hofstadter, *The Age of Reform*, 82–83.

55. Dobkowski, *Tarnished Dream*, 122.

56. Baltzell, *Protestant Establishment*, 113–128.

57. See John Higham, *Send These to Me: Immigrants in Urban America*, rev. ed. (Baltimore: Johns Hopkins University Press, 1984), 126–129. Also Baltzell, *Protestant Establishment*, 116–121.

58. Higham, *Send These*, 129; Baltzell, *Protestant Establishment*, 135–142.

59. Higham, *Send These*, 139.

60. Marcia Graham Synott, *The Half-Opened Door: Discrimination and Admissions at Harvard, Yale and Princeton 1900–1970* (Westport, Conn.: Greenwood, 1979). Also Marcia Graham Synott, "Anti-Semitism and American Universities: Did Quotas Follow the Jews?" in David Gerber, ed., *Anti-Semitism in American History* (Urbana: University of Illinois Press, 1986), 233–271.

61. Synott, "Quotas," 240.

62. See Morton Rosenstock, *Louis Marshall, Defender of Jewish Rights* (Detroit: Wayne State University Press, 1965). Also Solomon, *Ancestors and Immigrants,* 204–205.

63. Higham, *Send These,* 139.

64. Louis Hartz, *The Liberal Tradition in America.* (Cambridge, Mass.: Harvard University Press, 1955).

65. See Higham, *Strangers,* chap. 6; and Baltzell, *Protestant Establishment,* chap. 4.

66. Baltzell, *Protestant Establishment,* 104.

67. Higham, *Strangers,* 155–157; and Baltzell, *Protestant Establishment,* 96–98.

68. Baltzell, *Protestant Establishment,* 114–116.

69. Steven Hertzberg, *Strangers within the Gate City: The Jews of Atlanta 1845–1915* (Philadelphia: Jewish Publication Society, 1978); and Leonard Dinnerstein, *The Leo Frank Case* (New York: Columbia University Press, 1968).

70. See Albert S. Lindemann, *The Jew Accused* (Cambridge: Cambridge University Press, 1991), 263. Also Dinnerstein, *Leo Frank,* chap. 1.

71. Hertzberg, *Strangers,* 162–163.

72. Ibid., 163.

73. Ibid.

74. Lindemann, *Jew Accused,* 243–244. Also Nathaniel Weyl, *The Jew in American Politics* (New Rochelle, N.Y.: Arlington House, 1968), 88–89.

75. Hertzberg, *Strangers,* 208.

76. Lindemann, *Jew Accused,* 264.

77. Hertzberg, *Strangers,* 213–214.

78. Martin Shefter, "Party, Bureaucracy and Political Change in the United States," in Joseph Cooper and Louis Maisel, eds., *Political Parties: Development and Decay* (Beverly Hills, Calif.: Sage, 1978), 230–231.

79. Ibid., 232–234.

80. Baltzell, *Protestant Establishment,* 189–192.

81. Arthur S. Link, *Wilson: The New Freedom* (Princeton: Princeton University Press, 1956), esp. chap. 13.

82. See Higham, *Strangers,* chap 8.

83. See John D. Buenker, *Urban Liberalism and Progressive Reform* (New York: Scribners, 1973), esp. 98 and 184.

84. Stanley Coben, *A. Mitchell Palmer* (New York: Columbia University Press, 1963), chaps. 11 and 12.

85. Paul Johnson, *A History of the Jews.* (New York: Harper, 1987), 459.

86. Higham, *Strangers,* 232–233; Cohen, *Palmer,* 239–245.

87. Buenker, *Urban Liberalism,* chap. 6.

Chapter Three

1. Naomi Cohen, *Not Free to Desist: The American Jewish Committee, 1906–1966* (Philadelphia: Jewish Publication Society, 1972).

2. Dan Oren, *Joining the Club: A History of Jews and Yale* (New Haven: Yale University Press, 1985), 177–178.

3. For an excellent history of black-Jewish relations, see Jonathan Kaufman, *Broken Alliance: The Turbulent Times between Blacks and Jews in America* (New York: Mentor, 1988).

4. See Jill Donnie Snyder and Eric K. Goodman, *Friend of the Court* (New York: Anti-Defamation League, 1983), chap. 1.

5. Samuel Walker, *In Defense of American Liberties: A History of the ACLU* (New York: Oxford, 1990), 220.

6. Ibid.

7. Bill Stanton, *Klanwatch: Bringing the Ku Klux Klan to Justice* (New York: Grove Weidenfeld, 1991).

8. Richard Alba and Gwen Moore, "Ethnicity in the American Elite," *American Sociological Review* 147, no. 3 (June 1982): 373–383.

9. Steven Fraser, *Labor Will Rule; Sidney Hillman and the Rise of American Labor* (New York: Free Press, 1991).

10. Geoffrey C. Ward, *A First-Class Temperament: The Emergence of Franklin Roosevelt* (New York: Harper, 1989), 254.

11. See Samuel Hand, *Counsel and Advise: A Political Biography of Samuel I. Rosenman* (New York: Garland, 1979).

12. See Michael Parrish, *Felix Frankfurter and His Times* (New York: Free Press, 1982). Also Joseph Lash, *Dealers and Dreamers* (New York: Doubleday, 1988), chaps. 13–17.

13. Jerold Auerbach, *Unequal Justice: Lawyers and Social Change in Modern America* (New York: Oxford, 1976), chap. 6.

14. See Benjamin Ginsberg and Martin Shefter, *Politics by Other Means: The Declining Importance of Elections in American Politics* (New York: Basic Books, 1991), 80–85.

15. Fraser, *Labor*, chaps. 17 and 18.

16. Martin Shefter, "Party, Bureaucracy and Political Change in the United States," in Joseph Cooper and Louis Maisel, eds., *Political Parties: Development and Decay* (Beverly Hills, Calif.: Sage, 1978), 240–241.

17. Ibid., 242.

18. Mark Lincoln Chadwin, *The Hawks of World War II* (Chapel Hill: University of North Carolina Press, 1968), chaps. 3 and 4.

19. Ibid., chaps. 7–9.

20. Liva Baker, *Felix Frankfurter* (New York: Coward-McCann, 1969), 240–241.

21. Arnold Forster, *Square One; A Memoir* (New York: Donald Fine, 1988), chap. 1.

22. Ibid., 57–59.

23. Cohen, *Not Free*.

24. Ibid.

25. Hollywood's role is discussed in Clayton R. Koppes and Gregory D. Black, *Hollywood Goes to War: How Politics, Profits and Propaganda Shaped*

World War II Movies (Berkeley: University of California Press, 1987), chaps. 1–3.

26. Myron Scholnick, *The New Deal and Anti-Semitism in America* (New York: Garland, 1990), 66.

27. "Jews in America," *Fortune* (February 1936).

28. Scholnick, *New Deal,* 82. Also Donald S. Strong, *Organized Anti-Semitism in America: The Rise of Group Prejudice during the Decade 1930–1940* (Washington, D.C.: American Council on Public Affairs, 1941), chap. 8.

29. Scholnick, *New Deal,* 152.

30. Ibid., 153.

31. See Chadwin, *Hawks,* 210. Also Geoffrey S. Smith, *To Save a Nation* (New York: Basic, 1973).

32. Chadwin, *Hawks,* p. 210.

33. Wayne S. Cole, *Roosevelt and the Isolationists, 1932–45* (Lincoln: University of Nebraska Press, 1983), 308.

34. Neal Gabler, *An Empire of Their Own: How the Jews Invented Hollywood* (New York: Crown, 1988).

35. Chadwin, *Hawks,* 215–219.

36. Glen Jeansonne, *Gerald L. K. Smith: Minister of Hate* (New Haven: Yale University Press, 1988), 65.

37. Scholnick, *New Deal,* 68–69.

38. Ibid., 88–89.

39. Ibid., 72–73.

40. "Jews," *Fortune* (1936).

41. On Coughlin, see Smith, *To Save a Nation,* chaps. 1 and 2.

42. Chadwin, *Hawks,* 213–217.

43. Sander Diamond, *The Nazi Movement in the United States, 1924–1941* (Ithaca: Cornell University Press, 1974).

44. Gabler, *Empire,* chaps. 9 and 10.

45. Ronald Radosh and Joyce Milton, *The Rosenberg File* (New York: Hall, 1983), 353–354.

46. Ibid., 355.

47. Ibid., 356.

48. Ibid., 357–358.

49. Walker, *Defense,* 212.

50. Glen Jeansonne, "Combatting Anti-Semitism: The Case of Gerald L. K. Smith," in David Gerber, ed., *Anti-Semitism in American History* (Urbana: University of Illinois Press, 1986), 152–166.

51. Gabler, *Empire,* 382–383.

52. See Kaufman, *Broken Alliance,* chaps. 1–3.

53. Ginsberg and Shefter, *Politics,* 86; Shefter, "Party, Bureaucracy," 243–254.

54. Ginsberg and Shefter, *Politics,* 87; Shefter, "Party, Bureaucracy," 243–254.

55. Ginsberg and Shefter, *Politics,* 87–88; Shefter, "Party, Bureaucracy," 243–254.

56. Ginsberg and Shefter, *Politics,* 88–89; Shefter, "Party, Bureaucracy," 243–254.

57. Ginsberg and Shefter, *Politics,* 88–90; Shefter, "Party, Bureaucracy," 243–254.

58. Doris Kearns Goodwin, *Lyndon Johnson and the American Dream* (New York: St. Martins Press 1976), chap. 11.

59. Stephen D. Isaacs, *Jews and American Politics* (Garden City, N.J.: Doubleday, 1974), chap. 7.

60. *New York Times* staff, ed., *The Watergate Hearings: Break-in and Cover-up* (New York: Bantam, 1973), 593–595.

61. *The Impeachment Report* (New York: Signet, 1974), 200.

62. See Ginsberg and Shefter, *Politics,* chap. 1.

63. Ibid., 94.

64. Ibid.

65. Ibid., 95.

66. Ibid., 90–92.

67. Ibid., 92–93.

68. Ibid., 93–97.

69. Isaacs, *Jews in American Politics,* chaps. 1–3.

70. See Sidney Blumenthal, "The Annointed," *New Republic,* February 2, 1992, 24–27. See also "Who's Who in President-Elect Clinton's Transition Team," *Washington Post,* November 13, 1992, A25.

71. See Larry Yudelson, "Some Politics Is Local: Spoiled by the Glare of the National Spotlight, Jews Are Urged to Return to Their Grass Roots," *Washington Jewish Week,* March 5, 1992, 3.

72. See Geoffrey Brahm Levey, "Towards an Adequate Explanation of American Jewish Liberalism" (Paper presented to the Annual Meeting of the American Political Science Association, Washington, D.C., August 29–September 1, 1991).

73. Oren, *Joining,* chaps. 10–12.

74. Ibid., chap. 13.

75. Data are reported by Steven Cohen, *The Dimensions of American Jewish Liberalism* New York: American Jewish Committee, 1989).

76. Ibid., 44.

Chapter Four

1. Jonathan Kaufman, *Broken Alliance:* The Turbulent Times between blacks and Jews in America (New York: Mentor, 1988).

2. Naomi Cohen, *Not Free to Desist: The American Jewish Committee, 1906–1966* (Philadelphia: Jewish Publication Society, 1972).

3. For a review of recent poll data, see Seymour Martin Lipset, "A Unique People in an Exceptional Country," in S. M. Lipset, ed., *American Pluralism and the Jewish Community* (New Brunswick, N.J.: Transaction Publishers, 1990), 3–30.

4. Nat Hentoff, "Strange Speech on Campus," *Washington Post*, May 21, 1991, A21.

5. See Joseph Epstein, "Racial Perversity in Chicago," *Commentary* (December 1988): 27.

6. John Tierney, "For Jeffries: A Penchant for Disputes," *New York Times*, September 7, 1991, 28.

7. Glenn Loury, "Behind the Black-Jewish Split," *Commentary* (January 1986): 23–27.

8. On this point see Henry Louis Gates, Jr., "Black Demagogues and Pseudo-Scholars," *New York Times*, July 20, 1992, A15.

9. Epstein, "Racial Perversity," 31.

10. Kaufman, *Broken Alliance*, 136.

11. Ibid., chap. 4; Diane Ravitch, *The Great School Wars* (New York: Basic Books, 1974), 251–380.

12. Kaufman, *Broken Alliance*, 142.

13. Ibid., 146.

14. Joseph Berger, "Exodus Leads to More Female and Hispanic Principals," *New York Times*, October 8, 1991, B1. See also Philip Gourevitch, "Jews Feel Pinch of Racial Policy," *The Forward*, July 12, 1991, 1.

15. Kaufman, *Broken Alliance*, 154–156.

16. Frederick Dicker, "Anti-Semitism Lecture Shocker," *New York Post*, August 5, 1991, 16.

17. Frederick Dicker, "Jeffries Drove Away Jewish Prof," *New York Post*, October 7, 1991, 14.

18. See Susan Chira, "CUNY Ousts Chief of Black Studies," *New York Times*, March 24, 1992, 1.

19. For a recent discussion of the place of Jews in American universities, see Suzanne Klingenstein, *Jews in the American Academy* (New Haven: Yale University Press, 1992. Also Stephen Joel Trachtenberg, "Achieving the Unthinkable: Jews as Leaders in the Academy" (unpublished paper, February 1993).

20. Letty Cottin Pogrebin, *Deborah, Golda and Me: Being Female and Jewish in America* (New York: Crown, 1991), Chap. 11.

21. The Lester case is discussed in Dinesh D'Souza, *Illiberal Education: The Politics of Race and Sex on Campus* (New York: Free Press, 1991), 203.

22. Edward Alexander, "Multiculturalism's Jewish Problem," *Congress Monthly* (November/December 1991): 9.

23. Ibid., 7–10.

24. Edward Alexander, "Race Fever," *Commentary* (November 1990): 45–48.

25. Alexander, "Multiculturalism," 7.

26. Nat Hentoff, "Why Do They Hate Us?" *Village Voice*, May 28, 1991.

27. Alexander, "Multiculturalism," 21.

28. Peter Goldman, *The Death and Life of Malcolm X*, 2d ed. (Urbana: University of Illinois Press, 1979), 14.

29. See Lena Williams, "Blacks, Jews and This Thing That Is Suffocating Us," *New York Times*, July 29, 1990, E5.

30. Leonard Dinnerstein, *Uneasy at Home; Anti-Semitism and the American Jewish Experience* (New York: Columbia University press, 1987), 239.

31. Kaufman, *Broken Alliance*, 71–72.

32. Ibid., 77.

33. For a discussion, see Adolph L. Reed, Jr., *The Jesse Jackson Phenomenon* (New Haven: Yale University Press, 1986).

34. Alison Mitchell, "Prosecutor Cites Problems in Crown Heights Inquiry: Says Stabbing Suspects Can't Be Identified," *New York Times*, April 15, 1992, B3.

35. Evelyn Nieves, "Students Rally to Protest Spath Verdict," *New York Times*, February 13, 1992, B1.

36. Jim Sleeper, *The Closest of Strangers: Liberals and the Politics of Race in New York* (New York: Norton, 1990), esp. chaps. 1 and 11.

37. Mark Mooney, "Rangel Gives 3G to C. Vernon Mason's Rival," *New York Post*, August 14, 1991, 5.

38. After the Crown Heights Affair, Dinkins had some difficulty restoring his support among New York Jews. E.g., see Todd S. Purdum, "Dinkins, at Synagogue, Defends Handling of Crown Heights Clash," *New York Times*, April 10, 1992, B3. Later, to demonstrate to his critics in the African-American community that he was not a puppet of the Jews, Dinkins denounced a group of Hasidic men who had beaten a black man they accused of seeking to burglarize the headquarters of the Lubavitch sect in Crown Heights. After Dinkins called the beating a bias crime, he was sharply criticized by many Jewish organizations. See Laurie Goodstein, "Dinkins Caught in Racial Cross-Fire," *Washington Post*, December 6, 1992, A10. In response to this Jewish censure of Dinkins, the mayor's close ally, Representative Charles Rangel, warned Jews to cease their criticism lest they provoke an anti-Semitic backlash. Delivery of this warning gave Rangel an opportunity to demonstrate that he, too, could stand up to the Jews. See Martin Peretz, "Durable Ideology," *New Republic*, January 4, 1993, 42.

39. Vinette K. Pryce, "Activists Criticize Dinkins on Lynching Statement," *Amsterdam News*, September 14, 1991, 1.

40. Ibid.

41. Ibid.

42. Ibid.

43. *New York Post*, August 27, 1991, 4, cols. 5–6.

44. David Evanier, "Invisible Man: The Lynching of Yankel Rosenbaum," *New Republic*, October 14, 1991, 22.

45. Paul Schwartzman, "Dinkins in Church Plea for Peace," *New York Post*, August 26, 1991, 4.

46. Paul Schwartzman, "Dinkins: I'm Not Going to Denounce Sharpton or Carson," *New York Post*, August 28, 1991.

47. *New York Post*, August 27, 1991, 4, col. 6.

48. Jonathan Rieder, "Crown of Thorns," *New Republic*, October 14, 1991, 29.

49. Loury, "Behind," 26–27.

50. Sleeper, *Strangers*, 246–247.

51. Pogrebin, *Deborah*, chap. 11.

52. Loury, "Behind," 26.

53. Harold Cruse, *The Crisis of the Negro Intellectual* (New York: Quill, 1984), 147–170.

54. Lenni Brenner, *Jews in America Today* (Secaucus, N.J.: Lyle Stuart, 1986), 228.

55. Alan Dershowitz, *Chutzpah* (Boston: Little Brown, 1991), 82–83.

56. The Greenberg story is told by a number of sources, including Kaufman, *Broken Alliance*, 81–120.

57. Alexander, "Multiculturalism," 8.

58. Mizrui, e.g., likes to argue that the conventional use of the term "Holocaust" is "Judeo-centric" and should not be "reserved exclusively for the Jewish experience." See Eric Breindel, "Whose Holocaust?" *New York Post*, June 27, 1991, 31. See also David Rossie, "Is Scholar Taking SUNY for a Ride?" *Binghampton Press and Sun-Bulletin*, June 11, 1989.

59. Of course, many blacks are aware of the underlying commonality of interest between themselves and Jews. See Ethelbert Miller, "Blacks and Jews Must Reunite against Injustice," *New York Times*, August 3, 1992, A18. In recent months, the Rev. Jesse Jackson, too, has focused on the importance of restoring a measure of political cooperation between blacks and Jews. See Paul Montgomery, "Jackson Condemns Anti-Semitism in a Conciliatory Speech to Jews," *New York Times*, July 8, 1992, 1. See also Debra Cohen, "Jackson Reaction," *Washington Jewish Week*, July 16, 1992, 5.

60. There are, of course, exceptions such as Professor Michael Levin of CUNY. Generally, however, Jewish organizations go out of their way to emphasize the interdependence of blacks and Jews and look for opportunities to point out contributions that each group has ostensibly made to the welfare of the other. For an example of such an effort by Jewish groups, see Jeffrey Goldberg, "The Exaggerators: Black Soldiers and Buchenwald," *New Republic*, February 8, 1993, 13–14. Also Larry Cohler, "AJCongress Reaches to Former Foes," *Washington Jewish Week*, December 17, 1992, 6.

61. Blacks have put anti-Semitism back on the political agenda in the same way that insurgent political parties and factions often bring new issues into the political arena. See Walter Dean Burnham, *Critical Elections and the Mainsprings of American Electoral Politics* (New York: Norton, 1970), 30. See also Craig Horowitz, "The New Anti-Semitism," *New York*, January 11, 1993, 21–27.

62. William Buckley, "In Search of Anti-Semitism," *National Review*, December 30, 1991, 56.

63. A. M. Rosenthal, "Victory for Buchanan," *New York Times*, February 14, 1992, A29.

Chapter Five

1. For a discussion of this offensive, see Benjamin Ginsberg and Martin Shefter, *Politics by Other Means* (New York: Basic Books, 1991), chaps. 4 and 5.

2. David A. Vise and Steve Coll, *Eagle on the Street* (New York: Scribners, 1991).

3. Ibid., 205.

4. Sarah Bartlett, *The Money Machine* (New York: Warner Books, 1991), 257–259.

5. Vise and Coll, *Eagle,* 275–289.

6. Ibid., 336.

7. For an excellent analysis of the dilemmas involved in regulating insider trading, see Jonathan Macey, "The SEC's Insider Trading Proposal: Good Politics, Bad Policy," *Cato Policy Analysis,* no. 101, March 31, 1988. Also Jonathan Macey, "From Fairness to Contract: The New Direction of Rules against Insider Trading," *Hofstra Law Review* 13, no. 9 (1984): 9–64.

8. Connie Bruck, *The Predators' Ball* (New York: Penguin, 1988), 331.

9. Bruck, *Predators' Ball,* 15. The event was the 1985 Drexel Burnham High Yield Bond Conference, which had come to be known as the "Predators' Ball."

10. Stephen Isaacs, *Jews and American Politics* (Garden City: Doubleday, 1974), chap. 1.

11. Norman Podhoretz, *Breaking Ranks* (New York: Harper, 1979). Also Norman Podhoretz, *The Present Danger* (New York: Simon and Schuster, 1980.

12. Nathan Perlmutter and Ruth Ann Perlmutter, *The Real Anti-Semitism in America* (New York: Arbor House, 1982), 157.

13. Walden Bello, "Little Reagans," *The Progressive,* January 26, 1986, 25–27. Also Robert Kuttner, "Unholy Alliance," *New Republic,* May 26, 1986, 19.

14. Quoted in Paul Findley, *They Dare to Speak Out* (Westport, Conn.: Lawrence Hill and Co., 1985), 29–30.

15. Ibid., 28–29.

16. Elizabeth Drew, "Washington Prepares for War," in Micah Sifry and Christopher Cerf, eds., *Gulf War Reader* (New York: Times Books, 1991), 180–193. On Solarz's role see Peter Hellman, "The Hawk," *New York,* February 18, 1991, 43–45.

17. See Edward Pound and David Rogers, "Roles of Ex-Pentagon Officials at Jewish Group Show Clout of Cold-Warrior, Pro-Israel Network," *Wall Street Journal,* January 22, 1992, A16.

18. See Alexander and Leslie Cockburn, *Dangerous Liason* (New York: Harper, 1991).

19. Ibid., chaps. 9 and 10.

20. Frank Donner, "Courting Disaster," *The Nation,* October 6, 1984, 324.

21. The fundamentalists are discussed in Wolf Blitzer, *Between Washington and Jerusalem* (New York: Oxford, 1985), chap. 9.

22. Perlmutter and Perlmutter, *The Real Anti-Semitism*, 157.

23. Gore Vidal, "The Empire Lovers Strike Back," *The Nation*, March 22, 1986, 352–353.

24. See Andrew Silow Carroll, "Mike Wallace: Just the Facts?" *Washington Jewish Week*, March 5, 1992, 4.

25. For examples, see Stephen Karetzky, ed., *The Media's War against Israel* (New York: Shapolsky, 1986). Also Jim Lederman, *Battle Lines: The American Media and the Intifada* (New York: Holt, 1992). In addition, Andrea Levin, "PBS Does It Again," *Commentary* (July 1992): 51–53. Also Andrea Levin, "The Voice of NPR," *Commentary* (January 1993): 50–52.

26. Anthony Lewis, "A New Life," *New York Times*, June 28, 1992, E17.

27. See Thomas L. Friedman, "U.S. and Israel at Sea: Both Sides Searching for New Basis for Ties in Post-Cold-War World," *New York Times*, March 22, 1992, 1.

28. See Michael Saba, *The Armageddon Network* (Brattelboro, Vt.: Amana Books, 1984). Also Blitzer, *Between Washington and Jerusalem*, chaps. 3 and 4.

29. The best discussion of the Pollard case is Wolf Blitzer, *Territory of Lies* (New York: Harper, 1989).

30. Ibid., chap. 12.

31. Ibid. Apparently the activities of Jews were conceived to pose a far greater threat to the nation's security, and thus to require more stringent punishment, than those of other groups. During the same period, for example, a Gentile FBI agent convicted of spying for the KGB only received a twenty-year prison term. An individual who sold antitank missile and radar technology to Poland and another who sold the names of CIA agents to the Soviet Union received eighteen-year terms. A man who sold U.S. stealth technology to Iraq was sentenced to less than four years in prison. As far as is known, Weinberger made no personal effort to intervene in any of these cases. Some observers asserted that Weinberger was motivated to seek a harsh sentence for Pollard by what one acquaintance called "a deep, visceral hatred for Israel." Others suggested that Weinberger was seeking to distance the United States from Israel and its Jewish allies. See Douglas Bloomfield, "Petty in a Big Way," *Washington Jewish Week*, January 7, 1993, 15–16. Subsequently, Representative Gary Ackerman (D.-N.Y.) intimated that Weinberger's eagerness to see Pollard imprisoned for life might have been linked to secret information that Pollard gave to Israel on America's dealings with Iran and Iraq. Weinberger was, of course, later indicted for withholding information from Congress on his involvement in the "Iran-Contra" affair, escaping prosecution only because of a presidential pardon granted him during Bush's final week in office. Ackerman promised that future congressional hearings on the Iran-Contra affair would touch on the Pollard sentence. See Larry Yudelson, "Weinberger Pardon Recalls Pollard," *Washington Jewish Week*, December 31, 1992, 13.

32. See Larry Yudelson, "Court Rejects Pollard's Appeal," *Washington Jewish Week*, March 26, 1992, 8.

33. Quoted in Ellen Bernstein, "D.C. Board of Rabbis Calls for Pollard's Release," *Washington Jewish Week*, September 24, 1992, 5. Bush was described as "indifferent" to requests that Pollard's sentence be commuted. A prominent Republican with access to the White House, working on Pollard's behalf, correctly predicted, ". . . it's not going to happen. This administration simply doesn't like Jews." See Bloomfield, "Petty," 15.

34. Blitzer, *Territory*, chap. 14. Others have also reported that in the wake of the Pollard case, Jews working in the Pentagon have lost jobs and faced career obstacles. See ibid., 16.

35. For one example, see Ellen Bernstein, "Soviet Emigre Breaks Barrier," *Washington Jewish Week*, October 15, 1992, 6.

36. See Larry Cohler, "For Israel, Push Comes to Shove," *Washington Jewish Week*, September 19, 1991, 4–5.

37. Michael McQueen, "Voters Support Bush's Hard Line on Israel Aid," *Wall Street Journal*, September 26, 1991, A20.

38. See Robert S. Greenberger, "Hard Line on Israeli Loan Guarantees Reflects Anti-Aid Mood, Bush's Aim to Pressure Shamir," *Wall Street Journal*, March 11, 1992, A16.

39. Patrick Buchanan, "The Bush-Israel Showdown," *New York Post*, September 18, 1991, 21.

40. Andrew Rosenthal, "Bush Acts to Calm Israel Aid Uproar," *New York Times*, September 20, 1991, 1.

41. Ibid.

42. See Thomas Friedman, "Uneasy Debate for Jews in U.S. on Loans Issue," *New York Times*, March 2, 1992, 1.

43. Larry Cohler, "The End of the Road: Supporters of Israel Loan Guarantees Face a Deadline of Tough Choices," *Washington Jewish Week*, March 5, 1992, 1.

44. See Patrick Tyler, "U.S. Asserts Israel Broke Arms-Transfer Law," *New York Times*, April 2, 1992. Also A. M. Rosenthal, "Missile-Mongering," *New York Times*, April 10, 1992, A37.

45. See Carroll J. Doherty, "Bush, Lawmakers Shuffle Blame as Israel Loan Talks Crumble," *Congressional Quarterly Weekly Report*, March 21, 1992, 733–735. Also Clyde Haberman, "Israel Confronts the Idea of Life without Washington," *New York Times*, March 22, 1992, E5. For an analysis of the impact of the struggle on the American Jewish community, see "Coming Apart at the Seams," *Washington Jewish Week*, March 19, 1992, 1.

46. Patrick Tyler, "No Evidence Found of Patriot Sales by Israel to China," *New York Times*, April 3, 1992, 1.

47. Cynthia Mann and Larry Cohler, "Yes to Loan Guarantees," *Washington Jewish Week*, August 13, 1992, 4.

48. Larry Yudelson, "Rabin Questions Role of American Jews," *Washington Jewish Week*, August 20, 1992, 6. Rabin was also reacting to AIPAC's ties to the former Likud government.

49. "The U.S. vs. Israel," *Wall Street Journal*, Marcy 6, 1992, A48.

50. Thomas Friedman, "Senators Press Baker on Help to Israel," *New York Times*, February 26, 1992, A6.

51. See "Bush Conciliatory Efforts Questioned," *Jewish Observer*, April 16, 1992, 21.

52. Marianne Goldstein et al., "Baker's 4-Letter Slam at U.S. Jews," *New York Post*, March 6, 1992, 2. Through a spokesperson, Baker denied the report. However, most informed Washington sources supported the original account. See, e.g., William Safire, "Blaming the Victim," *New York Times*, March 19, 1992, A23. Also Mark Helprin, "Baker Should Resign," *Wall Street Journal*, April 15, 1992.

53. For a discussion, see Thomas L. Friedman, "Midwest Exercises: Talks Resume Today, But Are Parties Ready to Do More Than Limber Up?" *New York Times*, April 27, 1992, 2.

54. See Cynthia Mann, "Effect of Clinton's Pro-Israel Rhetoric Unclear," *Washington Jewish Week*, November 12, 1992, 8. Also, Robert I. Friedman, "The Wobbly Israel Lobby," *Washington Post*, November 1, 1992, C2. Indeed, AIPAC President David Steiner was compelled to resign in November 1992 after boasting of his organization's clout with the new administration.

55. Larry Cohler, "Top Clinton Aid 'No Enemy,' " *Washington Jewish Week*, November 12, 1992, 9.

56. See Fred Barnes, "They're Back!: Neocons for Clinton," *New Republic*, August 3, 1992, 12–14. Also Larry Cohler, "Returning to the Fold," *Washington Jewish Week*, July 16, 1992, 4.

57. See Cynthia Mann, "Safer in Bush's Hands?" *Washington Jewish Week*, August 20, 1992, 4.

Chapter Six

1. See Norman Podhoretz, "Buchanan and the Conservative Crackup," *Commentary* 93, no. 5 (May 1992): 29–34.

2. See Sidney Blumenthal, "Tomorrow Belongs to Me," *New Republic*, January 6 and 13, 1992, 24–26. Also Jacob Weisberg, "The Heresies of Pat Buchanan: Anti-Semitism and Conservativism," *New Republic*, October 22, 1990, 22.

3. Thomas Edsall, "The Rebel Yell against a White-Gloved GOP: Buchanan and Duke Woo Democrats and the Disaffected," *Washington Post National Weekly Edition*, March 9–15, 1992, 16.

4. See ibid.

5. Fred Barnes, "Heir Apparent: The New Right and Buchanan," *New Republic*, March 30, 1992, 22.

6. John Fund, "The Protectionists behind Buchanan," *Wall Street Journal*, March 3, 1992. Also John Judis, "The Tariff Party: The GOP Rediscovers Protectionism," *New Republic*, March 30, 1992, 23–25.

7. See Joseph Sobran's attack on the neocons in response to William

Buckley's *National Review* piece on anti-Semitism. "Letters," *National Review*, March 16, 1992, S4–S8. Also Joseph Sobran, "Invidious Curse of Ismism," *Washington Times*, March 5, 1992, G3.

8. For a summary of Buchanan's comments, see James Perry, "Buchanan, Fighting Bush, Is Himself Attacked," *Wall Street Journal*, February 13, 1992, A20.

9. John Judis, "The Conservative Wars," *New Republic*, August 11 and 18, 1986.

10. Blumenthal, "Tomorrow," 26.

11. Douglas Harbrecht and Richard S. Dunham, "A Tattered GOP Starts Thinking about Tomorrow," *Business Week*, November 16, 1992, 41. On Robertson, see Michael Lind, "The Exorcism," *New Republic*, December 14, 1992, 20–21. Also Cynthia Mann, "Republican Identity Crisis," *Washington Jewish Week*, December 3, 1992, 13.

12. See Jack Anderson and Michael Binstein, "GOP: The Coming Night of the Long Knives," *Washington Post*, November 5, 1992, C7.

13. Barnes, "Heir Apparent," 21.

14. Ari Goldman, "Quayle Honors Victims of Holocaust," *New York Times*, April 27, 1992, B3.

15. Andrew Rosenthal, "G.O.P. Courts Jewish Voters with Eye to the Future," *New York Times*, April 8, 1992, A9.

16. Thomas B. Edsall, "GOP Unity Session Ends in Discord," *Washington Post*, November 18, 1992, 1. Angela Buchanan is quoted in Douglas Bloomfield, "Whose Nation Is It, Anyway?" *Washington Jewish Week*, December 3, 1992, 19.

17. On the Duke Candidacy, see Julia Reed, "His Brilliant Career," *New York Review*, April 9, 1992, 20–24.

18. See John Maginnis, "The Hazards of Duke," *New Republic*, November 25, 1991, 25–29.

19. Richard Hamilton, *Who Voted for Hitler?* (Princeton: Princeton University Press, 1982), 377.

20. "Jewish Actions Minimized in Duke Defeat," *Jewish Observer*, November 28, 1991, 13.

21. Larry Yudelson, "Despite Defeat to Edwards, Duke Shows Real Strength," *Washington Jewish Week*, November 22, 1991, 1.

22. Donald Beachler, "The South and Divided Government" (Ph.D. diss., Cornell University, 1992).

23. For the social and economic division of the vote, see Peter Applebome, "Blacks and Affluent Whites Give Edwards Victory," *New York Times*, November 18, 1991, 1.

24. Peter Appelbome, "David Duke Battling in Dark as Spotlight Trails Buchanan," *New York Times*, March 6, 1992, A1.

25. Dirk Johnson, "Colorado Klansman Refines Message for the '90s," *New York Times*, February 23, 1992.

26. Alan M. Schwartz et al., *Hate Groups in America* (New York: Anti-Defamation League of B'Nai B'rith, 1988), 18.

27. On the use of direct mail by conservatives, see Steven Holmes, "The Checks Are in the Mail," *New York Times*, February 24, 1992, A16.

28. Martin Gottlieb, "Minor Candidate's Fund-raising Turns Spotlight on Party," *New York Times*, January 1992.

29. Larry Cohler, "Winning over the New Congress," *Washington Jewish Week*, November 5, 1992, 6.

30. Yudelson, "Despite Defeat," 5.

Index

Pickens, T. Boone, 192, 194
Pingree, Hazen, 95
Plahve, Wenzel von, 57
Plessis, Armand-Jean du (Cardinal Richelieu), 16
PLO. *See* Palestine Liberation Organization
Podhoretz, Norman, 204, 208
Pogrebin, Letty Cotton, 162
Poland, 12, 32, 33, 35, 55
Political action, Jewish: in Communist state building, 27–33; in liberal state building, 19, 20–21, 22, 25, 26–27, 39; in U.S., 1, 137–38, 139, 225–26. *See also* Administration of government, Jews in
Polk, Frank, 109
Pollard, Jonathan, case of, 215–18, 262n.31, 262nn.33 and 34
Populism. *See* Radical Populist anti-Semitism
Posner, Victor, 192
PPI (Progressive Policy Institute), 138
Presbyterian Church, 227
President's Commission on Higher Education (Truman), 100
President's Committee on Civil Rights (Truman), 100
President's Committee on Income Security (FDR), 108
Preuss, Hugo, 25, 29
Princeton University, 2, 84, 97
Progressive Policy Institute (PPI), 138
Progressivism, 7, 61–62, 91–96
Protective function of state, 9, 11–13
Protocols of the Elders of Zion, 163, 164, 178
Prussia, 9, 17–19, 28, 29
Public Citizen, 137
Public interest movement, 133–39, 225–26
Public Utility Holding Act of 1935, 105
Publishing, Jewish influence in, 19, 22, 26, 103. *See also* Journalism, Jewish influence in
Pulzer, Peter, 43

Qaddafi, Muammar, 177
Quayle, Dan, 232, 234
Quinn-Oliffe Act (New York, 1948), 99

Rabin government, 3, 214–15, 222–23
Race and Settlement Office (Nazi), 49
Racism: Jewish, 152–53, 182, 260n.60; in Republican party tactics, 187. *See also* Anti-Semitism, history outside U.S.; Anti-Semitism in U.S; Discrimination; Radical Populist anti-Semitism
Radek, Karl, 30, 53
Radical populist anti-Semitism: current, 4–5, 10, 236–43; future growth of, 224, 239–43; in 19th-century U.S., 60–61, 75, 76–78, 81–82, 87–91, 240; outside U.S., 33, 38
Radio journalism, 110–11, 113, 117, 123, 124
Railroad construction, 68–70, 73, 74
Rakosi, Mathias, 32
Rangel, Charles, 171, 176, 259n.38
Rankin, John, 2, 120
Rathenau, Walter, 26–27
Ravitch, Diane, 155
Raynal, David, 21
Reagan, Ronald: economic policy under, 188, 189–99, 200, 227, 230; and future of anti-Semitism, 228; general foreign policy under, 185, 199–202; media attacks on, 137; policy on Israel under, 166, 199, 205–7, 209–13, 214, 227; social programs under, 185–86
Reconstruction era, 6–7, 65–68, 74–75, 252n.24
Red Scare (post–World War I), 7, 93–96, 119–25
Regan, Donald, 190
Regulatory agencies, 135–36, 137, 185, 186, 226
Reich, Robert, 139
Reichkristallnacht, 48
Reinach, Baron Jacque de, 20, 39, 74
Reinach, Joseph, 21
Reisman, Yuli, 31
Religion in government, world history of, 14, 16, 21, 34, 37, 39, 40, 45–47, 56
Religious freedom and school prayer, 2, 100–101, 185
Representative, The, 77